KU-482-234

Call Me Mrs. Brown

Brendan O'Carroll is an Irish writer, producer, comedian, actor and director. He is best known for playing Agnes Brown in the BAFTA award-winning sitcom *Mrs. Brown's Boys*. He has written four films and nine comedy shows, including *The Course* and *The Last Wedding*. He has also published seven novels, including *The Mammy*, *The Scrapper* and *The Young Wan* - a number of which have been translated into twelve languages. He lives between Dublin and Florida with his wife, Jenny.

Call Me Mrs. Brown

BRENDAN O'CARROLL

MICHAEL  JOSEPH

PENGUIN MICHAEL JOSEPH

UK | USA | Canada | Ireland | Australia
India | New Zealand | South Africa

Penguin Michael Joseph is part of the Penguin Random House group of companies
whose addresses can be found at global.penguinrandomhouse.com

First published, 2022
001
Copyright © Brendan O'Carroll, 2022

All images courtesy of the author, with on set photography by Graeme Hunter.

Every effort has been made to trace copyright holders and to obtain their permission for the use of copyright
material. The publisher apologizes for any errors or omissions and would be grateful to be notified of any
corrections that should be incorporated in future editions of this book.

The moral right of the author has been asserted

Set in 13.5/16pt Garamond MT Std
Typeset by Jouve (UK), Milton Keynes
Printed and bound in Great Britain by Clays Ltd, Elcograf S.p.A.

The authorized representative in the EEA is Penguin Random House Ireland,
Morrison Chambers, 32 Nassau Street, Dublin D02 YH68

A CIP catalogue record for this book is available from the British Library

HARDBACK ISBN: 978–0–241–48366–4
OPEN MARKET ISBN: 978–0–241–48367–1

www.greenpenguin.co.uk

MIX
Paper from
responsible sources
FSC® C018179

Penguin Random House is committed to a
sustainable future for our business, our readers
and our planet. This book is made from Forest
Stewardship Council® certified paper.

My entire life has been blessed and shaped
by strong women.
Today I am surrounded by really strong
yet compassionate women
who make every day a joy for me.
And to these wonderful women I give my thanks
and I dedicate this book.

Annie Gibney
*

Fiona Gibney
*

Éilish O'Carroll
Marian O'Sullivan
*

Emily Houlihan
Helen Spain
Edel Fitzgerald
*

Sandra Twomey
Valerie Keating
Annette Dolan
Jo Kennedy Valentine
*

Amanda Woods
Marian Sheridan
and
Fiona O'Carroll
*

Finally, of course, she who gives me wings,
Jennifer O'Carroll

Just a note from me to you . . .

Peterboro, just outside Toronto, Canada
4 April 2020 – the day I started this book

My sister Fiona died today.

My heart is broken.

I'm not short of sisters; I have five. I also have four brothers. A big family by today's standards but not in 1955 when I was born.

My sister Maureen is the eldest of the family. The age difference between her and me is eighteen years. To be quite honest, we were kind of three families, if you like. There were the eldest five, then the twins, Fiona and Finbar, in the middle, and then Micháel (pronounced mee-hall), Éilish and yours truly.

Those of you who come from big families will know that although Mammy is Mammy and Daddy is Daddy, it's the older children that really raise the younger ones. Fiona raised me. Don't get me wrong, I had a wonderful mother, who did all the mother stuff. But my first visit to the beach? Fiona took me. Every visit to see Santa Claus in Cleary's store? Fiona took me. My first visit to the zoo, my first museum, art gallery, train trip, swimming lessons, movie, everything – Fiona took me. Fiona was kind, gentle, funny and had an amazing personality, and I often remarked that if you didn't like Fiona, there was something wrong with you.

1

She named one of her sons Brendan.

I named my daughter Fiona.

It would be easy to say that Fiona was proud of me when watching my career take off and blossom. She *was* proud that I have written four novels, seven plays, and thirty-six episodes of the *Mrs. Brown's Boys* TV series. But she wasn't waiting for these to be proud of me.

When my daddy died just after my ninth birthday and I held in the tears because I didn't want to upset Mammy, Fiona told me she was proud of me for being a 'big man'.

When I was ten and sent away to a private school recommended by a judge, she didn't judge me nor make me feel bad.

She was proud of me as she stood in the cold on the sideline when I scored my first goal for Home Farm FC. I was just twelve.

Fiona had dreams. She was never going to settle in Ireland. Fiona was always going away. She emigrated to Canada in 1968. Too soon for me. But I got aerogramme after aerogramme from her each month, keeping me up to date with her life. If you don't know what an aerogramme is, then google it. She made a wonderful life for herself in Canada and married an amazing man in Larry Gowland. If you have read *The Mammy* or any of its sequels, you will already have guessed that Agnes's sister Dolly in Canada is based on Fiona.

In the last ten years Fiona and Larry would come down to Jenny and me in Florida each December until the following March, getting away from the cold and snow of Toronto. It was snowing when Jenny and I arrived in Toronto this morning. It was a red-eye flight, arriving in Toronto at 3 a.m. The car rental didn't open until 6 a.m., so Jenny and I sat in silence for the three hours and waited. I arrived at Fiona's bedside just in time. Fiona's nurse tells me that she had asked him time after time to 'just keep me alive until Brendan gets here'.

Larry, her wonderful husband, met me at the door with a hug and cautioned me not to expect too much as she slept most of the time. When I got to Fiona's bedside, I leaned over her and said, 'I'm here.' Her eyes opened and she smiled. Within minutes I had her laughing, and together we even sang 'These Boots Are Made for Walking'. She got tired then. I held her hand and we did our usual exchange. I said, 'I love you.' She replied, 'I love you more.' I smiled and said, 'I love you the most.' That was usually the end of the ritual except this time Fiona added, 'Forever and ever.' She closed her eyes.

Fiona died and my heart is broken.

I had wanted to open this book with a funny story and a laugh. But I needed to put the above to bed. This way I can get on with things and continue to make my sister Fiona proud. So then. Here we go!

FOR FIONA.

Preface

Maureen O'Carroll gave birth to ten babies. The last of those, myself, arrived when she was forty-two years of age. Mammy told me once that I was 'one more time for old times' sake'. I laughed at this. I knew it was a joke for I never felt unwanted, although at that time Mammy was a member of the Irish parliament and chief whip of the Labour Party, so I'm sure I was about as welcome as a fart in a spacesuit.

In the early part of this story of mine please keep in mind that I am writing the memories of a child and, as with all childhood memories, I remember things not always as they were, only how I recall them, or in some cases maybe as I wished them to be – I'm not sure. What I am sure of is that I was loved.

Mammy gave me many lessons over the years before she left me, little nuggets of her wisdom that she would plant in my brain and which sometimes would not be clear to me until I got much older. Like, 'Never ask for advice but take all that's given.' If you ask someone for advice, she would say you put them on the spot, so they now must come up with an answer. If advice is offered unasked for, it has been thought out or is based on experience, so take it. There were many of them – enough to fill this book – but probably the most important lesson she ever gave me was when I became a father and began to doubt that I could do that job properly. When I confessed this to her this is what she said: 'The most important thing you can teach your children is to not be afraid. Not afraid to lose. Not afraid to fail. But equally not afraid to win or to succeed. The main thing is not to be afraid to TRY.' I have failed so many times in so many ways, but I have never, ever failed to try. I have three wonderful children, Fiona, Danny and Eric. They are not afraid.

I am very lucky to have had some success. I have worked hard for it. I have found happiness, not in the success of what I do, but in the journey to where I am and in the joy of doing what I do with the people I do it with. I have six amazing grandsons, which any grandparent will tell you can fill any gap in your heart. But my deepest happiness comes from waking up each morning beside Jenny. Jenny has saved me in the darkest of times and I hope I have saved her right back. I have never felt such love as the love I feel for her.

What you are about to read is some of my story as I recall it. It's a helter-skelter of a story about the helter-skelter journey of a scrawny kid from Finglas in Dublin to TV screens in Ireland, the UK, Australia, the USA, Canada, Romania, South Africa, Mexico, Italy, Spain and France. In Ireland and the UK they know me as Brendan O'Carroll; in all those other countries they call me Mrs. Brown.

I

When I was a child my mother said to me, 'If you become a soldier, you'll be a general. If you become a monk, you'll end up as the Pope.' Instead, I became a painter and wound up as Picasso.

PABLO PICASSO

The Mammy is the title of my first novel but more importantly it is what I called my mother. She who gave me life, confidence, direction and more than one clip across the ear.

I was named Brendan Desmond Jarleth Francis O'Carroll (I know, a lot of names) and christened in Berkley Road church in Dublin on 25 September 1955, eight days after my birth in what was then a private hospital and is now a hotel.

My brother Micháel, who was then six years old, had saved up five pennies to give to my mother to buy a little brother. He owns me. My sister Éilish was just four and now went from being THE baby to just another kid. I was the new BABY. Éilish recalls being furious that I was born . . . that was just last week!

I was thirteen when I found my mother's diary collection in the attic of our house on Casement Grove in Finglas West. She had them well hidden.

They were in a cardboard box marked DIARY COLLEC-TION. Clever.

I fully admit that I am a nosy fucker, so when I found the box and saw all the diaries, I sat on an old suitcase and I browsed through a few of them. For two hours. I devoured them. Why? Well, apart from the fact that I adored my mother's beautiful script-style handwriting (she used ONLY a fountain pen, never a ballpoint) my mother Maureen was a very, very interesting woman.

So there I am in the attic browsing the diaries and loving it. I opened Mammy's diary for 1954 and flicked through it. All boring stuff really, until I came to *the* entry for 28 December. There were a few entries but the one that stuck out was 11 a.m. It read, in beautiful script: *Appointment with Dr Fine for test results. He thinks it's either a growth or I am pregnant. I hope it's a growth.*

My jaw dropped. It was me! She was pregnant with ME. How could an entry hinting at the possibility of having ME arrive not be surrounded with love hearts and the page stained with tears of joy? I dropped through the hatch from the attic and made my way downstairs to the sitting room where Mammy was sitting by the fire knitting.

'Look what I found,' I announced. I held it up like a referee with a red card.

She didn't even look up from her knitting. 'What did you find?' she asked.

I was indignant. 'I found your 1954 diary,' I said.

'My private 1954 diary?' she asked accusingly.

I got defensive. 'It was in the attic, in an open box; you could have no expectation of privacy.' I had heard this said on *Perry Mason* on telly. It felt good to have a chance to say it.

Mammy gave me one of her sharp sideways looks that often terrified me. 'I'm just asking which one. I'm not asking if you have a forking search warrant,' she said.

'This one,' I said. As I was already holding it up, I held it up higher as if that would emphasize my disgust.

Mammy stopped knitting and looked up at me, her youngest son, standing now like the Statue of Liberty. 'So?' she simply said.

I opened to the page and read aloud. 'On 28 December you wrote, "Appointment with Dr Fine for test results. He thinks it's either a growth or I am pregnant. I hope it's a growth".'

I awaited her apology, but she just picked up her two Aero number-eight needles and went back to her knitting. Over the clickety-click she said, 'You were a growth . . . and you're malignant.'

There was a pause. She looked at me and I held her stare. Then we both burst into laughter.

Now, I know you are thinking: *he's just skipped thirteen years*, but quite honestly does anybody really care about the early years of someone else? Really?

(Editor's note: *Yes, that's what we're paying you for.*)

OK. Fine. Well, let me tell you as much as I remember as I remember it. Now that I think of it a lot of things happened in those thirteen years that shaped all I am now and probably all that I will ever be. I will tell you in episodic style, as my life has truly been a collection of episodes rather than a linear timeline that's continuous and never-changing. Within these episodes there are moments that made me stop, think and completely change the direction of all that I believed or where I was going. So where to begin?

I'll start with a few THINGS ABOUT ME.

I'm a hugger

Anyone who knows me knows this. I hug when I greet, and I hug when I say goodbye. I do give a good hug, though. Like most influences in my life, I get this from my mother. I'm not talking about a kiddie hug you give to your parents as they are sending you off to bed. I'm talking about a real hug, a man hug. By the time I got to my teenage years there was only Micháel and Éilish left in the house with Mammy and me. I do not remember a goodnight or a good morning with either of them without a hug. I couldn't understand that this wasn't the case with every family, or indeed every person. When I meet someone new I automatically go for a hug. I forget that not everybody hugs, and I have had the strangest reactions. Some just keep their arms straight down, so that I'm now hugging a lamp post. Some attempt to hug back but pat me on the back as if I were a horse. Some turn sideways so I get a kind of one-armed hug (the one I hate the most). But then some people hug me right back, and there is no feeling like it in the world.

When I was about fifteen years old I remember Mammy and me were having one of our many late-night cuppas and a crack at the *Irish Times* Crosaire crossword. During a pause, and out of the blue, I asked her, 'Mammy, why do we always hug?'

She answered, 'Because it's nice and it breaks down barriers with people.'

I shrugged. 'I suppose.'

She could see that I wasn't entirely happy with the answer. So she ploughed on. 'OK. We hug when we greet someone to show that we are genuinely happy to see them.'

I smiled. 'True,' I said. 'But what about the goodbye hug?'

'Ah.' She sat up now, always a sign the question interested her. 'That is the most important hug of all.'

I didn't understand that there was a difference. 'Why?'

Obviously there was a story to go with this. 'Well,' she began, 'you know when your sister Fiona comes home from Canada for a trip, and when her holiday ends and we leave her at the airport?'

I nodded, feeling a bit sad. 'I hate that bit.'

Mammy nodded as well. 'Me too. Don't you give her an extra-special hug when she's at the departure gate?'

Of course I did. 'Yes,' I said.

'Why?'

What a silly question. 'Because I know I won't see her again for a long time, maybe a year. Isn't it the same for you?'

Mammy shook her head. 'No, son. I hug her in case I never see her again. It's a strange world we live in. I hug her as if she were a soldier going off to war.'

I was back with an answer. 'But she doesn't have to be going away for that to be the case. She could live down the road and the same thing would apply.'

Mammy smiled. 'Exactly,' she said, and gave me one of her winks as she tapped the side of her nose. 'Never forget that with anybody.'

I hope I never have. So when I hug you goodbye it's in the hope we meet again.

By the way, if I don't hug you goodbye, it's probably because I hope I never fucking see you again.

I'm OCD (at times)

This is about the supermarket shopping. Look, you have to plan in reverse.

The items you are going to buy go on to your kitchen shelves in a certain order. So it's only natural that they should come out of the car in an order that matches that.

So if they are to come out of the car in a certain order they must GO INTO the car in a certain order.

To make this easier to do in the small car park they must be bagged in a certain order.

To be bagged in that order they must be put on to the conveyor belt in reverse order.

And, of course, for this all to happen, you start at the start by putting your groceries into the shopping cart in a certain order.

(Christ, now that I have typed that out it looks fucking ridiculous.)

I exaggerate . . . sometimes

In a wonderful book entitled *The Night Listener*, the author Armistead Maupin introduced me to the 'Jewelled Elephant Syndrome'. He explains it with a beautiful story that I won't repeat here. This is the way *I* tell it to anyone who will listen. A young woman, let's say she was from Doncaster, met a young man, he was from New Delhi, and they fell in love. He proposed marriage to her and she accepted, and the date was set for the wedding that was to be held in India. Her parents went to India for the wedding and on their return they were out one night for dinner with some friends. Naturally the friends wanted to know how the wedding had gone and the father of the bride began to tell them. 'It was amazing. The ceremony was beautiful with many people in traditional Indian dress, a rainbow of beautiful colours. The temple where they were married was surrounded by beautiful flowering trees and the scent of jasmine filled the air. Our daughter then arrived on an elephant covered in sparkling jewels and as she walked down the aisle she did so on a bed of flower petals.' The friends were impressed and happy for the couple.

Later, as the couple drove home, the wife commented on how well he had described their daughter's wedding, but she added, 'I was there, and I don't remember a jewelled elephant.'

He smiled. 'No,' he said. 'But it makes the story much more interesting.'

Sometimes when I tell a story . . . there just might be the odd jewelled elephant in there. Thank you, Armistead.

I don't keep things

I'm not a collector, never have been. I tried it when I was a kid with stamps, but it wasn't for me. You had to stick them into an album using this little strip of what looked like gummed greaseproof paper. As I sit here typing in my kitchen, if someone knocked at the door and asked me for something 'Mrs. Brown', I swear I wouldn't be able to find anything. I don't keep merchandise or souvenirs of the places we have been. I don't keep anything. There was one time I did. I collected thirty crisp bags and sent them away to an ad agency. It was a promotion, and the prize was a *Man from U.N.C.L.E.* kit, which included a decoder. By the time I had made it to thirty bags it was past the closing date. But I sent them off anyway. Whoever opened my late entry in the advertising agency, God bless their hearts, because I got my *Man from U.N.C.L.E.* kit, decoder and all. But, other than that, I was never a collector. To me stuff is just stuff, and if it goes missing or gets damaged, I never fret. It really is just stuff. As long as it's not my children or family or friends that are harmed, I really don't bother.

I am a magnet for trivia!

When I come out with a trivial fact when we are in company, like 'Children's dreams are shorter than adult ones', Jenny rolls her eyes and says, 'The winters just fly by with him around.'

I cannot help it, I swear to you. Trivia is not just information to me; these facts are like little nuggets of gold that swirl around my head and give me a high that I'm sure only drug addicts could identify with. I'm not even sure if the stuff my brain collects is true, but I don't care.

Here's one, for instance, that I delighted in reading and adore telling. Winston Churchill's father, Lord Randolph Churchill, was up in Scotland on a holiday with his son, the future prime minister of the UK. While there, one afternoon the boy Winston was swimming in a local lake when he got into some difficulty. A local farmer saw this and dived in, swam to the boy and dragged him out, saving his life. When Lord Churchill heard about the rescue, he called to the farmer's house to offer his thanks and to reward the farmer for his bravery. The farmer was adamant that he wouldn't take any reward, telling Lord Churchill that he had a son too and he would hope that were his boy in difficulty somebody would do the same for him. Lord Churchill had an idea. He suggested to the farmer that if he would not take anything for himself, maybe as a reward he would allow Churchill to set up a trust for the education of the farmer's son. After some thought the farmer agreed to this kind offer and the boy went through a full education, his specialty being science.

That boy was Alexander Fleming, who years later, in 1928, discovered penicillin, and one of the first people penicillin was used on to treat an infection was the now adult Winston Churchill.

Alexander and his Greek wife Amelia subsequently joined the Greek resistance during the Second World War, for which Winston Churchill is credited as leading the Allies to victory.

How could you not fall in love with that story?

Well, as much as I don't collect stuff, I do collect trivia and I love it more than any stamp collection. Here are a few treats for you.

- Half the six million parts on a Boeing 747 aircraft are fasteners.
- The gym on the *Titanic* had a mechanical camel. Why?
- Wembley Stadium is the building with the most toilets at 2,600.
- Lips are a hundred times more sensitive than fingertips.
- It took nearly forty years for radio to reach fifty million users. The internet took just five.
- Pharaoh Pepi II had his slaves covered in honey to keep the flies off HIM.
- In Canada the post code for Santa Claus is HoH oHo.
- An average family of four uses two trees' worth of toilet paper a year.

Now I'll bet you are feeling good after reading those. The winter nights just fly by if you have me for company.

The coincidences

I cannot over-exaggerate the coincidences in mine and my family's lives. I swear that if my car broke down on a country road in Ireland at 3 a.m. on a winter's night, the next vehicle to come round the bend would be a tow truck (actually happened). There are too many to recount in a single book, but let me give you three examples that illustrate how they impact our lives.

Forbidden marriage

In 1911, when just a nineteen-year-old, my grandma Lizzy O'Dowd fell in love with a local man, Michael McHugh. They were mad about each other, which was great except for one little detail. Michael, at thirty-five, was just eight years younger than Lizzy's father. So her father was not having it. He forbade Lizzy from seeing Michael.

Although she promised it would end, they continued their romance in secret. A year later he proposed and she said yes, and, as sad as it made Lizzy, she knew her father would not agree to this marriage, so the couple decided that they would elope to America. Over a few weeks Lizzy sneaked her clothes bit by bit out of the house until the fateful week came. Michael had purchased the tickets and they were all set to go by the week's end.

However, Lizzy got very depressed at the thought of saying goodbye to her mother one morning as if she were off to work and knowing that she would probably never see her again. So, late one night when she couldn't sleep, she was sitting in the kitchen with a cup of tea when her mother, all concerned, joined her. Lizzy blurted out the whole thing and her mother was shocked. Lizzy's mother begged her daughter to let her wake her dad and tell him. 'If he knew you two were so serious about this that you would elope, he will accept it.'

After some persuasion Lizzy agreed. But her father went NUTS! He screamed and vowed to not just kill Michael but to hang, draw and quarter him. Then he calmed down. Once calm, he implored Lizzy to stay and get married in Dublin.

Lizzy went and told Michael what had happened, the two men shook hands and they agreed not to elope. Michael now went and sold the tickets, which were two train tickets to Queenstown in Cork, and two tickets to travel from Queenstown to the USA on a beautiful new ship named the *Titanic*. He sold the tickets to a police officer who bought them for a honeymoon trip. The police officer survived the disaster, but his wife passed away. Fast-forward forty-six years and this same man, now a high-ranking officer, helped my mother get the formation of the women's police force across the line.

A deadly night

16 October 1920. Manor Street in Dublin can be a busy thoroughfare, but not tonight. Firstly it was 2 a.m. and secondly there was a curfew on Dublin due to the 'troubles'.

The locals took the curfew seriously as the British militia, known as the Black and Tans, terrified them. The Black and Tans were made up of British gangsters and thugs, or sometimes prisoners that were given the choice to serve time or serve in the militia for Britain in Ireland. They got their name from their uniforms or, should I say, non-uniforms. When these men arrived in Dublin, they went to a warehouse on the docks to be kitted out. There they found heaps of uniforms of both the army and the police all jumbled together.

The men just picked whatever fitted them, be it army or police. So some had police trousers and an army top or the other way round, thus 'black and tan'.

Back to the story . . . The quiet of the night was broken by the screech of an army truck pulling up outside of number 83 Manor Street, a small hardware shop. Soldiers emerged from the truck and banged on the door. It was opened by my grandfather, Peter O'Carroll. The soldiers demanded to know where Peter's three elder sons were, the sons being volunteers in the Irish Republican Brotherhood.

Peter, who was himself secretly an intelligence officer with the IRB, shrugged and said he didn't know. The sons were actually upstairs in bed, but the soldiers did not search the house, only said they would be back later and that if he didn't know by then, he would be arrested. The soldiers didn't search because the only reason they called was to ascertain if Peter himself were home.

An hour later a civilian car pulled up at the shop. Four MI6 types emerged from the car. A stocky man led the way. He limped slightly because of his wooden leg. He had been sent from Britain for the sole purpose of assassinating my grandfather. They banged on the door and again my grandfather opened it.

This time he was not alone. He held the hand of his nine-year-old youngest son. Without any talk the one-legged man pulled out a .22 pistol and shot my grandfather in the head. He then shot the boy. Then he got back in the car and drove off.

Nobody would come out of their homes for fear of getting shot, so the bodies of my grandfather and his young son lay half in, half out of the doorway to the street for over an hour. It was a journalist who was coming from a late shift and had a curfew pass that came upon them on his way home. He quickly realized that Peter was dead, but the boy still had a slight pulse. He scooped him up in his arms and carried him to the Richmond Hospital, which thankfully was just a few hundred yards away.

Once the boy was being seen to, the journalist made his way home, arriving just in time to have breakfast with his family. He recounted the story to his wife and his seven-year-old daughter, who was particularly taken with it.

So the coincidence? Thirty-five years later that seven-year-old girl became my mother, and the nine-year-old in the hospital?

He became my dad.

Johnny Seven

It was Christmas 1965. The first Christmas following my father passing. I was ten years old. Of course I still believed in Santa Claus. I still do now.

On the run-up to every Christmas my friends and I would be trying to pick the right thing to ask from Santa. Various old canards would be trotted out. Meccano? Airfix? Or if you were rich like the Matthews (I'll come to them later), maybe Scalextric! All the speculation ended one night just before the start of *The Late Late Show* on television. There was an advert. It was for the most amazing thing that any boy could have . . . a Johnny Seven.

The Johnny Seven was a rifle, but not JUST a rifle; it was a pistol, grenade launcher, rocket launcher and, in fact, as its name suggests, it did seven different things. The following day every kid on my street wanted a Johnny Seven and so did I. Actually I had never wanted anything more, *ever*, than I wanted that Johnny Seven. I wrote my letter to Santa and very clearly wrote in all capital letters 'JOHNNY SEVEN'. I had no idea how much it cost; cost wasn't a factor when you were talking to Santa Claus. I also had no idea that we were poor.

On Christmas Eve I could barely sleep. But I did. I woke so fucking excited. I crept downstairs. The light was off in the front room, but the room was lit with all colours and had never looked more magical. I went to the chair where my stuff would be, and it wasn't. I don't mean my stuff wasn't there; my Johnny Seven wasn't there. Instead, there was a torch that changed colours and two silver Lone Star pistols and red holsters, a frilled cowboy hat with a foiled piece of paper stuck on the front that read 'Sheriff' and a plastic pin-on badge confirming that I was the sheriff.

My heart sank, though I knew enough to pretend to be delighted just in case Santa Claus was still watching – you never know with Santa, or as I referred to him 'fat fucker'. It was still dark as I made my way down to eight o'clock mass. In the church I was surrounded by Johnny Sevens.

My brother Micháel nudged me and whispered, 'You're the only sheriff here.'

I stared daggers at him. 'Fuck off,' I thought I whispered back, but I'm not great at whispering. The hand of one of the church clerks grabbed my collar and dragged me out of the church.

But you know what? Santa Claus works in many ways. About ten days later it was back to school. I got my first bus, the number 40, to Hart's Corner and made the ten-minute walk towards St Peter's church where I would get my second bus. As I turned round Doyle's Corner I could clearly see there was something going on up at my next bus stop. There were three fire engines and the road was half blocked. I now ran to see what the story was.

The fire engines' hoses were all leading down a narrow lane, so I followed them and when I emerged at the other end there were the burnt ruins of what I'm sure was a warehouse. I wandered around the building, the horrible smell of watered burnt wood choking me. Then I saw it. I could not believe my eyes. A pallet – the stuff on it was half burned but some of it was unharmed. A pallet full of Johnny Sevens. I could hardly speak. I inched across the road, just staring at them.

From behind me a voice boomed. 'Son?'

I jumped with fright. It was a big burly fireman. 'Should you not be in school?' he asked.

'I'm just on my way now,' I answered, and went back to staring.

The fireman poked me in the shoulder. 'Go on, son. Help yourself.'

I couldn't believe it. I ran to the pallet and pulled a box out from near the bottom where they were OK. As I came back towards the fireman I was crying. 'Are you OK, son?'

I nodded and just said, 'Thank you so much.'

He smiled. 'You can take a couple if you want?' he offered.

I shook my head. 'No, thanks. This'll do.'

I did not go to school. I went straight home and had an entire day with just me and Johnny Seven.

But again, this is not the coincidence. I promise you'll find it later in the book.

2

My mother should never have been elected to the Irish parliament.

Maureen McHugh began her adulthood as a novice nun in Gortnor Abbey in Galway. She got a BA degree from Galway University. Then, one weekend, on a visit back to her home in Dublin, Sister Maureen attended a local dance where she met my father, Gerry O'Carroll. He was a wonderful dancer and my mother *loved* to dance. In the following months she began to doubt her vocation. To the great surprise and shame of her parents, shortly after my mother renounced her vows and returned to civilian life and home. At that time the only thing worse than not having a family member in the Church was to have one that had been in and got out.

Nevertheless, Maureen carried on with life (and with Gerry – take that whatever way you like) and became a teacher of languages, in particular Latin. This is when her first battle arrived.

On 14 July 1936 Gerry and Maureen married and my mother was fired. You see, at that time in Ireland a married woman could not hold a civil service or teaching position, which is why most people of my generation remember being taught by either a nun, a spinster or a man. Well, my mother wasn't having this. So she pushed the Teachers' Union to force the government to abandon this practice and in the process was very outspoken about it. This captured the attention of the press, and she was very adept at getting column inches.

Maybe it was to keep her quiet, but for whatever reason she found herself appointed to the Lower Prices Council, the consumer protection agency of the time. Here again she excelled at drawing attention to price gouging . . . and herself. So it was that in the upcoming election of 1954 the Labour Party, of which she was a member, had a bright idea.

We have PR voting in Ireland, proportional representation. The way this works is that say the number of votes in a constituency is 50,000 and there are three seats, then the 50,000 is divided by three and one is added, so in this case the quota would be about 16,667. Let's say there are nine candidates for three seats. When the first votes are counted, if none of the candidates have reached the quota, then the one that received the least votes is eliminated. Their votes are now distributed and on and on until there are only three left. The distribution is done on the basis of who the eliminated candidates voters picked as their second choice, then third, fourth, fifth and so on.

So here was the plan. For the Dublin North Central constituency Labour wanted Mickey Mullen to be elected. A stalwart of the cinema branch of the Irish Transport and General Workers' Union (ITGWU), and truly a great man. The plan was to run Maureen along with Mickey, so the billboards would read *Vote Mickey Mullen and Maureen O'Carroll 1 and 2*. The belief was that my mother would get the housewives' vote and that when she was eliminated her votes would pass to Mickey and he would get over the line. My mother was aware of the plan and was delighted to take the hit. She adored Mickey and truly believed he was the man for the job. She campaigned well and they both pressed a lot of flesh. Then came election day . . .

OK, here's the thing. I am a scriptwriter. So if you will bear with me, I am going to write the election stuff as a script. I hope it fills in the colour for you.

ELECTION DAY IN DUBLIN
The polls, which are held in every local school in Ireland, are busy. Maureen O'Carroll, a candidate for the Labour Party, is outside the polling station, far enough from the entrance to be legal, handing out flyers and shaking hands with voters as they make their way to the polling station.

EXT. POLLING STATION AT AUGHRIM STREET - DAY
Maureen is tired. It has been a hard-fought campaign and she had little sleep last night. A woman pushing a pram with a baby in passes Maureen. Maureen drops a flyer into the pram.

MAUREEN
Vote Labour one and two.

WOMAN
Fuck off, you and your flyers, missus.
The woman crunches up the flyer and throws it on the ground.

MAUREEN (*POINTING*)
There is a waste bin just there.

WOMAN

What are you running for? Fucking litter warden? It's your flyer, not mine, ya brasser*.

The woman pushes the pram away and Maureen kinda thinks she won't get that vote. Maureen looks at her watch. Polls close in thirty minutes. She gives a long exhale of relief.

INT. A HOUSE IN MANOR STREET, DUBLIN – CONTINUOUS

Gerry O'Carroll has been busy since his arrival home from his cabinetmaker's job. He had cycled the three miles from his workplace and carried the bicycle on his shoulder through the house past his eight children, some of whom were doing homework and some of whom were just playing. Out back, he leaned the cycle against the outside toilet and locked it. He then cooked dinner, fed the brood, got them washed and put to bed. He then sat in his chair and clicked the radio on as he polished the sixteen shoes that would be worn the next morning.

For half an hour he relaxed, listening to the news and sports on the radio. Then, after a quick glance at his watch,

---

* *Brasser* is slang for prostitute.

he rose and went out back again where he got the large tin baby bath. He half filled it with water and placed it on the stove where it covered two gas jets. He lit the jets and waited for the water to heat. He glanced again at his watch and now lit the back gas, placing the kettle on it. The kettle had just boiled when he heard the front door open. He smiled to himself at the accuracy of his timing as he poured the boiling water over the tea in the teapot.

CUT TO:

THE SITTING ROOM

MAUREEN
I'm home, Gerry.
She flops into her chair. She is exhausted.
Gerry enters with a steaming mug of tea, places it on the side table beside the ashtray. He leans over and kisses her. Just a peck.

GERRY
Tired?
Gerry is a man of few words. Very few. When he was just a child, he had witnessed his father being assassinated and indeed has been shot and left for dead himself. From that day on Gerry spoke with a pronounced stammer. He found

*it less stressful to speak as little as
possible.*

MAUREEN
I'm exhausted.
Gerry exits to the kitchen.

MAUREEN (CONT'D, *CALLING*)
It's not looking good for Mickey. Most of
the voters couldn't give a shit who wins
as long as they make some effort to make
things better.
*Gerry arrives back in the room, now
carrying the tin bath, which he places at
Maureen's feet. He has a box of Epsom
salts nearby and he begins to pour them
into the bath as he stirs it with his
hand.*

MAUREEN (CONT'D)
I just saw Mickey briefly at the
polling station in Phibsboro. He
looked just as tired as I am. But he
kept up the smile and the handshaking.
He's a good man.

GERRY
He . . . eh, eh, is.
*Gerry now puts his two hands up Maureen's
skirt to undo her suspender clips.*

MAUREEN
Hey, I don't need your vote that badly.

*They both laugh as Gerry slides off her
nylon stockings. He lifts Maureen's feet
and places them into the bath and kneels.
He begins to massage her tired feet.*

> MAUREEN (CONT'D)
> I don't think I did enough to get my
> deposit back.

*Maureen has had to pay a ten-pound
deposit to put her name on the ballot,
which she borrowed from Gerry.*

> MAUREEN (CONT'D)
> I don't know how I'm going
> to pay you back.

Gerry looks up at her and smiles.

> GERRY
> I'll th-th-think of some-something!

*He winks and Maureen giggles like a young
teenager.*

INT. GERRY'S WORKPLACE - NEXT DAY
The radio beside Gerry is playing
classical music.

Gerry has been working on a roll-top
desk all day. He prides himself that every
inch of it is handmade by him and that
not one nail or screw was used. He is a
true cabinetmaker. He has French polished
and sanded the desk at least eight times
and it shines like a tanned mirror.

Gerry's boss approaches him.

BOSS

Lovely job, Gerry. The customer will be
very happy.

The boss runs his hand over the desk.

BOSS (CONT'D)

Beautiful, just beautiful. I hear the
radio on there. Any news yet?

*Gerry looks at his boss, a puzzled look
on his face.*

BOSS (CONT'D)

The election. Any word on Maureen?

*Gerry has become so absorbed in the work
that he has forgotten all about the
'count'. He runs to the yard, straddles
his bike and takes off in the direction
of Bolton Street College where the count
is taking place.*

*When he arrives at the college, he
locks his bike to the railings and makes
his way up the steps. At the top he is
stopped by a large Garda.*

GARDA

Where do you think you're going?

*Gerry stands there, his overalls dirty,
sawdust in his ginger hair, unshaved, and
now has to speak.*

GERRY

I-I'm just che-checking.
My wi-wife is a can-can-di-di-date.

The Garda looks him up and down.

> GARDA
> Is that right now?

Gerry nods.

> GARDA (CONT'D)
> And who would she be?

> GERRY
> Mau-Maureen O . . . O'Carroll.

The Garda smiles.

> GARDA
> Is that right now?
> Tell me, do you own a suit?

*Gerry does. It is taken out every Sunday
for mass, and as soon as he gets back is
put back in the wardrobe again.*

> GERRY
> I-I do.

> GARDA
> Well, now, why don't you go home and put
> it on? Your wife is going to be elected
> in about an hour.

*Gerry cycles home as fast as he can.
The tears stream across his face.*

Well, as he was massaging Maureen's feet that polling night, the wink that Gerry gave Maureen had a whole lot of meaning to it. She didn't have to pay back his deposit, but they did celebrate and the result of their 'celebrations' arrived on 17 September the following year, 1955. It was an incredibly beautiful baby that they named Brendan Desmond Jarleth Francis O'Carroll.

It was me.

3

It's true. Everyone can remember a year that they would rather forget. I'll bet you can recite one. A year when it seemed everything went wrong, or things happened around you that you had no control of? When no matter how hard you tried to be happy, life seemed to conspire against you? Unlike King Midas for whom everything he touched turned to gold, everything you touched seemed to turn to shit. I have had a few. Yet as bad as they were, something seemed to come out of them. A seed maybe or a growth? I don't know exactly how to explain it, but I know that after each one of those damned years my life took a huge leap and I seemed to grow a little more.

The first one, the first I remember anyway, was 1965. As the world moved into that year, I was nine years old. I was attending St Gabriel's National School on Oxmantown Road.

In 1955, when I was born, we had lived in Kirwan Street Cottages, just off Manor Street where my mother and father had grown up. It was a two-bedroomed artisan home where the twelve of us lived. I was just a baby and have no memory of it. Once Mammy had been elected to the Dáil life got better, and my parents were able to buy a four-bedroomed house on Ballymun Avenue. Four years later, in 1959, Mammy lost her seat and they couldn't afford the mortgage, so we then moved to a corporation (council) house in Finglas West. This is where I grew up. Casement Grove, Finglas West, Dublin 11.

To get to St Gabriel's from my home in Finglas I had to get

two buses, walking about two miles between them, and it would take me an hour to get there. There were three schools within a half-mile of my home. But I ended up in St Gabriel's, an hour away. So why was that? Well, when we first got to Finglas four of my siblings, Éilish, Fiona, Finbar and Micháel were all attending. They were too close to finishing primary to move them, so it made sense to let them finish it there. But someone had to take *me* to school – Fiona obviously – so I was enrolled there and when they all left it was just me.

I loved living on Casement Grove. I loved living in Finglas. I will write more on Casement Grove later, but for now I want to get back to 1965.

My father, Gerard, or Gerry as my mam called him, was not a tactile person. I remember a time just after Granny, my mam's mammy, died – I think it was the night of her funeral in 1965. It was late and I was coming out of the toilet into the back hall. It was dark but the light was on in the front hall and Daddy was hugging Mammy as she wept about the loss of her mother. He was hugging her tightly and saying, 'There, there, there.' When he saw me standing in the back hall, he pushed Mammy away from him and grumbled, 'What are you doing awake? Get up them stairs to bed.'

I have no memory of ever getting a hug from him. No memory of him ever wiping my tears away. Nothing. As I get older, I am looking more and more like him, but my children will never say that I didn't hug them. I do, at every opportunity.

In 1965 I knew he was sick. He had been in and out of hospital a lot. This had the whole house disrupted as the only income my mother had was from her working children and the Canadian dollars that came from Fiona. I was having a hard time in school. For some reason we had a series of 'temp' teachers. I say 'for some reason' but I suppose it was the school. I went back to St Gabriel's school on a visit a few years ago and it is now a modern, clean, brilliant place of learning. But back in 1965 it was a hellhole. Teachers did not *come* to St Gabriel's; they ended up there. Some of them were the most sadistic and angry people I have ever met.

Coming up to the summer break, the teacher we had then called me up to the front of the class and accused me of something I had not done. I protested and was steadfast in my innocence (mainly because I knew who was guilty), but he was adamant that it was me and my protests only angered him more. He roared at me to put my hand out. The going punishment was one whack of his bamboo cane on each hand. (I am sick now, thinking back, that there was a teachers' store in Dublin that sold these canes whose only function was to beat children.) I put out my hand and he lashed the cane across my palm. The sting shot up my arm and for a second I was dizzy. I stretched out my other arm and opened my hand. WHACK, this one was even harder, and my arm shot down to my side. With my hands now tucked under my armpits I turned to go back to my desk.

'Hey,' he screamed. 'Get back here. I'm not finished with you yet.'

I wasn't sure what he meant. Not finished? Gingerly I made my way back to where I'd been standing.

'Hand out,' he barked.

'But, sir?' I mumbled.

He grabbed my arm and pulled it from my armpit. 'HAND OUT.' He was mad now.

So was I. I stared right into his eyes as I slowly uncurled my hand. To this day I can remember my thoughts as clear as if it were today. *You will not make me cry.* I said it with my eyes and I said it with my body, which now stood straight and stiff and defiant.

He whacked each hand two more times. I didn't cry. He had caned me, but I had beaten *him*. I won. Although my hands were numb after the first two slaps and I had barely felt the others, the pain that followed lasted over a week. I couldn't hold a pencil. My mother asked me why my hands were sore. I told her, and like millions of mothers all over Ireland back then her answer was 'You must have deserved it.'

The summer break came at last. I don't want to do the old-man shit, but the days were sunnier and the air was cleaner. It was a fabulous summer. My best friends, Jimmy Matthews and John Breen, and I had a wonderful time roaming the fields, kicking footballs on the streets and staying out late and sitting under the lamp posts telling stories. It was a dream.

The heist when we did it was wrong right from the start.

The very first supermarket in Dublin's suburbs was opened in Finglas. Superquinn's supermarket was a revelation. It was the brainchild of Fergal Quinn, who had returned from America with a plan to copy the supermarkets there. It was a huge success, and he opened more branches over the years. But he never forgot Finglas and twenty years later he wrote about the change he had brought to Finglas and indeed Ireland in an article entitled 'From Bread and Jam to Avocado Pears'. Myself, Jimmy and John loved going down to Superquinn's for errands for our mothers or neighbours. I know it's hard to believe but up to this point all stores kept goods behind a counter, so I can't overstate the amazement of being able to touch stuff before you bought it. We didn't know what it was called then but we began shoplifting.

We were caught. I was obviously the worst thief in the world. I had a small roll of Sellotape, two Oxo cubes and a bicycle lock. I have no idea why I took those. I had nothing to tape, no food to season and certainly no bicycle. Whether it was to make an example of me or what, I don't know, but the Garda were called and we were spoken to very harshly, then our names and addresses were given and we were allowed to go. I thought that was the end of it. It wasn't.

As the summer moved on my daddy was again back in hospital, but to be honest he had been so detached from my life that I barely missed him. Mammy had now set up a home for abused women and children and spent most of her time there, so I had a lot of freedom. But September was coming and on the Monday of the second week in September I was due to go back to the hellhole school. I was dreading it. So you can imagine my delight when without reason Mammy said I wasn't going back 'yet'. Instead, I was sent to stay with my Aunt Florrie, my favourite aunt.

Aunt Florrie lived just two minutes from St Gabriel's, so in the evenings I saw lots of my classmates. The latest news was that the class had yet another new teacher. But so far he seemed OK, in that the boys told me that he had not even taken the cane to any kids yet.

By the time my birthday came on the seventeenth I still had not been back to school. That morning my mammy picked me up from Aunt Florrie's. On the bus she filled me in on what my birthday 'day' was going to entail. We would visit my daddy in hospital, we would go to Bewley's café for morning coffee and then she was going to take me to an amusement arcade. It was a cracking day's plan and I was so excited.

We walked down to Finglas village where we got a number 34 bus. The bus took us to the Richmond Hospital. My mother pointed out the place outside the hospital where my father's elder brothers had set up and manned the barricade in the Easter Rising of 1916. They had eventually been overrun by the British forces, captured and sent to Frongoch prison camp in Wales. We climbed up the red-stone steps of the hospital. My daddy had been there for a couple of months by this time. I say 'this time' because he had been in and out of hospital a few times over the previous few years. Amazingly the Richmond Hospital was the very same hospital that my daddy had been taken to when he had been shot as a young boy.

I didn't like the place. It was dark and a bit gloomy. I didn't go into the ward. Mammy sat me on a bench in the corridor and she went in. A few minutes later they both emerged. My da was wearing a tartan dressing gown. He had his hands in the pockets and a Carroll's Number One cigarette hanging from his toothless mouth. (He wouldn't wear false teeth.) He sat down beside me and took his hand from his pocket. He had his Ronson lighter in his hand. It was a silver one and looked like a rocket. It was a Christmas present from my sister Fiona. He lit the cig, took a drag and blew out the smoke. 'So, how are you getting on in school?' he asked.

I looked at Mammy, and her eyes said 'lie'. So I did. 'Great. I love it.'

He patted my head. 'Good man.' I felt so strange. He took his other hand from the pocket and handed me two shining silver half-crowns. I was thrilled. 'What are you going to do with that now?' he asked.

I didn't even have to think about it. 'I'm going to buy two pigeons.' I wanted to keep pigeons like so many boys in Finglas did.

'Really?' He sounded surprised. 'Well, I'll tell you what. When I get out of here, I'll build you the best pigeon loft in Finglas.' I was thrilled, because I knew he could. He was an amazing woodworker. I really would have a pigeon loft that was the envy of every boy in Finglas.

Mammy smiled and shooed me towards the door. 'Go on, I'll follow you down.'

I left and stood outside, in my mind designing what was

going to be the best pigeon loft in Finglas. Mammy joined me after about twenty minutes and we went to Bewley's.

Let me describe Bewley's café.

Every table had a crisp tablecloth. The waitresses all dressed like maids you would see in a period TV series on BBC. And the smell of coffee . . . Oh, that smell. To this day nothing raises the hair on the back of my neck like that smell.

There's something else I want to drop in here. Growing up I had my own knife, fork, teaspoon, cup and saucer, dessert spoon and plate. They *were* mine. Each of them had *BOC* either engraved on them or printed on them. It wasn't until my first visit to **B**ewley's **O**riental **C**afé that I realized that my mammy had stolen them there. I didn't care.

We sat at our table. I call it 'our table' because it was the table we always sat at. Well, when I say 'always', I had only been there three times before. On my seventh, eighth and ninth birthdays. My birthday was the only day I was allowed a cup of coffee. I should tell you right now that I love – no, adore – chocolate eclairs. To this day I cannot pass them. Well, here's the thing. When you ordered coffee and cakes in Bewley's they would bring a three-tiered cake stand with two of every pastry they had, including two eclairs, which on my birthday I was allowed to devour.

My mother gave the pretty waitress our order. Within minutes the frothy coffee had arrived, and along with it the waitress brought the cake stand. As usual it had two of each pastry. I waited for the nod from Mammy and slowly devoured, with relish, both chocolate eclairs. When I had finished the last morsel my mammy giggled at me licking my lips, and pointed out the chocolate on the tip of my nose. 'Come here,' she said. Then she did the thing I hated most, especially in public. She took out her handkerchief, spat on it, and roughly wiped my face down with it. I pulled away and she laughed. As she put her hanky away, she asked, 'Are you looking forward to the amusements?'

I smiled. 'Sure, but not as much as I'm looking forward to THE BEST PIGEON LOFT IN FINGLAS.' I said it out loud too. I wanted everyone in Bewley's Oriental Café to know.

Mammy sipped her coffee, looking at me over the rim of her diamanté glasses. 'Yeh, pigeon loft,' she said quietly.

Daddy died a week later.

It was a Saturday night. It was raining so my cousins and I were all sitting in watching TV. Aunt Florrie's front door was very busy that evening. I keep referring to it as being Aunt Florrie's, but it was actually her husband, Uncle Sean, that was my mother's brother, but he was rarely there so I will just stick with Florrie.

There were lots of callers that evening, including my mammy's sister Auntie Éilish and her husband Uncle Bill. Uncle Bill was the only relative I knew that had a car. A light blue VW Beetle. The odd thing about the callers was that nobody came in. All conversations were held either outside on the pavement or in the 'hallway' of Aunt Florrie's house, which I swear to you was no bigger than a phone box. I went to bed when told to and next morning I was told that Uncle Sean and Aunt Florrie would take me to mass and afterwards that Uncle Bill and Auntie Éilish would take me home to Finglas. I was thrilled. I hadn't seen my mother since my birthday the previous week. During the mass I heard my daddy's name being read from the altar. 'Hear that, Aunt Florrie? They're praying for me daddy to get better.' Aunt Florrie squeezed my hand and smiled.

On the way to Finglas in Uncle Bill's car, I had the back

seat all to myself and slid from side to side. 'Sit the fuck easy, yeh fidget,' Uncle Bill said to the rear-view mirror.

It was when I saw his eyes in the mirror looking at me that I realized it was aimed at me. Auntie Éilish slapped him on the shoulder with the back of her hand. 'Bill,' was all she said. His eyes squinted at me in the mirror and I stopped sliding.

On the way Uncle Bill stopped for petrol at a Shell garage. I knew from television adverts that Shell was doing a promotion that if you bought £5 of petrol or more you got a free key ring. I watched as the attendant pumped the petrol, the numbers rolling in the pump window. When it went to £4.17.6 (google it), I was transfixed by the numbers. The pump started to slow down and slowly made it to £5. 'Yes!' I exclaimed.

Auntie Éilish got a start. 'What is that about, Brendan?'

I leaned between the two front seats. 'Uncle Bill just got enough to get a free key ring.' Bill Monaghan, my Uncle Bill, was a big man. One look and you would not dream of messing with him.

Auntie Éilish said flatly, 'Ask for the key ring, Bill.'

Bill stared at her for a couple of seconds. 'Key ring me arse.' He waved her off.

Auntie Éilish slapped his shoulder with the back of her hand again. 'Get the key ring!' Uncle Bill was big, but Auntie Éilish was the boss.

Uncle Bill turned the chrome window handle and the window rolled down about six inches. He passed the five-pound note through the gap and asked, 'I think I get a key ring?' The young attendant shook his head. 'Nah, you have to get *over* five pounds. You just made it to the five pounds.' It was as if the young man hadn't even spoken. Uncle Bill just rolled the window down another inch. 'Get me a fucking key ring.'

I played with the key ring all the way to our house. When we pulled up, I noticed many of the neighbours about but when they saw me they kinda bowed their head or looked away from me. I swear, despite all the signs, I had not got a clue what was happening. There was a small card pinned to the front door; it was outlined in black. I couldn't read what was written on it. As I went into the hall, I saw that the beautiful mirror my dad had hand-carved was now turned in to the wall and I could see into the sitting room, where although it was not yet midday the curtains were closed.

I went into the room. Mammy was sitting on the end of the sofa. She was dressed all in black and had a black mantilla over her perm-styled hair. She saw me. 'Brendan, darling.' She opened her arms wide, and I hugged her. Her hug was tight and a little longer than usual. When she released me, she took me by both shoulders and in a soft voice said, 'Daddy is gone to Heaven.'

I couldn't believe it. A tear ran down my face. I could barely speak at first, but I sobbed and then: 'So no pigeon loft then?'

My Auntie Éilish smiled and, first leading me away from my mam, she picked me up and hugged me. 'Let's give your mammy some space,' she whispered in my ear. I loved Auntie Éilish. She was warm, kind and gregarious, and within six months she too had passed away. I couldn't believe it when Mammy told me. 'Why is everybody leaving me?' I asked. Mammy just hugged me.

My daddy was buried on 28 September. I was not allowed to attend as apparently I was too young. I wasn't. On the twenty-ninth I released the two pigeons I had bought with my daddy's birthday gift. They flew into the blue sky and began circling the house. They then landed on the roof. I heard them cooing to each other. I think they were saying, 'This place is a fucking dump.' Because they took off towards the Dublin Mountains and I never saw them or Daddy again.

*

I am often asked when my 'comedy' started. When did I become a 'joker?' Until recently, I would give different answers because I couldn't really remember. It wasn't because I was bullied; I wasn't. It wasn't because I was shy for sure. It's only when I began reliving moments in my life for this book that a possible answer came to me.

It was about two weeks after Daddy died. Our toilet was downstairs. I was in bed one night when I needed a pee. I quietly made my way down the stairs and in the dark did my pee, nearly all in the bowl. As I was sneaking back up the stairs, I could see under her door that Mammy's light was still on. She loved to read in bed, so I presumed that she was reading. But as I got closer, I heard her crying. Sobbing. I sat on the stairs and listened, quietly crying myself. I now remember that sitting on those stairs I decided that my job, for the rest of my days, was to make Mammy laugh. I think I succeeded ninety-nine per cent of the time.

They say that for every yin there is a yang. What by that September of 1965 had seemed like an appalling year, having lost Granny and then Daddy, was to take an amazing turn – in fact, more than one. This was the year I got my Johnny Seven *after* Christmas.

The Monday following my daddy's funeral I was sent back to school. I wasn't keen, and I was terrified of meeting the new teacher. I sat with the class waiting for my first glimpse of this new horrible person to arrive. Then in walked this young, maybe twenty-something, man with horn-rimmed glasses. I hadn't expected him to look like *that*. I didn't expect him to be smiling like he was delighted to be there in St Gabriel's. And I certainly didn't expect him to change my life.

But he did.

4

Apparently Billy Flood had been in training to be a Christian brother. They are kind of like a male nun. Chastity and a life dedicated to the Lord and the education of young boys was their thing. De La Salle Brothers, many of them. Deranged torturers, most of them. Ask any man who has been taught by them and you will hear some horror stories. They did not have the title of 'Father'; instead they were called 'Brother' and were referred to as Christian brothers.

Billy Flood must have decided that this life was not for him. So he instead became a layman teacher. He was very young, and I have no idea how he ended up in our school because the rest of our teachers were on their last legs.

Billy Flood's first lesson stunned me.

'OK,' he began with a huge smile. He pulled from his inside pocket a tuning fork, tapped it on the desk and touched the point of it to the wood. It hummed musically. I thought it was a magic trick. He did it again and now he joined in by humming with it, matching the fork's hum perfectly.

'OK, boys, everyone hum like the tuning fork.' He tapped it again. 'Go,' he ordered.

A very low sporadic hum came from the desks. Not me. I hummed as loud as he did. He pointed at me. 'Well done, O'Carroll.' No teacher had ever before said 'Well done, O'Carroll'. I beamed and he had me. 'Now, come on, all of you.' He did it again. This time everybody hummed, some melodically, some sounding like a cheap Honda 50 motorbike burning oil.

He then broke us into three groups; there were forty-four boys in the class, so it was fifteen, fifteen and fourteen. He soon had us singing 'Three Blind Mice'. He got the first group to start and had the second group start after the first group had sung the first line, 'Three blind mice', and the third group to start when the second group had sung that line. When we had finished, we all laughed. We were amazing.

This was not school as I knew it. This was fun. This was relaxing. All my anxiety left me. Everyone in the class was smiling. Mr Flood smiled too when we finished the song, then he very humbly said, 'Thank you for singing for me, boys.'

We then took out our maths books and started the day with enthusiasm.

Thank you for singing for me? I would do anything for him. This was fourth class. I had Mr Flood for the whole year and every word that came out of his mouth was a drip of gold to me. I couldn't believe that he had stayed and in my prayers every night (yes, I said my prayers at night) I asked God to keep Mr Flood at St Gabriel's Boys' National School.

Obviously our school had very few resources. We had no PE or equipment. We played other schools in GAA, Ireland's national football game. Mr McGrath was in charge of this; he was coach, manager and ball boy. It was an after-school thing so he did it voluntarily. None of us appreciated him. The first time I played for the school Mr McGrath slapped me on the back and said, 'Aha! You are wearing your brother Finbar's jersey.' Finbar had worn this jersey eight years before. I don't think it had been washed since Finbar had worn it. Mr McGrath dreamed of winning a Schools' Cup and he was disappointed every year. The year I played for the team, he was disappointed yet again. Ironically St Gabriel's made it to the final some years after Mr McGrath retired. But he went to the game in Croke Park and had a heart attack during the game and passed away. St Gabriel's went on to win that final and I am often sad when I think that Mr McGrath never got to see them win it.

Anyhow, back to Mr Flood. We had no equipment but Mr Flood did his best to fill the gap. For instance, our 'yard' was entirely enclosed. You could not get out; it was akin to an exercise yard in some of the older prisons. Mr Flood got a local grocer to hang on to his empty onion sacks for him and when he had enough he stitched them together and using two of the long window-opener poles and chalk he made a volleyball court in the yard. We loved it. I swear to you that when I saw my hero Robin Williams in *Dead Poets Society* I was convinced it was Mr Flood's life story.

There was a fair cross-section of kids in our class. The school was flanked by two Irish Army barracks. Arbour Hill Barracks to the south and McKee Barracks to the north. Both barracks had living quarters, so there were more than a few soldiers' kids in the class. The Irish troops were serving in the Congo at the time, so, needless to say, the kids were anxious if not plain scared. Of course we had great names for some of our classmates. One was 'Barreller', as he was a small chubby kid shaped like a barrel. Another had two nick-names. He continuously had mucus dripping from his nose. So in the summer his nickname was 'Number Eleven' and in the winter he was 'Bubbles' for obvious reasons. Then there was 'Buddha' – nothing to do with any religion; he had a stammer. So when the teacher asked him a question he would always reply with 'But, eh, but, eh, but, eh' before he began any answer. Oh, we were cruel.

Mr Flood started a library in the class. It was a cardboard box filled with books he either had or bought himself. Cleverly he put the two toughest troublemakers in charge of it.

They responded very positively to the job, as does anyone you treat with respect. They kept the notes of who had what and you always returned your book if you knew what was good for you. The first book I took out was *Treasure Island*. It took me a long time to read it, but I loved it. Every second time I took out a book from the 'library' it would be *Treasure Island* and I would read it over and over again.

It wasn't just me; Mr Flood had some effect on lots of the kids. But I took every word he spoke as gospel. For example? Well, we were in the middle of class one day and Mr Flood was on a roll, speaking, when he noticed one of the boys chewing gum. 'Are you chewing gum?' he asked the boy.

The boy nodded, expecting to get thrashed. 'Good for you,' Mr Flood said, and finished whatever he had been saying. He went back behind his desk and thought for a moment. Then he began to go off on one of his tangents (which I loved). 'Boys, have any of you ever thought about what it is that measures a life?'

There was silence.

'What I'm saying is, how come some people live to be ninety and yet other people die at forty?'

Silence in the class.

'What measures it?' He put his finger to his lips as if he were thinking.

'It could be blinks. Maybe we are only allowed to blink ten million times and, puff, your time is up?'

Nobody in the class blinked.

'It could be farts!'

We all giggled. Mr Flood now walked down the classroom.

'Maybe you're allowed ten thousand farts? You'd be in trouble, O'Reilly.'

Now we all laughed. Including O'Reilly. Then it came.

46

'What if it's chews?' He now stood beside the boy with the gum but didn't look at him.

'What if –' he paused – 'you're only allowed to have so many chews before your time is up? Wouldn't chewing gum be a killer?' Mr Flood turned and made his way back to his desk. Behind him the boy spat the gum into a piece of paper. Mr Flood then called out, 'Now, where was I?' and the class went on.

Since that day to this I have never had any chewing gum, ever. And when I see people chewing gum, I cringe and feel sad for them. That's the effect Mr Flood had on me.

And I remember just the day before we broke up for the summer break Mr Flood was trying to explain statistics to us. How they can be helpful but sometimes so wrong. He pointed out that if two people were sitting in a room, one earning £10,000, the other earning £2,000, then the average wage in that room would be £6,000, but it wouldn't reflect anything real. We kind of got it. He went on, and I think he was trying to warn us really to be careful over the summer. 'Statistics show that point nine per cent of children die in an accident during summer holidays.' He opened his arms wide. 'So statistically speaking one of you will not be back after the holidays.'

We laughed, but during that summer one of the boys died when he fell off a bus platform as the bus was moving. As I say, Mr Flood's word to me was gospel.

I should have had Mr Flood for three years except for a tiny glitch. Let me start by explaining something that every September baby already knows. Children begin school in what we call in Ireland 'low babies' at four years of age. However, school always begins in the second week in September. So if you, like me, were born on 17 September you can start in September at the end of your third year or the following

47

year when you would be five for all but days of your school year. I started when I was three and became four just days later. But this follows you throughout your schooling. So it was that during the summer holidays after my second year with Mr Flood I was only eleven years old. I was swinging on my gate early one sunny morning and my friends who were all a year older than me came out of their houses at the same time and headed up the road. I asked one of them, John Dunne, where were they going? John told me that they were all going to do an entrance exam for a new secondary school that was just down the road.

'Hang on,' I said, 'I'll go too.' I jumped off the gate.

'You can't – you have to be in sixth class; you're only in fifth class.'

I winked at him. 'They won't know that.' I went into the house, got a pen and ruler, which is what they had been told to bring, and joined the lads. I just wanted to be with my mates. When I got there I filled out the form and sat the exam, which was piss easy. A few weeks later my mother got a letter telling her that I had got in the top ten in the exam and could start in the September.

She was delighted. 'This is fantastic, Brendan. It's close to home. You can cycle there on your bike.'

I was nearly twelve and I *did not* have a bike. 'I don't have a bike, Mammy.'

She smiled. 'I wonder what you're getting for your birthday?'

I whooped.

Having got the place, the problem now was could I actually leave primary at St Gabriel's at eleven years old? Primary school started two weeks before the secondary, so I went back to school at St Gabriel's as normal and on the first day my mother told Mr Flood the situation. His advice was that

I should tell nobody, finish the week and he would just write that I had transferred to another school.

On the Friday of that week only Mr Flood knew I would not be coming back. Neither of us made a big deal of it. He dismissed the class and on the way out of the door he handed me a brown-paper parcel.

I didn't open it until I got on my first bus to home. It was the book. *Treasure Island.* Mr Flood had written inside:

> *Best of luck, Brendan.*
> *'When the young hand took the old book'*
>
> *We stood aside*
> *and our wonder grew,*
> *that such a small head*
> *could hold all he knew.*
>
> *Do great things.*
> *Billy Flood*

I hope I have made him proud and that when he reads this he truly understands how much he means to me.

Mr Flood eventually transferred to a school in Finglas East where he taught Derek Reddin, who now plays Dr Flynn in *Mrs. Brown's Boys.* He then became principal of a school in Portrane where he taught my son-in-law Martin Delany, who plays Mrs. Brown's missionary son Trevor. The world is a village if you are Irish.

5

When my mother lost her seat in the Dáil we apparently could no longer afford the mortgage on the big house in Ballymun. So we had to move. I'm sure it was through Mammy's connections that we were put into a corporation house. We were moved just a few miles to Finglas West. Our new address was 43 Casement Grove, Finglas West, Dublin 11.

It was a satellite suburb, brand new. Finglas had been just a small village north of Dublin city. Very quickly a village that had a population of about 400 in 1955 had a population of about 40,000 when we moved there in 1960. There was no church in Finglas West, although there was a beautiful one, St Canice's, in the village. So they built a temporary church out of corrugated sheets, which gained the obvious name of the 'Tin Church'.

I was just four when we moved there. I have very little memory of my first four years on Ballymun Avenue, except that when I misbehaved Mammy would hang me up on the kitchen door by my pant straps. Of course Fiona, when she would arrive home, would take me down and cuddle me. But I do remember moving to Casement Grove.

On our street the homes were in blocks of six. So you had four terraced homes with a semi-detached at each end. I loved Finglas West, still do. And I just adored living on Casement Grove. On the street the odd numbers were on one side of the street and the evens on the other. Our block went from 37 to 47. Number 37 was the home of the Matthews family. Jim and Anne were the parents and they had three children. Jimmy, who was one of my two best friends, his sister Betty and the youngest, David. Next to them, in number 39, were the Egans. They scared the bejaysus out of me. The family was made up of Mr and Mrs Egan, who looked about a hundred years old, and two adult daughters, Hannah and Eileen. For some reason I was scared of them as they behaved differently to other adults I knew. On reflection I think they were probably autistic. God love them, but nobody knew what that was back then, or if they did they didn't tell the Egans. In number 41, next door to us, were three lovely spinster sisters, the McCormacks. My mother affectionately referred to them as Essie, Bessie and Tessie. My daddy used to do little house repairs for them. Years after he died I went in to fix an electric outlet for them and they stood round me as I did it, commenting.

Essie: 'Great pair of hands.'

Bessie: 'Wonderful tradesman.'

Tessie: 'Just like his father.'

On the other side of our house, which was 43, was number 45. In here lived the Reddins, the most wonderful neighbours anyone could hope to have. Jimmy senior and Nelly were the parents, and they had four kids, Margaret, Jimmy, Philomena and Deirdre when we moved in, and Ann who was born later. Jimmy Reddin senior, or Gem as he was called, was just the kindest, most wonderful man you could want to meet. Both Gem and Nelly were townies. They had lived in the city centre and their heritage was a long line of dealers. Now, when you say 'dealers' in this era, you usually mean drug pushers. They were NOT drug pushers; they were stallholders in one of the market streets in Dublin city centre. I suppose 'inner-city traders' would be a good term for them. Streets like Meath Street, Moore Street, Francis Street or The Hill were alive every day with the chatter of people and the melodious cries of the women traders. They mainly sold second-hand clothes and shoes, but at Halloween they would be our source of fireworks or 'bangers'. At Christmas the stalls would be full of colourful toys. One of my favourites was 'Cheeky Charlie'. This was a small monkey puppet. Christmas was not Christmas until you heard the cry of 'Get the last of your Cheeky Charlies' or 'Wrapping paper, five sheets for a shilling'. These dealers were honest, hardworking people, mostly women, and can trace their lineage back to Molly Malone. It is on these wonderful women that I based Agnes Brown.

For now let's get back to Gem Reddin. Gem was so very good to me, and God knows I didn't deserve it. Along with my brother Micháel we pulled many pranks on him. One I remember in particular was hilarious. Gem had a shop/van that was parked outside his house. It was our local shop for anything from cigarettes to ice cream and it was our hangout spot too. Gem was always very flush and *always* had beautiful cars. A Consul or a Zephyr or the like. Gem was the first person we knew to get a Japanese car, a Honda. Before he got it he would wax lyrical about how the Japanese would take over the car market and tell us that this new Honda he was getting would get fifty miles to the gallon, 'Probably more.' I remember the first day he got the car I was about seventeen and my brother Micháel and I were coming back from our local pub, the Cappagh House. We had gone there after our soccer training and, as we rounded the corner at the top of our road, we saw the Honda in the garden. It was beautiful and shining like a new car is.

In script form, this is what happened.

THE HONDA

EXT. CASEMENT GROVE, FINGLAS – EVENING

Brendan and Micháel stroll slowly on
their way home from the pub. They have
gone there for a shandy after football
training. They speak about the upcoming
game they are to have the following
Sunday against bitter rivals Clapton
United, also based in Finglas.

                    MICHÁEL
          I don't fancy us coming out of
             this game with a result.

                    BRENDAN
          I'll be happy to get out of it
                with both me legs.

*They laugh. They are still laughing as
they round the corner at the top of their
street, Casement Grove. It is Micháel that
sees it first. He stops in his tracks.*

                    MICHÁEL
                   Holy fuck!

*Micháel points down the street to the
garden of their next-door neighbour Jimmy
(Gem) Reddin.*

               MICHÁEL (CONT'D)
          Mr Reddin got the new car,
               the fuckin' Honda.

*Brendan can see it now. A gleaming brand-
new Honda is parked in Mr Reddin's*

garden. He has converted the garden to a
driveway. The closer they get to it, the
more beautiful the car looks. Shining
red. Metallic finish. Glistening chrome.
They stop at the entrance to Mr Reddin's
driveway.

                    MICHÁEL (CONT'D)
              It's beautiful, isn't it?
Brendan is just completely taken by it.

                    BRENDAN
              Gorgeous. I'd love a car
                 like that someday.
Michael laughs.

                    MICHÁEL
         You wish. The bus conductor will
           always know your first name.

                    BRENDAN
                 Fuck you.
They stare in silence for a moment. From
behind them a voice booms.

                    GEM
           What do you think, boys?
              Isn't it beautiful?
They both turn to see Mr Reddin leaning
out of the hatch of the shop/van that he
owns. That van has kept the area in
supplies for years and it kept Gem in
fancy cars for years too.

                    BRENDAN
         It's beautiful, Mr Reddin.
              Fair play to yeh.

                      GEM
         Thanks. Do yous want to have
              a look inside?
*As he finishes this sentence, Mr Reddin
ducks back in through the hatch and
emerges with a set of keys. He tosses the
keys and Brendan catches them. Brendan
and Micháel go to the car. They don't open
it immediately; first they walk round it.*

                   MICHÁEL
         It really is beautiful.

                    BRENDAN
         Yeh. *(Calling to Gem)* What's
              this chrome thing?

                      GEM
         It's an aerial. It pulls up.
         It's an aerial for the radio.

                    BRENDAN
         How much extra was the radio?

                      GEM
         Nothing! It comes with the car.

                    BRENDAN
         Fuck off! You're kidding me?

                       55

                         GEM
          I'm not. It came with the radio.
          And a cassette thing as well.

                       MICHÁEL
               What's a 'cassette'?

                         GEM
         I don't know, but that fucking car has
                one. And built-in seat belts.
          The boys open the car now and look
          inside. If the outside of the car has
          wowed them, the inside is even better.

                       BRENDAN
              Headrests? What are they for?
          Gem shrugs.

                         GEM
          I dunno. Maybe in case you have to
         sleep in the car. You know my Nelly,
                maybe I will some nights.
          The three laugh.

                       MICHÁEL
            Well, you were right, Mr Reddin,
           if they keep giving free stuff like
          radios and cassettes, seat belts and
         that with their cars, the Japanese WILL
               take over the car market.

                    GEM
          And you're looking at about
           forty miles to the gallon.

                  MICHÁEL
          No way! An Austin A40 only
            gets about twenty.

                    GEM
          I'm telling you that car there
               is the future.

          BRENDAN (*CLOSING THE DOOR*)
       Well, long may you drive it, Mr Reddin.

                    GEM
                Thanks, lads.
*The two boys now climb over the garden
fence to their own garden and go into the
house.*

INT. O'CARROLLS' HOUSE – LATER
Brendan wakes with a start. Micháel has
been shaking him to try to wake him up.
Brendan is bleary-eyed.

                  BRENDAN
       Where am I? What the hell, Micko.
                I was asleep.
*Brendan then realizes he is not in bed
but in an armchair by the fire. The TV
broadcast has ended, and a test card is
now displayed.*

                    MICHÁEL
              Do you want tea?

                    BRENDAN
        Yeh, sure. How did that film end?

                    MICHÁEL
      It doesn't matter. We were both asleep
          before it really got started.
    Brendan follows Micháel out to the
    kitchen and sits himself at the kitchen
    table. Micháel is filling the kettle.

               MICHÁEL (CONT'D)
          I have an idea for the craic.

                    BRENDAN
              Yeh? What is it?

                    MICHÁEL
      I saw a thing on the telly that someone
      did to a friend that got a Japanese car.
          I'd love to try it on Mr Reddin.

EXT. MR REDDIN'S DRIVEWAY – MOMENTS LATER
Micháel and Brendan are crouched in the
dark beside the Honda. Brendan is
fiddling with the petrol cap of the car.

                    BRENDAN
            I have it. It's open.
He leans back. Micháel now moves to the
petrol tank with the cap removed. He is

*carrying a one-gallon tin of petrol. The
boys keep it in their shed to fuel the
lawnmower they use to mow lawns in the
area as supplemental income.*

> BRENDAN (CONT'D)
> I hope this doesn't fucking blow up.

*Micháel hasn't removed the cap of the
tin yet.*

> MICHÁEL
> I'll tell you what might reduce
> the chances of that. Put out your
> fucking cigarette.

*Brendan quickly stubs the cigarette out
but keeps the remains of it. It is only
half smoked.*

> BRENDAN
> Sorry.

*Micháel pours the petrol into the Honda's
tank. Brendan replaces the car's petrol
cap and they sneak back to their house.
Over the week, Micháel and Brendan do this
four times.*

EXT. MR REDDIN'S VAN – EVENING
Micháel and Brendan are returning from
the pub yet again, following their post-
training shandy. As they pass Mr
Reddin's shop/van, Gem pops his head
out.

GEM
Sixty!

The two boys stop.

BRENDAN
What's that, Mr Reddin?

GEM
Sixty miles to the gallon. That's what
I'm getting out of the Honda. I kid you
not! Sixty fucking miles to a fucking
gallon.

BRENDAN
Wow, that's amazing. Are you sure?

GEM
Positive, I haven't put petrol
in it all week.

MICHÁEL (*UNDER HIS BREATH*)
We have.

Brendan elbows Micháel.

BRENDAN
That's great, Mr Reddin.
I'm delighted for you.

INT. O'CARROLLS' HOUSE – LATER
Brendan and Micháel are looking out of
the window at Mr Reddin, who is showing
off the Honda to Mr Pimley, another
neighbour.

                        BRENDAN
        I can read his lips . . . Look,
      he's saying 'sixty fucking miles'.
                   We have to stop.
*Micháel nods. He has come to the same
conclusion.*

                        MICHÁEL
       Yeh. Jaysus, I didn't think
           it'd work that good.
*So they stop that night. Never touching
Mr Reddin's tank again. But it got worse.
Every time either Brendan or Micháel
would pass the shop/van Mr Reddin would
have a new number for them.*

EXT. MR REDDIN'S VAN – MONDAY

                          GEM
                   Seventy-five!

EXT. MR REDDIN'S VAN – TUESDAY

                          GEM
                      Ninety.

EXT. MR REDDIN'S VAN – THURSDAY

                          GEM
        I filled it up for the first time
      since I got it today. I'm embarrassed to
        tell you what mileage I got out of it.
Brendan smiles.

                          BRENDAN
                        That's great.

                            GEM
        I phoned the Honda salesman and told him.
         He wouldn't believe me. He asked me to
        bring it back so they can have a look at
          it. I told him to fuck off; it's mine
          now and he's not getting it back. He's
        sending his mechanics up to look at it.
        Brendan goes pale.

                      BRENDAN (*MUMBLES*)
                   Oh, sweet, loving Jesus.

INT. O'CARROLLS' HOUSE – TWO DAYS LATER
Brendan and Micháel are looking out of
the window as two mechanics pore over the
Honda engine. A very proud Gem stands,
hands in pockets, watching them with a
big smile on his face.

                          MICHÁEL
                         Oh fuck.

                          BRENDAN
We can never tell Mr Reddin what we did.
Ever.

We never told Jimmy Reddin, but I'm sure he figured it out.
Back to Casement Grove. The last house on our block
was 47 and housed the O'Briens. A quiet family. I never
knew the parents except as Mr O'Brien or Mrs O'Brien.

                            62

Mind you, if me mam heard me address any of the adults on our road by anything but 'mister' and 'missus', I would get a slap. The O'Brien kids were Peter, David, Janet and Damien. Peter was such a brilliant artist that when he would show us some of his sketches we would be amazed; it was hard to believe that anyone in Finglas had that kind of talent. Many of them were of naked women, which only made sense later in my life when Peter became one of the leading fashion designers in Ireland and the UK. So then that was our block.

My best friends on Casement Grove were Jimmy Matthews from my block and John Breen who lived across the road from me in number 52. We did everything together. We all three of us played for Home Farm FC: Jimmy was a goalkeeper, John was a star player tipped to go on and play professional, and I was an old-fashioned number seven outside right. It took two buses to get to the club for training every Tuesday night, but it was worth it.

When we were all thirteen years old I took up a secret hobby; I didn't even tell John or Jimmy. Knitting. I did get myself into a bit of a pickle at Home Farm trying to keep my secret hobby secret. *The Monkees* had just started on television and in the much-loved series Mike Nesmith wore a woolly hat we all now called a Monkee hat. I decided to knit myself one in the Home Farm team colours: blue and white hoops, with a tassel made from blue and white wool. The first time I wore it to training it was a huge hit with the guys, who all asked, 'Where did you get that?'

I was too embarrassed to say that I had knitted it. 'My mother made it for me,' I lied. I thought I'd got away with it until the next Saturday when we met for our match at our home ground on Mobhi Road. Some of the boys had brought a sixpence with them and gave it to me and asked me to get my mam to make them one. My hands were cramped making those fucking hats.

Jimmy, John and I had been friends from five years old. We attended three different schools. I list them here in order of the standard of education each offered. From the bottom up they were me at St Gabriel's, John at St Peter's in Phibsboro and Jimmy at St Vincent's in Glasnevin. I cannot remember us ever falling out. We three boys were stuck together like glue.

I got myself a nickname, BOCK. If somebody today says, 'Hiya, Bock,' I know they're from Finglas. It's fairly obvious the name came from my initials B. O. C. A bit lazy, I suppose.

I was reasonably popular around our area. But everybody knew John Breen. He was a stunningly handsome boy. If the three of us met three girls, all three of them ignored Jimmy and me and went for John. His talent as a footballer was undisputed and he was an 'A' student. John was one of those rare kids that could excel at whatever he decided to do.

Jimmy Matthews was a whole different kind of boy altogether. Jimmy was quieter than me; most kids were. He was also a cautious boy and would steer clear of trouble. He was much loved by his mam and dad. Although Jimmy's dad, Jim, was a humble truck driver, Jimmy and David always seemed to have the best of everything. They were the first to have Meccano, the first to get Scalextric, Jimmy even had the James Bond Scalextric car that had a pop-up shield on the back window and working headlights. Needless to say, both David and Jimmy got Johnny Sevens for Christmas, as did John.

We had many happy summers and winters. We went on 'adventures' together across the fields beside our home. Catching tadpoles and searching for nests that we would check every now and then until the chicks were born, then we would follow their progress up to their first flight, which was more like a tumble from the nest. We would search for rabbits the way kids today search for a Wi-Fi signal. We had wonderful times.

As that summer of 1966 was coming to an end, I was sent to stay with one of my older sisters in London – 'To keep me out of trouble.' With the pocket money my mother had given me I bought three IR (International Rescue, from *Thunderbirds*) hats down at Walthamstow High Street. One each for Jimmy and John and one for me. I also fell in love with the Willie the lion mascot for the England football team, which went on to win the World Cup that year. When I returned to Ireland I gave Jimmy and John their IR hats and we set out to save the world. We would knock at elderly people's doors, announce ourselves as International Rescue, and offer to run errands for them. Surprisingly they let us. We would cycle to Finglas village, me on a borrowed bike as I didn't have my birthday bike yet. Mammy had made the hire-purchase application and we were waiting with our fingers crossed for credit clearance. International Rescue would cycle down to the pharmacy to fill someone's prescription for them and speed back as if we were carrying lifesaving drugs. But all too soon that summer ended and we all had to go to our first year in our respective secondary schools. Jimmy to the St Vincent's secondary, John to Beneavin College in Finglas East and me to Patrician College.

6

The new secondary school was a ten-minute cycle away on my birthday bike. I would cycle down Kildonan Road past the rent office and Collins's shop, then through the car park of the Church of the Annunciation, where I served as an altar boy quite frequently, as it happened, because many of the priests insisted on saying the mass in Latin, even though English was creeping in. I could serve it in Latin. I'd then lock my bike and leave it in a spot that I could see from various classrooms.

The school was new. It was *really* new. The main school and classrooms were not built yet. Our classrooms were prefabricated huts. But it still had an elegance of a sort. For the first time I had to wear a uniform. In St Gabriel's I don't think they would have cared if you arrived naked. On that first day I looked amazing. Crisp white shirt, school tie, grey trousers and a navy blazer with the school crest on it. If memory serves me the crest was a mitre, a harp and a sprig of shamrock. Mammy told me that the school had helped her with the finance for the uniform and the books. I don't know how that worked; Mammy called it a scholarship. For all I know it could have all been stolen. Or maybe they were bought by my Uncle Vincent and Uncle Paul? Let me explain who they are.

They were two men from a charity called St Vincent de Paul. They called virtually every Friday night to my mother. I now know that they were helping Mammy pay electricity bills, gas bills and even rent. They would always give her a bag of broken chocolate, which she would pass on to me telling me that it was from my Uncle Vincent and Uncle Paul. So that's who they were. She told me when I was older who they were. We could not have lived without the help given by the Vincent de Paul. I vowed that if ever I could afford it, I would make sure to give back to them so they could help people just like my mammy. I have kept my promise.

Back to the school. The school was the Patrician Brothers School in Finglas. It was a good school, but I was a piss-poor student. Looking back on it, I think I was just too young, too immature, to understand that the school was offering me an education and that it was up to me whether or not I took advantage of it. I didn't. I remember only Brother Cormack and Brother Fideles. I think I had Cormack for Irish and maths, and I'm certain I had Fideles for Latin. My mammy had taught Latin when she was teaching, so she loved Brother Fideles. Me? Not so much.

I struggled through that first year and lost interest half-way through. I was quite surprised that I managed to pass the end-of-term exams. Mind you, I wasn't as surprised as my teachers were. We broke for summer, and I was free . . . for now.

7

As lucky as I was to have passed the end-of-term exams with all Cs, it still made Mammy very happy. She always believed that I was a genius anyway. I'm serious. I can remember her sitting me up on the kitchen table when I was only five years old, and when she finished tying my shoelaces she would pinch my cheek very gently and, looking into my eyes, she would say, 'You are a genius; you can be anything you want to be. All you have to do is keep working hard.' I loved the first part – not so much the second.

Anyway, as it turned out, my first week off was also Mammy's week off. That first morning Mammy woke me and said that to celebrate my exam results we were going to Bewley's. I jumped out of the bed, washed, dressed and was soon ready to head for the bus stop at the top of our road to get a number 40 into town. That is how we referred to Dublin city centre. We still do. The centre of Finglas was the village, and the city centre was town.

Mammy always dressed very elegantly. On this day she wore her lime-green coat and round her neck she wore her mink wrap. She had her diamanté glasses on and as we sat upstairs on the bus she smoked her all-white Consulate cigarette through a long cigarette holder. I was never embarrassed by her clothes; I loved her elegance. Before we got to town Mammy said, 'Ring the bell – we're getting off here.'

I was puzzled. 'I thought we were going to Bewley's?' I moaned.

'We are. But first we have something we have to do.'

I was now more than a little puzzled. It showed on my face.

'Do you remember last summer when you stole from Superquinn's?'

I nodded guiltily. 'Well, we have to deal with the consequences of that.' I had learned from Mammy a long time before this that every action has consequences, good or bad. We were going to the children's court. I swear to you that I was so terrified that I can remember very little of the court, except I remember a Garda being really nice to me and telling me not to worry. I do remember at one point Mammy's hand squeezed mine a little harder than usual, but it was only for a moment.

We left the court and got a bus into town and Bewley's. We sat at *our* table and when Mammy gave the waitress our order she covered her mouth with the back of her hand and mumbled something to our waitress. Soon the coffees arrived along with the three-tiered cake stand. But this time the cake stand was different. Where it usually had an assortment of pastries, not today. Today it was ALL eclairs. My eyes bulged with surprise.

Mammy nodded to the stand. 'Go on, help yourself.'

I did. I ate six eclairs. Mammy giggled at first and then began laughing as I scoffed the beautiful cakes.

Afterwards we walked around town for a bit, then we got the bus home. There I filled a basin with hot water and some Epsom salts. I unzipped Mammy's boots and she closed her eyes, putting her feet into the basin with a loud relaxed exhale. I began to massage her feet.

'We need to talk.' This is a phrase Mammy often used and what came after it was never good. I should have smelled a rat in Bewley's. Seriously, six eclairs? I should have smelled a rat, a huge rat.

I was more than a little apprehensive. 'OK,' I answered with a bit of a wobble in my voice.

Mammy went on. 'The court today decided that as I work full-time and you are on school break that you should be supervised during the holiday break.' She took a moment here to frame what she was about to say. 'You have to go away.'

The next day I stood outside the entrance to Pearse Street Garda station. My brother Finbar had brought me. It was a bright sunny morning, so Mammy had insisted that I wear short trousers. I didn't want to wear shorts. And they were short shorts. I was a skinny kid with snow-white legs; it looked like my torso was being held up by two number-eight knitting needles. Worse, even though I was only bringing a jumper, underwear and a pair of long trousers with me, I still needed a case. The only case we had in the house was one that had been left behind by my sister Fiona on her trip home for Daddy's funeral. It was a bright pink weekend case. So there I was, going to join a hoard of young thieves, muggers and, who knew, maybe killers, in my short shorts with my pink weekend case.

'Go on, in you go,' Finbar said, and gave me a little push.

'Are you not coming in with me?' I asked.

'No, I'm late for work; you'll be grand,' he said with another little push.

I climbed the first two steps and turned to look at him. He had gone. I pushed open the huge door and now so was I.

Believe it or not, I don't remember too much about my time there. Which is unusual as I'm sure it was traumatic. I remember that it was run by Christian brothers. I remember a brother asking me when was the last time I had been to confession. It was just days ago, so I was OK there. Then he asked when I had last been to mass.

I replied, 'Three times last week.'

The brother looked astonished, so I explained that I had been on Sunday and had served two masses for weddings on the Saturday. 'You're an altar boy?'

I nodded and he smiled. Life was about to get easier for me. I served mass a lot of mornings; I remember that. I also recall the first meal there. We sat at long tables, ten to a table. Every kid was older than me. One of the boys was about thirteen and I think had stubble (or that could be a dream). I had no sooner sat down than I was asked, 'So what did you do?'

I wasn't going to tell them that I had stolen two Oxo cubes and a roll of Sellotape. I quickly racked my brain for an answer that would get me 'cred' but be plausible. But what I blurted out was: 'I killed me father.' Inside I was screaming at my brain, *Plausible, I said, fucking PLAUSIBLE!*

It worked. The nine of them went 'whoa!' in unison.

Though I don't recall much of my time there, I do recall my last day. I was down by a pond in the grounds. It was a blistering sunny day. The pond was surrounded by tall reeds, and it was so beautifully quiet. My mother wrote me a letter every day and I would go there to read them and cry in private. I was a bit down this day because no letter had arrived from Mammy, even though if I was handed one in front of the other boys, I would roll my eyes and stuff it in my pocket. 'I wish she'd stop this writing shit.' But I loved them and couldn't wait to sneak away and read them. This was the day that I saw my first-ever dragonfly. I didn't know what it was, so I was startled at first. It was huge. It buzzed around the reeds and I followed it. One second it looked blue, then it looked golden. I was transfixed. It landed on a reed close to me and I slowly started to stretch out my arm to try to catch it. It started to move a little, so I froze. Then it took off and landed right on the back of my hand. It was beautiful.

As I stared at it a voice from behind me shook me out of my trance. 'O'Carroll, go and pack your bag – you're going home.'

I had expected to be there for the whole summer, but whatever Mammy had done I was going home after just three weeks. I was taken home by two Gardai in the back of a squad car, and here's something ironic: the reason I was sent there in the first place was because I would be unsupervised for the summer. But when the squad car and the two Gardai arrived at my house there was nobody home. I had no key, so I told them I'd check the back door. I climbed over the O'Briens' wall and went through the Reddins' back garden. The back door was locked but I had learned to pick locks a long time ago. Within seconds I was in, and the two Gardai stayed with me until my mammy got home.

I made them a sandwich and a cuppa, and we played cards. I remember the smile on my mother's face that day. I remember the kindness of the Gardai. I remember curling up in my own bed that night. But mostly, of that day and that time, I remember the dragonfly.

I returned to Casement Grove and soon life got back to normal – well, as normal as it could be in Finglas West. I found my first girlfriend, Mardi Deegan. She taught me how to kiss, properly. I was head over heels and every day seemed like spring for the whole three weeks before she broke it off. I only found out that she dumped me on the streets. I mean, literally on the streets. We used the chalk from plaster to mark out the streets for football or the girls used it for marking out the footpath for hopscotch. The girls would also use the chalk to declare who their beau was by writing their own initials, then under them they'd write 'XXX', for 'kiss, kiss, kiss' and under that they would write the initials of

their boyfriend. So I would see all over the streets *MD –
XXX – BOC*. It was an important part of the mating ritual.
Not that we were mating; I still didn't know what my penis
was for other than pissing.

So then, one day, I came out of my house and John and
Jimmy were up the road sitting on the O'Briens' railings.
They called to me to join them and I did. When I got to them
they pointed to the ground. 'Look at this,' said Jimmy.

I looked. Written in chalk was: *MD – XXX – BOT*.

I laughed. 'Mardi got my initials wrong. She put a "T"
instead of a "C".'

They shook their heads in unison. 'Nope,' said John with
a bit of a giggle in his voice. 'Brian O'Toole just stole your
mot.' ('Mot' was a Dublin term for girlfriend, or even wife, in
those days.)

I just shrugged and smiled. 'There's plenty of fish in the
sea,' I said, and we headed back down the road to Reddin's
van. I hope the look I gave over my shoulder to check that it
was a 'T' and not a 'C' didn't give away how fucking devastated I was. Because I was.

Speaking again of Reddin's, Gem's beloved wife, Nelly,
passed away that year and the family were very sad for a long
time. Young Jimmy, who we had nicknamed Redser, became
part of our gang, and we tried to keep him from getting too
sad. Gem himself went through a tough time and drank
more than usual. I became his conversation partner. Because
Mammy sometimes worked a night shift I would be alone in
the house. After the pub Gem would knock to check I was all
right and invariably he would say, 'Come on, Brendy, come in
to mine and we'll have a cup of tea.'

I'd make the tea. Gem liked it very strong and I swear his
own mug was as big as a bucket. Then we'd settle down for
a chat. We'd start with maybe football. I was and still am a

Liverpool FC fan, and he was, if I remember right, a United fan. Then we'd move on to local gossip or politics. It didn't matter because we always ended up talking about Nelly. Well, Gem talking about Nelly and me nodding and laughing in the right places.

Gem had five wonderful children; the eldest, Margaret, took on the motherly role and did it so well, though she couldn't have been more than fifteen or sixteen. The others were all younger than her and they adored their father, surrounding him with love. I learned a lesson from seeing this. Gem Reddin was surrounded by family and friends and yet he was lonely. That's why, I realized, my own mammy sometimes got down. Mammy had ten children, including me under her feet, all of whom would keep in touch with her, but she was lonely.

Anyway, back to Gem. The incident I want to tell you about happened during one of these late-night chats. The Reddins' home was amazingly beautiful. They had the best of everything. The living room where we had our chats had a big colour TV, a top-of-the-range stereo, a plush carpet and a three-piece suite to die for. There was a chandelier that had four bright bulbs and over each there was a golden leaf set into a mahogany base. The wallpaper was Shand Kydd, deep wine flock with a gold base, and there were the most beautiful red-velvet curtains edged with golden bobbins. This was a council house with interior design by Liberace. So me and Gem are sitting there in the lap of luxury one night, and he is talking about how beautiful pigs' cheek is if it's boiled and 'pressed' right when he stopped mid-sentence. He was staring at the bottom of the long curtains.

'What? What is it?' I asked.

He put a finger to his lips and shushed me. I followed his gaze to the bottom of the curtains and there it was, a mouse.

74

Not taking his eyes from the mouse Gem ever so slowly stood, then he leaned down to the fireplace and took up the poker and gradually stepped towards the mouse. Then he suddenly pounced.

I swear to you that what followed was chaos. Gem whacked the bottom of the curtain with the poker, missing the mouse but putting the poker through the plaster. As he tried to extract it, the mouse ran up the curtains to the wooden curtain rail. Gem retrieved the poker and now the mouse was tripping along the curtain rail. Gem swung at the rail, cracking it in two, and the mouse jumped on to the other curtain and ran down to the floor. The poker was now caught in the first curtain. Gem yanked it and the two curtains, and rail, fell on top of him. The mouse ran along the skirting board and Gem took off after him, now wearing the curtains like a cloak. The mouse ducked behind the stereo, and Gem swung again, putting the poker through the Perspex lid of the record player. The mouse (who I was surprised had not died of heart attack by now) darted out from behind the stereo, jumped on the floor and ran between Gem's legs. Gem turned but the broken curtain rail that was across his shoulders with the heavy curtains dragging from it was hindering his movements, so he lifted the rail like a weightlifter and threw it off. The rail now hung on the chandelier for a moment, then dropped, taking a light and a single golden leaf with it. The mouse now made to run under the couch, which I was sitting on. Gem slashed at it, missed, and ripped a hole in the upholstered arm. I stood up and, as the mouse emerged from the other side of the couch, it made to cross the room again. I swung at it as if I were taking a corner for Liverpool and luckily got my timing right. I caught the mouse square on and he flew against the wall and dropped to the floor, dead.

'Good man, Brendy,' Gem called out, as if I had scored a

goal. Then he stood in the middle of the room catching his breath.

We both stood there in silence.

I looked around the room; it was wrecked, debris everywhere.

Gem ran his fingers through his Brylcreemed hair and, extending his arms out, said, 'I know it's only a mouse, but look at the fucking damage they do.'

I pissed myself laughing then, I pissed myself laughing when I was telling Mammy and I'm actually laughing now as I write this. I loved that man.

For summer holidays Jimmy Matthews and his family would go to a Butlin's holiday camp. It was an amazing place, I believe. I would never get to see it. John Breen would go to relatives; I think they were in Wexford. In the years that we could afford it Mammy would rent the 'cabin' in Portrane. The cabin was actually a retired railway coach that had been converted into a kind of holiday caravan; it was a bit dingy but it was nearly on the beach so who cared.

Long before I was born, the family would come here or go to Courtown. Mammy told me stories of how she would get the bus out to Portrane with the two youngest, Michéal and Éilish, as they travelled free on the bus, then Daddy would ferry the others sometimes two at a time on his bike, going back and forth. It was a good six-mile cycle each way. For the next two weeks that would be his base and he would cycle to work from there while the family enjoyed the beach and the carnival in the town.

For me it was heaven twice a day. I'm an early riser; I always have been. One of the times I enjoyed the cabin was about 5.30 a.m. when the sun was just coming up. I would wake up, hop out of the bed and make a cup of tea. I would open the railway carriage door all the way and sit on the step as the sun rose and heated my face. There I would wallow in the quiet with only the rumbling waves of the sea for company. I would sit there for a couple of hours before anybody else got up. I would sit there and just dream. Then in the evening, as the sun was setting and all the day trippers had gone home, I'd sit on the sand dunes watching the waves crash and dream some more.

Without us realizing it, the 'gang' were seeing less and less of each other. Jimmy and John were in different schools and in their tough second year, so now had lots of homework. I was working and had now left Home Farm FC and was playing for Raven Athletic. I can't remember why, but I think it was because their matches were on a Sunday, and I only worked one Sunday a month. So this brings me to work.

But before I move on, I must tell you that John was diagnosed with leukaemia and died at sixteen. Jimmy and I were so, so upset. Then Jimmy, on the night of his engagement, was in a car crash on the way back from the celebrations. He died. He was eighteen.

Why does everybody leave me?

8

Brace yourself, as we're just about to take a short break to talk about planes . . .

To steal inspiration from *Goodfellows*, for as long as I can remember I wanted to be an airline pilot. Our house in Finglas West was right under the north–south landing flight path for Dublin airport. Sometimes the planes would be so low going over our house I could actually see people's faces in the windows. Or maybe that was a dream, but in any case we were just about a mile from the runway threshold as the crow flies. (I don't know why people say that. Every crow I've ever seen flies like they are pissed.)

Anyhow, I was convinced that I would be the youngest pilot Aer Lingus ever had, and I would be the best too. From about seven years old I would walk from our house, through the fields, to the end of the runway and spend hours just sitting in the long grass watching the planes either landing or taking off, depending on the wind direction. I knew every aircraft Aer Lingus flew from the Vickers Viscount to the BAC-111. I would get there early to see the transatlantic flights arrive: the Comet, the Dakota and then the Boeing 707, its four engines spewing exhaust as it passed over me, maybe 100 feet in the air. The planes would make a tiny screech as the wheels touched and then I'd be left with the beautiful smell of aviation fuel exhaust for a good ten minutes after. I loved it.

As I got older, two things happened that changed all of this a little not a lot.

The first thing was this. It was 1965, February. I was getting my annual health check-up in school. Everything seemed fine, then it came to the eye test. I had no problem with the chart. I read it all, including the printer's name on the bottom. 'Twenty-twenty vision,' the doc declared.

Then the nurse sat me down and produced a bunch of cards that were maybe eight by ten inches. They were all different colours. Red, green, yellow, blue, etc. She held up the first one. ' OK, how many spots do you see on this card?' she asked.

It was easy, as the card was blue and the spots were red. 'Eight,' I answered confidently. Then 'Six' and so on until she came to the final card.

She smiled and wrote something down and I was done and dusted. I went back to my class. When the school day ended I was about to leave when the teacher called me back. He gave me an envelope and said, 'Give this to your mother when you get home.'

I couldn't wait to get home and find out what was in the envelope. I gave it to my mammy as soon as I walked in the door. 'What forking trouble are you in now?' she asked, as she took a letter from the envelope.

I shrugged. 'Dunno.'

She opened the letter and I waited.

'It's nothing, just the result of your check-up.' There was a pause as she read on. 'You are as healthy as a pup.' She smiled and so did I. Then she did an 'uh-oh'.

I don't like uh-ohs. I preferred the smile. 'What? What is it?'

I was relieved when the smile came back. 'It's nothing really . . . but you're colour-blind.'

Nothing? Nothing? I was aghast. 'But that could be dangerous. I mean, when I start to drive how will I be able to tell traffic lights?'

Mammy tossed the letter to one side as she answered. 'I'll give you a hint, son, the red one is on the forking top.' I laughed. 'Look –' she wanted to calm me down – 'it's only on shades, mainly blue and green. You'll be fine.' I relaxed, as she lit another Consulate. 'Mind you, there are some jobs you won't be able to qualify for.'

'Like what?'

'Well, you won't be defusing any forking bombs for a start.' We both laughed at this. 'And let me think . . . Electrician, you won't be an electrician, or a telephone engineer. But you could be a plumber.' Again we both laughed. 'What else . . .'

A sudden foreboding came over me. My head started spinning. All that was running through it was *Don't say pilot, please. Please don't say pilot.* I held my breath.

'Astronaut.'

I nearly cried with relief.

'Or pilot obviously.'

I was so numb that I wasn't sure I heard it. I was speechless. I was so angry with her. It was as if it were her fault. It took me a long time to get over it. My dreams had taken wings and flown away, which was more than I could ever do.

The second thing I was to discover is that, as much as I adored aircraft, I was terrified of flying. I didn't know I was, but I was to find out when I was sixteen years old and had my first flight. My sister Fiona was living in Toronto so Mammy had a great idea: we would spend Christmas in Toronto with Fiona. A white Christmas. I was so excited – not about the trip – I was going to see Fiona. So, on a bitterly cold, windy and rainy December day, we boarded a chartered Aer Lingus 707.

I was buzzing. Soon I would be floating above the clouds. When the plane was fully loaded the beautiful air hostess (they were called that then) closed the door with a loud bang.

I jumped and I started to sweat a little too. Then the air hostess began a safety talk. It was terrifying. Everything she said I was answering in my head. She began by taking out a seat belt that wouldn't fit round my mother's thigh.

'You should now have your seat belt closed. To close it, insert the flat piece into the bigger piece and tighten it by pulling here.'

I checked my belt.

'In the unlikely event of decompression . . .'

I looked at my mother. 'What's "decompression"?' I asked.

'A hole in the plane. Now shush.'

A hole in the plane? A fucking hole in the plane? What the fuck is she talking about?

The hostess now held up a plastic thing over her head. 'Masks will drop down from above you.' She let go of the plastic thing and it dropped down, hanging from a curling of plastic tubing.

As it dropped, I involuntarily let out a little yelp. My mother gave me the evil eye. I looked up. *Mine is empty. I bet mine is fucking empty.*

'In the event of the aircraft landing in water –'

No. No. Fuck that. Aircraft don't land in water. They fucking CRASH in water.

'– there is a life jacket under your seat.'

I felt for it. It was there.

'Each vest has a light and a whistle.' She pointed them out.

I was aghast. Light? It was a Christmas-tree bulb. And a whistle, why? *Let me get this straight, I'm floating around in the dark in the freezing Atlantic with ten-foot waves crashing around me and the helicopter is going to see and hear me with a fucking Christmas-tree bulb and a whistle? Fuck off!* I'm sweating profusely now.

'Do not inflate your life jacket while in the aircraft as it may impede your exit.'

No it won't. And neither will YOU. You will have a size-eight footprint in the middle of your back as I stomp over you.

She then ended the horror show with: 'Now sit back, relax and enjoy our flight to Toronto.'

Relax? Are you mad, woman? Enjoy what, the hole in the plane or the plane turning into a submarine?

Mammy rummages in her handbag and fishes out a handkerchief and hands it to me. 'You're perspiring.' Fuck yeh, I was perspiring.

I could hear the engines whine as they started up. Again I don't know why, but I had imagined that the aircraft would be soundproof. Was it fuck. By the time all four engines were running I could barely hear Mammy snoring. Yep, she was asleep. A seasoned traveller, she popped off as soon as Miss Let-Me-Scare-the-Shit-Outta-You had finished her 'happy talk'.

I tried to relax; I really did. The plane began to taxi towards the runway. That's when I noticed it. The wing, it was flapping. Moving up and down at the tip.

I nudged Mammy. 'Mammy, the wing,' I said, pointing out of the window.

She didn't even open her eyes. 'Yes, love, it's supposed to be there. And there's another one over on that side.' She pointed.

'No, Mammy, it's flapping.'

She opened her eyes now. 'Flapping?' She was genuinely puzzled.

I pointed out of the window at the wing. 'That's not flapping. There has to be some give in the wing, so it doesn't snap off.' She closed her eyes again.

Snap off? What the fuck is this 'snap off' you speak of? I think before we get to the runway it's going to fucking drop off. For the next six hours I sat with one hand squeezed tight on the armrest, bent over, and the other hand ready to pull out my life jacket, while praying that my Christmas-tree bulb would work.

As awful as this was, I'm ashamed to say that it was not my worst performance on a flight. That came much later on a short flight from Heathrow to Dublin. I'll get to it in a minute, but first I want to impress on you what I mean by terrified of flying. In my day you booked your flights in a travel agent's. When I went to an agent's to book, by the time I had the tickets I would be drenched with sweat. I would then be on edge every day before the flight. If it were a flight to Spain for a holiday, I would spend the entire two weeks just being worried about the flight home. It was awful.

OK, let's get to that Heathrow to Dublin flight. I wasn't even a young teenager; I was in my late twenties, but I hadn't flown for a long time. It was a straightforward up-and-down flight home to Dublin. I sat beside this guy, who was about my age.

As we took off, he said to me, 'Nervous flyer?' He'd probably guessed because my fingernails were digging into his arm. He had it on the centre armrest.

I smiled. 'Yeh, a bit.'

He smiled back. 'I understand,' he said. I'm sure he was now wondering if his arm was bleeding.

Once up in the air the crew started serving drinks. They did in those days, and free too. I had a vodka with Coke, and he had a whisky with ginger ale. He chatted about flying. 'I take this flight at least six times a month, so you have nothing to worry about.' Believe it or not, I started to relax. 'Look,' he said, 'as we go over Birmingham the heat from the city rises up and it will get a bit bumpy, but it's very slight and nothing at all to worry about.'

I was so glad I had sat beside this guy. He was distracting me as well as relaxing me.

About twenty minutes into the flight the pilot makes an announcement. 'Ladies and gentlemen, I've just switched on the seat-belt sign as we might get a little turbulence. Thank you.'

Whisky and Ginger gave me a knowing nod. I smiled, thinking, *This guy is great*.

There was a little bump and shudder. I looked to Whisky and Ginger and he winked.

Now a senior crew person made an announcement. 'Ladies and gentlemen, we have some more turbulence ahead, so I would ask you to fold up your table and those that have drinks hold them in your hand.'

This was obviously the routine, so I folded my table and held my vodka. I turned to Whisky and Ginger with a smile, but he wasn't smiling. He was FROWNING.

'They've never said that before,' he said.

We got severely bumped around, overhead doors popped open, people's hand luggage fell out – it was crazy. It only lasted about three minutes, but it felt like a lifetime. When it had all calmed down Whisky and Ginger, with a laugh in his voice, said, 'That was something, eh?'

'Don't talk to me, you fucking liar,' I snapped at him. I was shitting myself. But the flight was not over. There was no more turbulence, but here's a couple of things I have learned. Number one is that when a 737, which is the aircraft we were in, reaches its cruising height it only stays at that height for a short time because it is such a short trip to Dublin. Just as it passes over Liverpool at cruising height it's possible for the flight crew to push the throttles to virtually idle and descend all the way across the Irish Sea and maybe not need to use power again until they are within sight of the airport. Nobody ever told me this. So I'm already on edge when I hear the engines wind down and down until I can't hear them and we begin to sink ever so slightly. Out of the window all I can see is blackness, as it is night, and we are over the Irish Sea.

This is when I learned my second thing. Which is this: if you laugh on an aeroplane nobody notices, but if you scream everybody joins in. I screamed at the top of my voice and then shouted, 'We're going down!' There were more than a few screamers in the chorus. Now, to my great shame, I began saying the Lord's Prayer at the top of my voice while repeatedly making a huge sign of the cross, making the downstroke all the way to my crotch. A purser made her way quickly to me and, pushing me into my seat, sat on me until I stopped crying. I was now having a complete meltdown.

Just as we landed Whisky and Ginger leaned over to me and, squeezing my arm, asked, 'Are you OK now?'

I looked in his eyes and when I spoke it was like *The Exorcist*. 'When we get off this plane I'm going to kill you.'

He recoiled, and I think he may have left the airport without picking up his luggage. Whisky and Ginger, if you remember this incident and you are reading this, I am SO sorry.

But I got over my fear eventually. It took years. I was very lucky to have had a neighbour, Kevan Johnson, who truly was one of the youngest captains in Aer Lingus. When I confided in him, he took the time to take me 'up' in the air, so to speak, any time the simulator was free in Dublin airport, and I'm talking sometimes at 3 a.m. He talked me through everything that can go wrong and how it is solved. He went to the trouble on his day off to hire a Cessna and take me up, even giving me the stick for short periods. I owe Kevan so much. I left *most* of my fear behind me, thanks to him. The last of my fears went on my first book tour in the USA for Penguin, promoting my first two books, *The Mammy* and *The Chisellers*. We appeared in nineteen cities in just twenty-two days so it was flight after flight after flight. By midway through the book tour I was so exhausted that I would board and just doze off. Now I fly without fear, and I have regained my love for aviation even more than before.

Having now reached a point where I am a fearless flyer here are some stories from some of my travels.

As a well-known person, and having met so many pilots through Kevan Johnson, I often knew many of the pilots flying the Aer Lingus flights I took, and pre-9/11 I was often invited to the cockpit for the landing. But prior to being well known I had an hilarious incident with an Aer Lingus captain and first officer.

I had been booked to do a couple of weeks of stand-up gigs in New York and Boston. I was to depart two days after the night I was due to be on *The Late Late Show*. That first appearance on *The Late Late* changed my life and, the day after, it now seemed that everybody in Ireland knew my name. So on boarding the 747 for New York the next day the cabin crew were all so nice and commented that they had watched the show and loved it. I was a bit taken aback but I tried to thank them gracefully.

About midway through the flight the purser was serving me a drink and said, 'The captain would love to meet you, Mr O'Carroll, so when you finish your drink perhaps I could take you to the cockpit?'

'Sure,' I said, and I was a little excited. Later I gave her the signal that I was ready, and she escorted me to the cockpit.

'This is Mr O'Carroll,' she announced to the flight crew. They were very courteous and pulled down the jump seat for me to sit in.

The first officer shook my hand and said, 'Can I just say my mother has been a fan for years. She loves your stuff, loves it.'

I was a little surprised. 'Well, please tell her thanks from me.'

He nodded. 'I will, I will.'

Now the captain spoke. 'So did you like Ireland?'

I didn't know what to say so I just said, 'I love Ireland and have done since the day I was born.'

He half smiled. 'Really? Well, that's very nice of you.'

I'm now fucking dumbfounded; then the first officer says, 'My mother's favourite of yours is the . . . whatcha call it . . .? What's the name of the song?' He now starts to sing: '*Oh my Papa, to me you are so wonderful.*' What's that one called?'

'It's called "Oh my Papa",' I answered.

He snapped his fingers. 'That's it. I'll tell you, when you play that on your trumpet my mother melts.'

I placed my hand on his shoulder. 'That's Johnny Carroll, not me.'

He looked at me. 'Oh,' he said, bitterly disappointed.

The captain, who must have been oblivious to all this, now piped in with: 'You don't sound Korean?'

I tried not to sound narky. 'Well, that's because I'm not Korean. I'm Irish born and bred.'

He looked at me, puzzled. 'Then why did Eileen say that you were a famous Korean?'

I twigged what had happened. 'She must have said "comedian" and you misheard?'

There was quiet now. The captain asks, 'So who are you?'

I hate that question. 'I'm Brendan O'Carroll.'

Quiet again. The captain now speaks to the first officer. 'Have you ever heard of him?'

The first officer shakes his head, then shrugs. 'No.'

'Me neither,' says the captain.

My turn to speak. 'Right, I'll be off then,' and I folded the jump seat back up.

'Enjoy the rest of the flight,' were the words I heard as I made my exit. I did.

Then there was the FAI flight.

I am very lucky that through some TV work and my links to the Football Association of Ireland I get to not just go to the away international games but on many occasions travel with the team. On the occasion I am about to tell you about the team were returning from an away game somewhere in Europe. The team, management and officials took up the front half of the aircraft and I sat with my son Danny, who was just ten years old at the time, and all the press guys down at the back of the aircraft. It was an uneventful flight, with a wonderful Aer Lingus cabin crew serving drinks and, of course, offering us the usual 'chicken or beef' choice of meal. The flight was captained by a pilot I knew personally.

About fifteen minutes out from Dublin one of the girls on the crew came to our seat, leaned in to me and whispered, 'Mr O'Carroll, the captain would like to know if you would like to join him in the cockpit for our landing?'

Let me point out at this juncture that the *only* time it's really any fun in the cockpit is either during landing or take-off. The middle bit is just plain boring. I was delighted.

I turned to Danny. 'Will you be OK, Danny?' He nodded and so I stood up.

I deliberately hung back a bit as the woman walked ahead of me down the aisle, saying quite loudly, certainly loud enough for the press guys to hear, 'Well, how sick is he?' Then I quickly followed her. As we got about midway down the aircraft I again called to her. 'Both of them sick? How can both of them be sick?'

As I made it to the cockpit door I could hear some of the players murmuring. 'What did he say?' and 'Sick? Who did he say was sick?'

In the cockpit I told the crew what I had done, and we had a good laugh. We were now about ten minutes out.

The captain said to me, 'Hey, do you want to make an announcement?' He handed me the microphone, so I did. Here's what I said:

'Good afternoon, everybody . . . eh, OK . . . I just want you to know that you are in good hands and we . . . eh . . . Would anybody who had either chicken or beef raise your hands so the cabin crew can see you?'

Danny tells me everybody put their hand up, including him.

'OK, thank you. Well, we will be arriving in ten minutes into Dublin airport . . . or thereabouts. In the meantime, please make sure your seat belt is fastened . . . tightly.'

As if it were planned, the aircraft now flew over Howth Head and I still had the mike on. A beep goes off in the cockpit and a robotic voice says, 'Terrain, terrain.' I think it's because of the sudden change from sea level to the height of Howth Head.

The captain simply pressed a button and the beeping stopped. To make things better or worse a sudden updraft raised and lowered the plane quickly.

I said into the mike, 'Whoa, ha ha! I won't be doing that again.'

Danny told me later that one of the press guys had called over to him. 'Can your dad fly a plane?'

Danny rolled his eyes. 'Of course,' he lied.

My last message to our esteemed passengers was: 'OK, here we go. Hold on tight and someone give Robbie Keane his soother and rattle.' (Robbie was new to the team and very young.) Obviously the captain greased the landing (*greased* is a term *us* pilots use to describe an exceptionally smooth landing) and at the gate I emerged from the cockpit, saying nothing to nobody, and Danny and I went on our merry way.

When we got into our car Danny asked me, 'Dad, did you really land the plane?'

I looked at him. 'I certainly did.'

He smiled and squeezed my arm. He was so proud.

He was only ten years old; what the fuck did you think I would say?

I often wonder if anyone who was on that plane still thinks I landed that plane that day. (Danny, if you are reading this, I did, I swear it, I did.)

9

And welcome back!

I may not have fulfilled that dream to become a pilot, but I have always worked. Even at ten years old I would scour the factories in the late evenings looking for a dumped pallet. I had a box cart I had made myself from an old box I found up in Unidare on Jamestown Road. I think it used to hold huge bottles of acid as when I 'found' it the box was full of straw. Another big hint was the printing on the side that read 'ACID'. (I should be a detective.) I also found a smashed-up pram in the Royal Canal near Cabra, the next suburb to Finglas. I took the two good wheels and axle off it, nailed it to the bottom of the box, used a couple of sturdy two-by-fours as handles and, voilà, I had a box cart.

Once I had found a pallet I would break it up into its parts with my hammer, load it in the box cart and take it home. There I would use one of Mr Reddin's old cleavers (he was also a qualified and very good butcher) and split the planks into strips about an inch thick. I would then break each strip to pieces about eight inches long. Finally I would get an old bicycle tube and cross-cut it into rubber bands. Then I would take six sticks and bundle them together, slip on the rubber band and fill the cart with these bundles. These were perfect for starting your fire, the only source of heating in the Finglas houses then. I would go door to door selling the bundles for a penny each. After a couple of hours I would sell out, with a decent pallet giving me fifty bundles and earning me about four shillings, which I gave to my mammy.

By twelve I was working as a lounge boy in the upstairs lounge of the Cappagh House, the quiet lounge. The job entailed serving drinks to the customers that were prepared to pay an extra penny per drink for the luxury of sitting in a carpeted room. The Cappagh also had a cabaret room, but only women were allowed to work in there, though I would sometimes sneak into the back of the room and watch Billy Hughes bash out the popular songs of the day and bring the house down every time.

Then there was Mr Wise.

When Mammy became a widow she qualified for a Widows and Orphans pension. This was paid out at the local post office every Friday. Along with the pension she would be given a 'turf' docket. In Ireland there are lots of bogs. The bogland was made up of a squishy, squashy turf. A government-owned company would 'cut' the turf into foot-long blocks and they would then be stacked at the side of the bog and left to dry out for months. When dry they were amazing fuel for your family fire. Mammy's docket entitled her to a hundredweight (two sacks) of turf per week. But you had to collect it yourself and supply your own sacks. Every area had its own turf depot; ours was behind the shops. It was a huge walled kind of warehouse. The best way to describe it is to imagine a squash court with a roof and big doors. The turf depot only opened on Saturdays and Wednesdays at 8 a.m. Mammy insisted on me getting it on Saturday. But I also had my soccer match on Saturday mornings. So to make sure I was top of the queue I would get there at 7.30 a.m. and park my cart right at the door with the empty sacks in it. Then I would go round the side and spend the next hour kicking a ball up against the big side wall, commentating to myself how O'Carroll was winning the World Cup for Ireland. One morning, as I was kicking away, I noticed a man watching me. It unnerved me, so I stopped kicking and went and sat on the side of my cart.

He came over to me. He had a slight accent when he spoke.

MR WISE'S FIRE

EXT. THE TURF DEPOT, FINGLAS - EARLY MORNING

It is 7.30 a.m. Brendan, a strikingly handsome young boy (it's my script so fuck off), is kicking a plastic football against a huge wall. The wall is the side wall of the turf depot. Brendan has already parked his box cart round the corner, up against the big doors of the entrance, to ensure he will be the first to be served when the depot opens at 8 a.m. as he has done every Saturday for months now.

Across the small green in front of the depot a man watches Brendan closely. Brendan has seen this man here before on the previous two Saturday mornings. As he kicks the ball up against the wall, Brendan is commentating to himself.

BRENDAN
O'Carroll takes the ball down on his chest . . . The referee looks at his watch; there cannot be any time left in this World Cup final. Is there one more chance to score the goal that

93

will bring this Ireland-Brazil
final into extra time?
Brendan takes the rebounding ball on to
his chest. It drops to the ground, and he
traps it.

BRENDAN (CONT'D)
O'Carroll must be exhausted;
it's his two goals that have kept
Ireland in this game.
Brendan side-steps an invisible Brazilian
player.

BRENDAN (CONT'D)
O'Carroll breezes past Pelé like he isn't
there . . . The referee puts the whistle
to his mouth . . .O'Carroll shoots . . .
Brendan waits for the ball to bang off
the wall.

BRENDAN (CONT'D)
He scores!
Brendan now jumps up and down and runs
around with his arms in the air, holding
his sleeve with the tips of his fingers
like Denis Law does. He is making the
noise of a crowd cheering. From the
corner of his eye he sees the man come
towards him across the green. Brendan
gathers his ball and goes round the
corner and sits on his cart. Seconds
later, the man appears. He stops short of
Brendan's box cart and points at Brendan.

MAN
You, boy!
*The man has a slight accent, maybe German
or Dutch?*

BRENDAN
Fuck off, yeh pre-vert.

MAN
Watch your language, and the word is
'pervert', but this is not a word that
should ever come from your mouth.

BRENDAN
OK, fuck off, yeh cunt!

MAN
Oy vey! My ears are too delicate for this
filthy language.
Brendan is a little embarrassed.

BRENDAN
What do you want?

MAN
I have been watching you.

- BRENDAN
I know yeh have, yeh, I know.

MAN
Every Saturday, always early,
always the same time.

BRENDAN
So?

MAN
This tells me maybe you are a dependable
boy. Are you? Are you a dependable boy?

BRENDAN
Leave me alone.

MAN
What's your name?

BRENDAN
What's YOUR name?

MAN
Wise. My name is Mr Wise.
Brendan isn't expecting an answer.
It catches him off guard.

MR WISE
So? What is your name?

BRENDAN
Brendan.

MR WISE
A nice name. Well . . .
Mr Wise takes a step forward.

MR WISE (CONT'D)
May I sit beside you?

BRENDAN (*STANDING*)
No.

MR WISE
How would you like to make a shilling?
Money? This perks Brendan's interest.

BRENDAN (*CAUTIOUS*)
What would I have to do?

MR WISE
Light my fire.

BRENDAN
Light your fire? Light your own fire.

MR WISE
I cannot. In my religion it is forbidden
to kindle a fire on the Sabbath.

BRENDAN
You want me to light your fire
on a Sunday?

MR WISE
Saturday.

BRENDAN
Sunday is the Sabbath.

MR WISE
Not in my religion. In mine
Saturday is the Sabbath.

BRENDAN

What kind of religion has Saturday for
the Sabbath?
Mr Wise is exasperated with this kid's
constant questions.

MR WISE

Do you want the fucking shilling or not?!
Wise immediately covers his mouth with
one hand. Brendan bursts into laughter.

BRENDAN

The depot opens in about ten minutes.
When I get me turf I'll light your
fire . . . for a shilling.

MR WISE

Good boy. I am in that house over there.
(*He points.*) The blue door.
Within minutes of the depot opening
Brendan fills his sacks with turf. As he
drags them out to his box cart the queue
is now thirty deep. He knows some of them
and acknowledges them as he passes them.
Once he has them loaded, he takes a deep
breath and heads for the blue door.

INT. MR WISE'S HOUSE – MINUTES LATER
Brendan is on his hands and knees. He has
rolled sheets of the *Irish Times*
newspaper tightly and places them on the
grate; he now is arranging the kindling
sticks in a criss-cross manner.

BRENDAN

You see, the tighter you roll the paper,
the better chance you have of getting the
fire to catch. The sticks are crossed,
but leave some gaps to let the air get at
the flame . . .

MR WISE

Brendan, I know HOW to light a fire;
I just cannot do it today.
So please just get on with it.
*Mr Wise now leaves the room and Brendan
begins placing pieces of coal strategically
on the sticks. He strikes a match and puts
it to the papers on the bottom. They
ignite. By the time Mr Wise has returned
the sticks have caught and give off a nice
crackle. Mr Wise is carrying a tray. On it
is a plate with two Marietta biscuits, the
plainest you could get, and a glass filled
with orange squash.*

MR WISE (CONT'D)

Here we go. This is for you.
He presents it like it's a royal buffet.

BRENDAN

No, no. You said a shilling.

MR WISE

It's on the plate.
*And so it is. Brendan smiles, devours the
Marietta and drinks the squash.*

99

BRENDAN
OK, I'm off.

MR WISE
See you next Saturday?

BRENDAN
Shilling?

MR WISE
Absolutely!

BRENDAN
See you next week so.
Brendan leaves.

CUT TO:

INT. MR WISE'S HOUSE – MORNING, SIX WEEKS LATER
Brendan sits at the window table. He is munching his Marietta and sipping on his squash.

BRENDAN (*LOOKING OUT THE WINDOW*)
I think it's gonna rain.

MR WISE
And that's the weather; now for the
traffic report!
They both laugh. Brendan looks closely at Mr Wise.

BRENDAN
Every Saturday, Mr Wise, you are always
in good humour. Always.

MR WISE
Why not?

BRENDAN
Do you NEVER feel down?

MR WISE
Brendan, every morning I get up, I put
the kettle on and while it is heating I
go across to the shop and get my *Irish
Times*. When I get back I make my tea, sit
at this table and open the paper.
He takes a sip of his tea.

MR WISE (CONT'D)
The first page I read is the
death column. If my name is not in
it . . . it's a great day.
The two of them laugh loud and long.

I lit his fire every Saturday morning until I was sixteen.
And every Saturday morning when I finished he would give
me a shilling and a glass of diluted orange squash. May God
bless him wherever he is now. I'll bet he's in Heaven. I'll bet
you a shilling . . . and a glass of orange squash.

My first 'real' job was to come in the summer of 1968 once I
had served my time with the Christian brothers. I had finished

my first year in Patrician College and we had broken up for the summer. Mammy had connections in the number-four branch of the ITGWU, the hotel and catering branch, and three of my brothers were chefs, all in the Gresham Hotel. I begged her to get me summer work but not in a hotel kitchen. She did. I was issued with a number-four branch union card and sent to get work in a hotel in Drumcondra, just beside Home Farm FC. The hotel was the Skylon Hotel; it hadn't long been open.

I first had to go for an interview with the head waiter. I was told the best time would be at eleven thirty, just before lunches started. I was there on time and, as instructed, I asked at the reception for Mr Gough, the head waiter.

The young lady on the desk called the restaurant, then hung up and pointed me in the right direction.

I gingerly entered the room. It was the most luscious room I had ever seen. Every table had a vase of fresh flowers in the centre. The cutlery and glasses sparkled. The carpet was softer than my bed. The restaurant desk was like a podium. All I could see behind it was the head and shoulders of this immaculately dressed man with a black bow tie. He had his head down and was writing on something.

I called up to him. 'Hello? I'm looking for Mr Teddy Gough.'

He looked up. 'Yes, I'm Teddy ... Where the fuck are you?' he asked, as he stepped out from behind the podium-like desk. I'm sure you won't believe this, but I was quite short. Maybe four feet tall? 'Ah, there you are. What can I do for you, young man?'

Without a word I proffered my union card. It said *Brendan O'Carroll, commis waiter, first year.*

He looked at me. He read the card again. 'Stay there, do not move.' Then he crossed the room to double doors which, when he went through them, I could see led to the kitchen.

When he emerged a few minutes later he had about ten men with him. Waiters. They were wearing wine-coloured jackets with long black lapels and black trousers with a wine stripe down the side. They looked class.

I could hear Mr Gough as he herded them down the room to where I was. 'Come on, come on, I want you all to see this.'

When they got to me the waiters stood round me in a circle. Teddy patted me on the head. He spoke to the waiters. 'OK, I asked the union for waiters and THIS is what they sent me. A fucking leprechaun!'

They all laughed and went back to what I later discovered was their lunch. I had failed. Miserably.

A customer appeared at the restaurant door and Mr Gough handed me back my union card. 'Start Monday ten sharp; white shirt, black trousers, black shining shoes.' He said it with a scowl, which immediately changed to a smile as he turned to the customer. 'Mr Phillips, lovely to see you again. I'll bring you menus in the lounge.' He saw that I was still standing there. 'You . . . out!'

I left the hotel high on life. I had a job.

Teddy Gough was to become the first of my many mentors.

Luckily I had black trousers from working as a lounge boy, and I had a couple of white shirts and black shoes that I wore with my school uniform. I arrived the following Monday at nine thirty just to be sure. Another commis waiter, Terry, brought me out to the staffroom and designated me a locker. I had a locker! I know that kids in America get lockers in school, but this didn't exist in Ireland. Nobody in Patrician College had a locker. Except, now, me.

My working day was what we in the hotel business called a 'split'. Ten a.m. to three p.m., a break for three hours, then six p.m. to ten p.m. The restaurant didn't close at ten, although last orders were at nine thirty, but under-sixteens were not allowed to work beyond ten. That first day was exhausting. As a first-year commis you are basically a runner, sidekick, packhorse. A piece of shit really.

I got home at about ten forty-five. Mammy asked me how it had gone, but I was too tired to give her the rundown. I just said, 'Fine,' and went to bed. I was asleep before my head hit the pillow.

The next day I had to do it all over again, and the next. I was off on the Thursday and spent most of the day in bed. I had training at Home Farm that evening and when we had finished training our manager said, 'See you all Saturday at 11 a.m. for the match. Have clean socks, clean knicks and clean boots. I'll be checking.'

Two things here. First I want to mention how disciplined it was at Home Farm. The club supplied the blue-and-white hooped jersey, but you had to get your own socks and knicks. And you got them from a specific store, Guiney's in Talbot Street, because we had a number on our knicks and no other team did. The other thing is, I WAS ON THE ROSTER TO WORK ON SATURDAY.

My heart sank. Nothing was more important to me than my football, so it looked like my days as a commis waiter were coming to an end, almost before they had started. I arrived at work the next day with the intention of quitting. I had no wages to collect as I had to work a back week, so I didn't have to join the queue that had formed at the accounts office. I went straight to the restaurant where Teddy Gough was alone.

This was my first-ever job. I had no idea how you quit a job. I went up to the podium where Teddy was working on his 'game plan'. This was his sheet of bookings and a list of who was getting what table, at what time, etc.

I began with a formal 'Good morning, Mr Gough,' and waited. He scribbled. 'Good morning, Mr Gough,' I said again. This time I said it louder, much louder.

'GOOD MORNING, BRENDAN,' he shouted back at me. 'I heard you the first time.' He scribbled on.

I stood there not knowing how to begin. I shuffled my feet.

Teddy eventually noticed me still standing there. 'What?' he barked.

I began. 'Eh, Mr Gough, I play football . . . for, eh, Home Farm.' I stopped.

'Good for you,' he said.

He went back to scribbling and again I stood looking at him. He noticed me again. 'Now what?' he asked, and I could see he was agitated with me.

I began to try to explain. 'I love my football. I play outside right for Home Farm. We're top of the Under 13B league and we're doing really well —'

Teddy raised his hand to stop me. 'I'm sorry, Brendan, my face has confused you. You think I give a fuck.' He went back to his notes.

This time I didn't wait for him to notice me. I just said it out straight. 'I have a match on Saturday.'

He didn't even look up. He just said, 'Really? I read the newspaper this morning and it never mentioned Home Farm's Under 13B match.' I think he was being sarcastic.

'It's at eleven a.m.'

Teddy closed his big diary and put it under his arm. 'You just make sure you're here for six. Lucky for you we don't do lunches on Saturday.' And then he walked away.

I could have cried with relief.

As tired as I was at the end of that first week, I got used to the work and the hours. There was something else too: I just

LOVED being a commis waiter. I loved it. In that first week I was not allowed to go near a table or serve anything, but by week two I was allowed to serve coffee. I would give everyone at the table a cup and saucer, and then, holding the silver coffee pot in my right hand, with my left hand and hand towel under the pot, I would pour. I practised for hours using a spoon and fork and became quite adept with them. All meals were silver service so the client would start with an empty hot plate in front of them and each main course and vegetables were delivered from silver platters using . . . you guessed it, a spoon and fork. By the end of my first month I was serving hors d'oeuvres, veg, dessert from the dessert trolley and coffee. I fucking loved it. My wages were £3.18s (google it), but I was handing up £4 a week to my mammy.

How did I do this? I was now getting tips! The Americans loved me. 'Look at the little leper-shawn serving us, ain't he cute?' I was cute all right, cute enough to make them laugh and to say thank you with humility when they pressed the few bob into my hand. I was taking about another thirty shillings a week on tips, nearly half my wages, so adding the extra two shillings to my mammy's money was no problem. All I needed was my bus fare each day, enough for some sweets through the week and twenty cigarettes for the week. Yes, I was smoking at thirteen. Don't judge me.

I was getting better and better at doing the job and I loved it. One interesting thing that happened was in my sixth week at the Skylon. We got a new head chef. I should point out that there was never any love lost between chefs and waiters. We looked upon them as overrated canteen cooks and they called us beggars with bow ties. But this was different. When I got into work on the day the new head chef was starting, I was met by Luke, an old-time long-time waiter.

'Did you see the new head chef?' he asked me.

'Eh, not yet,' I lied.

Luke leaned in as if to tell me a big secret. 'Word is, he's a bollix. I believe he cut a waiter's finger off in his last job.'

I just shook my head. The reason I said *I lied* was because the new head chef was my brother Gerry. Gerry was not a bollix, and he never cut anybody's finger off. In fact, Gerry was a brilliant chef. He even represented Ireland in the Hotel Olympiad in London. I said nothing to Luke. Gerry ran the kitchen like a Swiss watch and the Skylon Hotel were lucky to get him.

The summer was ending. It was getting time to pack all this in and go back to Patrician College. *Soon*, I thought to myself, *it'll be seven and a half hours a day of schooling, three hours every night of studying and no money* . . . Then I said my thought out loud: 'Fuck it! I'm not going back.'

The thought scared the shit out of me but excited me too. How would I tell Mammy? I came up with a plan. The plan was I *wouldn't* tell Mammy. What I told Mammy was that Teddy had asked me would I like to work as a casual (part-time) when I went back to school.

Mammy was concerned. 'Will you be able for it?'

I assured her that I would; it was only five nights a week from six to ten. I'd get my homework done before I went to work. I'd be fine.

She agreed to let me, provided I would quit if doing school and work became too much.

I didn't tell the school; I just didn't go back. So each morning I would put on my uniform with which I now wore black trousers – I explained to Mammy that the grey was only for first years and she bought it – then I would leave the house and lock my bike at the shops and get the bus into work. After doing lunches I would come home, pretend to do homework, and then go back to do the rest of my split shift. It worked like a charm. For two months.

Mammy loved shopping. One of her favourite stores was Arnotts in Henry Street. It was shopping there one afternoon that she spotted one of the teachers from Patrician College, Brother Fideles. She made her way to him and they chatted about this and that. As Brother Fideles had me for Latin and my mother had taught Latin, she eventually asked him, 'So, tell me, Brother Fideles, how is Brendan doing?'

He raised his eyebrows. 'I was about to ask you the same question.'

I arrived in from work that night to find Mammy waiting for me. 'Sit down, love, you must be tired. I'll get you a cup of tea.'

I was delighted. 'Thanks, Mammy.' I made myself comfortable in an armchair by the fire. Minutes later Mammy arrived with a lovely cuppa. I sipped on the tea, and she began her ruse.

'How did school go this week?' she asked very matter-of-factly.

'Great. I'm really starting to enjoy it, especially science.' I did not suspect a thing.

She played along. 'Ah, science, it can be so interesting. Thermodynamics, gravitational calculations, and chemistry — can you believe that neon, which lights Times Square in New York, is an inert gas?'

I rolled my eyes. 'Yeh, can you believe it?'

She smiled. 'Inert my forking arse!' Then she laughed and so did I, even though I had not a fucking clue what she was talking about. We both now sipped our tea. She lit up a Consulate. She blew the smoke out and asked, 'And how is your Latin coming along?'

I took another sip. 'Good, yeh . . . Good.'

She smiled. 'Good. Let me hear some tenses.'

I began to get red-faced. 'Eh, *voco, vocobo, vocobemis.*' I stopped and cleared my throat.

She leaned back in her chair. 'My God, I remember teaching that . . . IN FORKING FIRST YEAR! AND YOU DIDN'T EVEN GET THEM RIGHT!' I was stumped. 'The game is up, you forking little forking liar!'

I got flustered. 'I'm trying my best,' I protested, still not yet realizing that I had been caught.

'Oh, I'm sure you are, but you'd find it easier to *try* if you went to forking school.'

It suddenly dawned on me. Fuck! She knew – how did she know?

'I met Brother Fideles today. You made a complete cant of me, yeh, yeh little cant.'

I decided that the only way out was to throw myself on the mercy of the court. 'I'm sorry. I'm really, really sorry, Mammy. I was going to tell you.'

She sat up. 'Were you now? When were you going to tell me?'

'I dunno, when the time was right. I don't know.' I was crying now.

Mammy looked at her watch. 'Well, it's half past eleven. NOW would be a good forking time.'

So I told her. I told her how I had been struggling in school. How much I loved serving people, being a part of their night out. How I loved the work, even though it was hard work. I stood up. 'Wait,' I said, as I went to the kitchen. I came back with a spoon and fork. I leaned across her and gently picked her cigarette out of the ashtray. 'See! I'm good at this.'

She held her hands to each side of her face. 'That's amazing.' I didn't realize she was being sarcastic and stood there with a big smile. 'It's not exactly a forking juggling show.'

I sat down, dejected. We stayed in silence for a time.

Eventually she said, 'Sorry, that was good.'

I said 'thanks', but I didn't mean it.

Silence again.

'Let me sleep on it,' she said, and I went to bed.

Mammy slept on it for two days. I don't mean she *slept* for two days; I just mean it wasn't talked about for two days. I wasn't aware of it, but she was making calls and putting things in place. She had called Teddy Gough, she had called the union and, in the meantime, I went to work as normal.

Eventually she sat me down. 'You are finished at the Skylon.' My heart sank, but I said nothing. 'If you want to carry on training as a waiter, OK, but you are going to train properly, and if you, my son, are going to be a waiter, you will strive to be the best waiter you can be.'

I'm thinking, *Train? What does she mean, train?*

'The Skylon Hotel don't have any training programme in place yet, so you are going to change to a hotel that does.'

For the first time I spoke. 'Well, Mr Gough will not like that,' I warned her.

'It was Teddy's suggestion,' she answered.

I was gobsmacked. She went on with her plan for my future.

'You start at the InterContinental Hotel next week. You will also attend Cathal Brugha Street Catering College two days a week –'

I interrupted her. 'Where is that?'

She stared at me for a moment. 'It's on Cathal Brugha Street, the clue is in the name.' She was being sarcastic again, but I was serious – I wanted to know where Cathal Brugha Street itself was. I hoped it wasn't miles away so that I'd have to travel an hour or something each way. It wasn't. It was in town, just three minutes from where my bus stopped. I had probably passed it a thousand times and never knew what it was. So that was it – decision made. I wasn't staying in the Skylon, but I wasn't going back to school either. Bit of yin, bit of yang.

That night was my last night in the Skylon. Before I finished Teddy sat down with me. 'You will see very quickly when you get to the InterContinental Hotel, and the college, the kind of training your mother was talking about. We can't do that here, not yet.'

I nodded my understanding. 'Mr Gough, I am going to be a great waiter someday, and I'll come back and work for you.'

Teddy laughed. 'You buckle down and become a great waiter, but I don't think you'll be back here, Brendan.'

I thought he was giving me the 'get out and don't come back' brush-off. As I stood up, I was a little deflated. 'Fair enough, Mr Gough, if that's how you feel.'

He stood too and smiled at me. 'Brendan, you will be a great waiter, but then I just know that you will go on and do great things. I don't know at what, but I can feel it, and there is not a better launching pad than being a waiter. You'll be back here all right, but as a customer not a waiter.' He winked and then did something I had never seen him do in the restaurant before. He hugged me. A first-year commis waiter and the boss hugged me. Teddy, God rest his soul, sent me on my way with my head held up and my chest puffed out. I was off to do 'great things'.

As Teddy had predicted, the InterContinental was a whole different can of piss altogether. It didn't take long for me to realize this. There was a uniform for the commis. For the commis that worked in the Embassy Room, the main restaurant, the uniform was a red jacket, the same cut as the one worn by members of the Chinese Communist Party. Although the jacket was red it had a green stripe down the middle, under which the buttons were hidden, and the sleeve ends were trimmed in green. It was the same uniform if you worked at the Coffee Dock, which was a twenty-four-hour-diner-type room. If you worked in the Martello Room, the most exclusive room on the very top floor, you wore the same style jacket, but it was green with a red stripe and trim.

First I was taken to the linen room. Joe, the second-year commis that was giving me my briefing and the tour on my first day, explained the 'system' to me.

'There are five areas where you can work; they are the canteen, the Embassy Room, the Coffee Dock, the Ballroom and the Martello Room. It's possible to work all of them over your four years of training, but you will work in at least three of them.'

As I stood in the linen room getting measured for my uniform, I wondered where I would start. Would it be the red jacket with the green stripe or the green jacket with the red stripe? It was neither. It was a plain red jacket. The sleeve ends were frayed, there were old stains, which looked like gravy, that despite multiple washes, and believe me this jacket had multiple washes, did not come out. The head housekeeper helped me into it. I buttoned it up and there was a button missing in the middle. I pointed this out and she just said, 'It's fine.'

I looked to Joe. 'I can't wear this jacket serving people,' I whined.

He smiled. 'You can where you're going.'

Yes, you've guessed it. The canteen. Not the main canteen; it had a side room where the managers, assistant managers, accountants and heads of department ate – there were about fifty of them. I was to serve these on my own. To make it even harder they all came in at the same time.

Joe took me to the canteen and introduced me to the

woman who ran it. Let's call her Karen because she was. From the moment I met her I knew she was going to break my balls. Oh boy, over the time I was there she did. No matter what I did or how hard I worked I couldn't please her. She never once said 'Well done' or even 'I suppose that'll do'. I got to detest her; she was only as tall as I was, but she was a roaring bitch, to me anyway.

I was there for breakfast and lunch. Once lunches were finished at three o'clock, I had to clear all the tables to a washroom in the other canteen, wipe them all down, mop out the room, wait for it to dry, then set the entire room up for breakfasts and prepare my station table for setting up for lunches. Dinner plates, side plates, knives, forks, dessert spoons, soup spoons, butter knives – all had to be carried from the main canteen into the managers' canteen. I would finish at about 4 p.m. I can't remember how many times the bus conductor woke me to get off the bus at the terminus. I would get on the bus, head against the window, and pass out.

Another thing, the college I was supposed to be attending had classes from three thirty to five thirty, so the other commis attended during their split day break. Not me. I was still shovelling shit while those classes went on. Joe had told me that I would be there for the first couple of months. Seven months later I was still there. There were so many days that I went home so tired that I would cry all the way home on the bus.

So one night I went into my mother's bedroom and sat on the edge of her bed. We had many, many conversations with me sitting on the edge of the bed, us solving the world's woes. That night I told her I wanted to leave the InterContinental and burst into tears. She hugged me and asked me why.

I had never told her about my boss, Attila the Hun, and I

poured it out: how hard the work was, how badly this woman treated me, the whole shebang.

She listened and when I had finished simply said, 'OK.'

I was aghast. 'Really?'

'Sure. But it's not like you.'

I was puzzled but I was also wary. Mammy had a way of turning you round without you realizing it. 'What do you mean?' I asked.

'It's not like you to make a big decision like that without questioning the situation. But if you think leaving is the answer, then leave.' That was the end of the chat.

Next day in work I decided to question the *situation* and my first call was to visit our shop steward, Andy Burke. A long-time union man and a real 'no bullshit' sort, I told him that I had been in the canteen for months now and was missing the training in Cathal Brugha Street.

He listened, nodding in the right places. 'Leave it with me, Brendan,' was his reply.

I left him thinking that I wouldn't hear any more about it, but I was wrong. Andy got back to me within an hour. He had already spoken to the food and beverage manager and with personnel. They acknowledged that it was unusual for me to have been in the canteen for so long. However, it could be explained. At the end of each summer one or two fourth-year commis waiters would come 'out of their time' and be fully qualified waiters, but for some reason there had been a lag that year. The good news was that there was a fourth year due to qualify within three weeks and I would be moved to the Embassy Room then. I was thrilled.

Later that day I also, I think for the first time, had a real chance to talk to 'Attila', during which I told her of my impending move. 'Good for you,' she said. Then without a smile or any change in the flat tone she spoke in, she added,

'You are too long here, but you will be missed. The managers who dine here really like you. It's hard work what you are doing but you never took any shortcuts and always arrived on time. To be honest, you are probably the best commis I've ever had here.' With that she stood, wiped the table and left, leaving me with my mouth open and my jaw on the table. The managers might have *really liked* me, but in all my time there not one of them had ever tipped me.

As Andy had promised, three weeks later I was reassigned to the Embassy Room. The policy in the Embassy Room was that you were assigned to a waiter for all the time you would spend there. His roster became your roster, except for breakfasts when you would work with room service. I didn't have a waiter assigned yet.

The roster was weird and changed every few months. My first roster was: Monday – off; Tuesday – three to ten; Wednesday (long day) – seven to three, back at six to ten; Thursday (split) – eleven to three and back at six to ten; Thursday – off; Friday (split); Saturday (split); Sunday (short day) – seven to eleven. This meant that I would finish on Sunday at 11 a.m. and not be due back to work until Tuesday at three o'clock. Each time the roster changed, you just moved your starting day forward by a day.

Twice a week I was in for breakfast and room service. The continental breakfast trays were slotted in tall steel cabinets already set for either one or two people. The cabinets were sorted by delivery time: seven, seven fifteen, seven thirty, etc. The 'Full Irish' breakfasts for two were served on tableclothed trollies, the line of which was the length of the kitchen. The head breakfast waiter had a stack of cardboard orders that the night porters had collected during the night, and he would read the orders, then slide the card on an appropriate tray or trolley. It was all go. The commis added the preserves, hot croissants, coffee or tea and milk or cream.

On one morning I was preparing a tray when the head commis looked it over and said, 'You forgot to put condoms on that order.'

I laughed out loud. 'Have we changed to the InterContinental Brothel now?'

Everyone stopped and stared at me with disdain: chefs, still-room women, kitchen porters and, worst of all, waiters. I cannot tell you how much pride every member of staff took in working for the InterContinental. Any slight was taken personally.

It was a waiter that saved the day. Bart O'Brien. He laughed too. 'CONDIMENTS, Top Cat, not condoms.'

Now everybody laughed and for the rest of my time, not just at the InterContinental but in the hotel business, I was called either Top Cat or T. C.

Speed was essential on breakfasts. You were no sooner finished delivering two seven o'clocks, than the seven fifteens were due. I cannot remember exactly, but there must have been at least twelve commis there each morning, along with their waiters, so twenty-four of us running like fuck to get those breakfasts up to one of the seven floors of rooms. Once room service finished at 9.30 you had your own breakfast, and then the onerous task of clearing the floors would begin at 10 a.m. This was only done by the commis as the waiters were now assigned to lay the Embassy Room for lunch.

Clearing the floors was tough work. You took one of the steel cabinets to the floor you were assigned to, collected the trays that in many cases were left outside the door, or if not you used your master key to get them out of the room, stacked the cabinet and the two of you (we worked in pairs) would wheel the now heavily laden cabinet down the length of the corridor into the service lift, then out of it, drag it past the locker room, past the linen room (which was all uphill), then past the canteen. You would take a left at the canteen and drag it down another corridor past accounts, personnel and administration offices to yet another lift. Down one floor to the kitchen and across the kitchen to the washing station. Here you had to scrape and stack all the plates, separate the cutlery, bin anything that was unused, even if it wasn't opened (the hotel took hygiene and safety VERY seriously). We then would clean down the unit itself, clean all the trays, put a clean tray mat on each one and stack the cabinet ready for the next morning. We would take the cabinet over to the room-service area where other commis would be waiting to set them for tomorrow. It was tough, but I just loved it.

After my first week I was assigned to my waiter. I had met a few of them on room service and I already had a good idea of who I DIDN'T want. I struck gold. My waiter was Bart O'Brien, the very man who had christened me T. C. We hit it off brilliantly.

The head waiter in the Embassy Room was a tall, very handsome guy, Gerry Gallagher. He seemed to concentrate on running the restaurant and paid little attention to the commis; that was left almost entirely to your waiter. Bart was a great mentor. He encouraged me non-stop. On days when I had spent my break in the college he would question me on what I had learned there.

He was hilarious. Once he asked me what I had learned that day and I said the history of various dishes. 'Like what?' he asked.

'Like the, eh, history of the sirloin steak.'

Bart nodded. 'And what is the history of the sirloin steak?'

I tried to think. 'Eh, it was originally just loin of beef, then when it was cooked for a king of England one time, eh, he loved it. He loved it so much that he knighted it, so it became "Sir Loin".' I waited for him to react. I was now doubting myself. 'Is that right, Bart?'

He smiled. 'I haven't a fucking clue. But it's a good story and if it's not true, it should be.' That night as we served our station at dinner Bart got me to recite the story at every table. He would call me as they were on coffee. He would wink to them and say, 'Listen to this.' He would prime the customers by saying: 'T.C., tell these lovely people the history of the humble sirloin steak.'

I would then rattle off the story and the customers would do a little clap.

Bart would rub my head and dismiss me. Then he'd say to them, 'I taught him that. Well, someone has to look out for him – he's an orphan.' I got my share of the tips that followed.

Life with Bart was an adventure. I only had Bart for one year. I was informed at the end of my year with him that I was being promoted to head commis in the ballroom. I was very pleased until I found out that I was also the ONLY commis in the ballroom. This was the hardest work I had ever done. Setting up the room to the plan Eugene, my head waiter, had drawn. Putting out the seats. Then there would be a bar set up for the pre-meal drinks; this was a separate room that ran the full length of the ballroom and had six doors or so into the function room itself. If the meal was for, say, 600 people, when they went in to eat I would have only the length of the meal to clear this room of glasses and have it ready for the after-meal action. At night I would wake up crying having dreamed that I was surrounded by glasses and people were beginning to come into the room.

When I had eventually served my four years and qualified it was time to look for another place to work. A restaurant can only have so many waiters. My brother Micháel was now working in the Green Isle Hotel, out on the Naas Road. It was a busy hotel with rooms and chalets. I went for an interview and the head waiter told me he couldn't afford to hire a waiter, but as he knew Micko he was prepared to offer me a job as an improver. An improver is not a commis and not a fully qualified waiter, a kind of 'nearly' waiter. The money was all right and I would see Micko every day, so I took the job.

I am so glad to this day that I did, for three reasons that I will tell you about here. The first was the head waiter, Noel Smith. He was amazing. He was a total showman. Every Saturday night we would be fully booked out and Noel would turn on the showman. Juggling the tables, getting people in and out. We never had enough tables. I once bent over to tie my shoelace and Noel threw a tablecloth over me and said, 'Lay him up for two.' Nobody made Irish coffees the way he did. He would make them in a brass flambé pan. Once he did his first one of the night and the flame burst from the pan up into the air, orders for Irish coffees came thick and fast.

The second reason was that I met John Sweeney. John's brother Mick was the head barman and John was in the same boat as me in that he was an 'improver barman'. We got on really well. He was a great footballer and we both played for the hotel team in the Wednesday afternoon hotels' league. The importance of John was not just that he was a good friend but that many years later, when we were both thirty-five and he was the manager of the Rathmines Inn, he gave me my very first gig as a stand-up comedian. More about that later.

The third and final reason that I am glad I took that job is because every Saturday night in the Winter Garden, the ball-room of the hotel, a dinner cabaret was held. The bonus for me was that before the main act performed in the Winter Garden they did a thirty-minute spot in our restaurant. We had an organ there and a tiny dance floor. The organ was played all night by Tommy Dando, who would also accompany the act if it were a singer. Sometimes it was a magician and I'd watch as he set up his stuff, but many times it was a comic. Old-fashioned but so funny. I would 'look after' the act before they went on. I got to meet Cecil Sheridan, an amazing performer. When he would be waiting to go on I'd ask him if he needed anything. It was usually a glass of water, but he had such a bad stammer it took him a while to get it out. He would then go on stage and do his whole hilarious comedy routine, amazingly without stammering once. He really was funny too. I would go home every Saturday night and repeat the comic's routine to Mammy, and she would cry laughing.

But the best of all was the inimitable Hal Roach. Hal had the best timing I have ever seen in a comic then or since. He was shit-hot. The routine was virtually the same each time, but I would laugh every time. He had little comments he'd make between gags, which I also loved. The bonus for me was that I could imitate Hal's voice, so when I did his routine in front of Mammy she really howled.

I'd walk into her bedroom as if walking on to a stage and off I'd go:

'Father Murphy was giving it socks from the pulpit the other day. He told us the end of the world was coming and we must be prepared. "Stand up," he shouted, "all those that want to go to Heaven." Of course we all stood up right away. "Stand up all those that want to go to Hell." Nobody stood up except Muldoon. "Do you want to go to Hell,

Muldoon?" "No, Father," says Muldoon. "*I just didn't like to see you standing there by yourself.*"

'*Write it down, that's a good one.*

'*Casey went to the dentist. He said to the dentist, "All my teeth are turning yellow. What should I do?" And the dentist said, "Wear a brown tie!"*

'*Oh, you lucky people, I wish I could be out there with you listening to this. Fantastic stuff.*

'*My dear people, let me try to describe the Widow Quinn: a wild woman from the hills of County Kerry with a figure like six miles of bad road. Long red hair down her back, none on her head. An ugly woman, God bless her. When she went to the zoo the keeper would tell her, "Keep moving – we're stocktaking."*

'*Teacher asks the child, "Who in Greek mythology was half man, half animal?" "Buffalo Bill," says the child.*

'*Teacher asks the child, "If I lay six eggs over there and five eggs over here, how many eggs would I have?" The child says, "I don't believe you can do it, sir."*

'*I met a woman who recently had twins. "Are they identical?" I asked. She answered, "The girl is but the boy isn't."*

'*Things that an Irish mammy would say . . . "Shut your mouth and eat your dinner," or "If you fall and break your leg, don't come running to me!"*'

If a gag didn't get a laugh, Hal would say, 'That's a little one I pulled out of the air. I think I'll put it back – it needs as much air as it can get.' Or: 'Oh, good God, there's a day job staring me in the face right now.'

When I became a comic I got to meet Hal and befriend him. And when in 2012 he passed away I was so honoured when his lovely wife Mary asked me to write a piece as part of his obituary.

Hal communicated with laughter. Shortly after Hal had been ill (he had a lung removed), we met literally as we were passing in Dublin airport. I was returning from gigs in America and he was heading out to gig in Las Vegas.

I gave him a big hug. 'You look wonderful,' I said, and he thanked me for the compliment. 'I heard you had a lung removed?'

He smiled. 'I did, and do you know I'm feeling so good I'm thinking of having the other one out.'

I laughed, we hugged again and that was the last we saw of each other. My hero.

Thanks to Hal, I can still see myself pausing while Mammy recovered from the laughter and coughing, wiping her eyes with her hanky. Those nights on her bedroom 'stage' were the proudest of my young life. Those were my best-ever performances. I would give everything to have five minutes more with her to tell her just one more joke. Ah well.

I worked at the Green Isle Hotel for three of my happiest years in the hotel business. I won't bore you with my job-hopping, but here is a list of the places I worked:

The Skylon Hotel
The InterContinental Hotel
The Green Isle Hotel
The Shelborne Hotel
The Pot Pourri restaurant
Cleary's restaurant
The Night Owl restaurant
Ashbourne House Hotel

But one year in that business that I do want to tell you about is 1984. Not the George Orwell one, more the George Buckley one. This is when I worked for the outdoor catering department of Aer Lingus. George Buckley was the head waiter. My brother Gerry was at this point working in the flight kitchen for Aer Lingus and it was he who suggested once, when I was between jobs (unemployed), that I should take some casual work with the outdoor catering. So I did and it led me to some of the greatest adventures of my life.

The outdoor catering department of Aer Lingus catered for a huge range of functions like exclusive private weddings, horse auctions, the Dublin Horse Show, racecourses, private in-home functions for the very wealthy, boardroom lunches for the top companies in Ireland and golf; we catered for the Irish Open for many years. I got my biggest-ever tip at the Irish Open. I was head waiter in one of the corporate marquees. We would have twenty tables of twelve, most booked by a different company for each of the four days. Some, though, would be booked by the same company for each day, bringing a different group of clients each day. The tipping gentleman involved was the host of two tables that were booked for the four days by an Irish bank. On the very first day he came to me and asked if I would be looking after him for the four days. I assured him I would. Keep in mind that my salary for the four days would be about £40 a day, so £160 for the week. I escorted him as he looked over the tables and he seemed satisfied.

He took an envelope from his pocket and handed it to me. 'I assume you will make sure our guests are well taken care of?' I tucked the envelope into my inside pocket and assured him that there would be nothing for him to worry about. I got distracted with getting the waiters' stations organized, doing other last-minute odds and ends, and, before I knew it, the first of the clients started arriving. The day went brilliantly well. By the end of it I had made over £50 in tips and sat to have a cuppa before heading home. It was when I was counting my tips that I remembered the envelope. I took it from my pocket and opened it. Inside was a cheque. For £1,200. It took my breath away.

The next day I made a point of getting the host alone and thanking him profusely for his generosity. He simply said, 'Well, if yesterday is anything to go by, it's worth every penny.'

I had bussed my way to and from the golf every day that year. The day after it ended I bought a second-hand bright yellow Mini Cooper. Bernhard Langer had won the golf, but I had hit the jackpot.

Thanks to Aer Lingus, I got to serve some of the world's leaders. Let me explain. The Department of Foreign Affairs had from time to time used Aer Lingus Outdoor Catering for banquets for visiting dignitaries. Working on these, I served people like the crown prince of Japan, Helmut Kohl of Germany and Jacques Chirac of France. I even got to be on the team that looked after Robert Mugabe and his party, or henchmen would be more apt. If ever there was an evil-looking bunch it was they. Scary. Someday I may write another book and I can include more detail of my time in the hotel and catering industry, but for now I want to tell you about two particular heads of government that I have served. President Ronald Reagan and Prime Minister Margaret Thatcher.

Ireland had its third presidency of the European Council in 1984. During that time Mrs Thatcher came to Ireland for the first time. I served her first drink at Áras an Uachtaráin, the home of the president of Ireland. I stood beside the head waiter, George Buckley, as he asked her what she would like to drink, and she said, 'I always said that if I ever came to *southern* Ireland I would have an Irish whiskey.' I fetched the whiskey and strangely she asked me whether I had children. I said yes, I had two: Fiona, my eldest, and Danny who was just a baby then. Weird, but there you go.

During that visit we did various functions associated with the occasion. One was a lunch in Dublin Castle. George Buckley had impressed upon us that Mrs Thatcher was to make a speech that would be broadcast live on the one o'clock news, so we had to have everything served and be off the floor before then. We had to hurry without looking like we were rushing. It was a close-run thing. The dessert was fresh strawberries and we had just got them served as George was herding us out of the room. As I passed behind Mrs Thatcher she raised her hand, so I stopped. 'Could I have some caster sugar, please?' she asked. I had been supposed to bring that out with the strawberries and in the rush I had forgotten. Now, with just minutes to spare, I hurried to the kitchen, grabbed a bag of caster sugar, poured it into a dish and took it out to her.

I got back to the kitchen where there was a TV just as the intro music for the news was starting. The Taoiseach, Garret FitzGerald, spoke first and as he was speaking, out of the corner of my eye, I caught sight of the bag of sugar I had just used. It was a white plastic bag and written on the side of it in black marker was one word. *SALT.* I went pale. Now I was glued to the TV, not to hear Garret speak but to watch Mrs Thatcher as she waited to speak. Garret was going on and on, so Mrs Thatcher picked up a small strawberry, dipped it in the sugar/salt and bit into it. I was about to pass out. Her expression didn't change. She lifted her serviette as if to wipe her lips, but I knew exactly what she was doing – spitting out a strawberry. Soon after she stood and spoke at length.

When the meal ended I expected the chief of protocol, or at least George Buckley, to fire me. Nothing was ever said. She said nothing and neither did I. Finally, and I want to preface this by telling you that I am a democratic socialist – I was against everything that Mrs Thatcher stood for and

I was horrified by her treatment of the miners and unions in general – but here's the thing: I do like class.

On her last day, Mrs Thatcher sat with Sir Geoffrey Howe as they waited for their car or helicopter or whatever to pick her up and I was serving her tea or coffee – I can't remember which. Once I had it poured, Mrs Thatcher said this: 'Thank you, Brendan. I'll bet Fiona and Daniel will be happy to see you.'

I was aghast. As I said, I hated everything she stood for, but if you can remember a waiter's name and his kids' names after the few days she went through . . . well, that's class.

Now to good old Ronnie.

Ronald Reagan's great-grandfather came from a little village in Ireland named Ballyporeen. It was decided that he should come to Ireland on an official visit and during it take in Ballyporeen. Honestly, until President Reagan went to visit I had never heard of the place. The welcoming banquet was to be held in the main hall of Dublin Castle, and we were doing the catering. Security was ridiculously tight. All manhole covers along the president's driving route and within a mile of Dublin Castle were welded closed.

The day of the banquet started badly for me. I had to be there early and the first bus from Ashbourne, where I lived, wouldn't get me into the city in time, so I stood on the side of the main road with my suit cover over my arm, thumbing a lift with the other hand. Lots of cars passed me without stopping. Eventually a Volkswagen van pulled in and a hand out of the window called me on. I ran to the van's side window.

'Where are you going?' the guy in the passenger seat asked me.

'Just into town.'

He smiled. 'OK. Hop in.'

Someone slid open the side door. The van was packed. I kid you not, there must have been a dozen people in it. I squeezed in, they shut the door and off the van went, slowly at first, then it built up momentum and we were on our way.

The group started singing now. 'We're off to see the wizard . . .' I smiled and even joined in. As I sang along, I was looking around the van, smiling, and my eye caught a stack of square white cards – they were about two feet by two feet. The thought ran through my head that they would be perfect for a . . . protest. I stretched myself up slightly to try to read the writing on the topmost card. *Fuck Reagan*, it read.

Fuck me! I thought. *If I'm seen getting out of this piece of shit with these headcases, I won't be off to see the wizard; I'll be off to the fucking nick.* As we got closer to Dublin Castle the gang were now singing 'We're on the One Road'.

I shouted at the driver, 'Anywhere here will do me, thanks.'

He couldn't hear me. Now we are at the traffic lights at the bottom of the Christ Church Cathedral hill.

'Hello, just here is fine for me.'

There's no reply and he pulls away from the traffic lights. 'STOP THE FUCKING VAN!' I screamed.

They all went quiet. 'I'm not stopping halfway up the hill; I'll stop at the top.'

When the van pulled over, we were just 300 yards from Dublin Castle. I got out and shouted my thanks back to the driver.

There were four Gardai standing together twenty yards away. They watched me get out of the van. As the van passed them, the boys inside shouted out of the windows. 'Go fuck yourself' and 'Go on, yeh fuckin' state muppet.'

As I walked past the Gardai, I said, 'I'm not with them. I was just getting a lift, I swear.'

The Gardai couldn't have cared less. Not so the Secret

Service. They took their gig very seriously. We got a briefing from them before the meal. It was something like, 'Here is the way it happens. You stand away from the table, back to the wall. When it's time to approach, the appointed Secret Service guy will give the head waiter a signal, the head waiter will give you guys the signal, and you can approach the table. Do NOT approach the table without a signal from the head waiter.' We were transfixed and scared. My immediate thought was that the soup was consommé! Hard not to spill at the best of times, but when you are shaking, good luck!

One of the waiters made a good point. 'Sir, we're waiters. If someone is looking about, or raises a hand, our instinct is to go to them and ask can we help. What happens then?'

The Secret Service guy put a finger to his forehead and said, 'You'll have one hole here and ten bullets in that hole.'

Consommé, fucking consommé!! I thought.

The evening went off without a hitch, though, and I managed to get a lift from one of the aides who I had met earlier when we were both outside having a smoke. He gave me three cigars in aluminium tubes with the presidential crest on them and a few books of matches with the crest too. But the big score was as I was clearing out the 'green room' used by the aides and some Secret Service guys. I picked up a menu of the night's meal signed by the president. I had no idea where that menu went. But I did find it eventually.

On 9 May 1984, when my son Danny was just eight months old, my mother, who lived with us, took him up to her room for a nap. He fell asleep and she died. As I was fixing her, waiting for the doctor to pronounce her dead, I noticed something sticking out from under her pillow. I smiled to myself as I pulled it out; it was the menu.

Mammy had been a nun, a teacher, a member of parliament, a wife and a mother. She had lived many lives in one lifetime. She was tired. It was time to rest. To close her eyes and go quietly into the night.

Her funeral was spectacular. The hearse stopped outside the Irish houses of parliament and the tricolour was lowered to half mast. From Blackrock to her resting place in Deansgrange Cemetery, about six miles, women of the Garda force lined the route, each of them saluting as her flag-draped coffin passed. At her graveside, a bugler sounded the Last Post as she was laid to rest. It was beautiful.

I did not cry. Not once. I thought it was because between Mammy and me nothing was left unsaid. She knew how much I loved her, and I knew how much she loved me. So I didn't cry. Not then.

IO

Incredibly, as much as I loved the hotel life, over the next few years I tried my best to get out of it. Somewhere in my mind I envied those people who worked nine to five and had every weekend off. Mammy called me Heinz Fifty-seven because she believed I had that many jobs. I was a window cleaner, a sportswriter, an advertising salesman, a cartoonist, a chef, a painter and decorator. One of the most interesting was when I was a presenter on a pirate radio station called Alternative Radio Dublin or ARD 257. I had two shows. On Friday evenings from seven to nine I presented *257 World of Sport,* and on Sunday mornings from eight to eleven I was *Uncle Bren the Kiddies' Friend,* a phone-in show where I also got to play whatever music I liked. In those days I had a perm like Kevin Keegan (hey, I can hear you fucking laughing). Really I had! When playing football I wore a headband to keep the hair out of my eyes.

I did both shows for about two years, but I never thought of myself as an entertainer. I had great fun. The children's show was hilarious as kids, if you give them the space, will say anything. But as funny as it was, the sports show gave me the most laughs. Read the following scripts of two interviews and one 'exclusive' and you'll see what I mean.

The first is with Synan Braddish, who was a young Irish footballer from Finglas. He was picked up by Liverpool FC. This was a huge thing for his father, who was a fixture of Finglas football, and also a cause for celebration for the whole of Finglas. I knew Synan and had both played with him and against him. He was a lovely, mannerly young man, and still is. When the news hit the papers, I had Synan in for his first-ever radio interview.

SYNAN BRADDISH

INT. ARD 257 STUDIO - EVENING
Brendan is presenting and they have just come back from a record.

> BRENDAN
> That was 'Three Times a Lady', and right now with me in the studio is one lucky gentleman. Synan Braddish, you are welcome to *257 World of Sport*.

> SYNAN
> Thanks, BOCK.

> BRENDAN
> Well, what a week this has been for you.

> SYNAN
> Yeh. I'm over the moon, over the moon.

> BRENDAN
> I'll bet you are. And a wonderful day for your dad too, who I think I have seen on the sideline of every game you have played?

> SYNAN
> Yeh. He's over the moon, over the moon.

BRENDAN
Where were you when you got the news?

SYNAN
Well, they've been talking for a while, but
when it was all agreed I was over the moon.

BRENDAN
I'll bet you were. I'm sure you'll be
somewhat nervous. Liverpool is a big
club.

SYNAN
Yeh, but, listen, I'm over the moon, I
am. Over the moon.
Brendan *stops for a moment. Silence.*

SYNAN (CONT'D)
Over the moon.

BRENDAN (*SURRENDERING*)
Well, we here on 257 and the whole
of Finglas, indeed Ireland, wish you
the very best, Synan.

SYNAN
Great, thanks. I'm –
Mic is cut.

BRENDAN
OK then, that was Finglas's own Synan
Braddish, off on his greatest adventure

to Liverpool Football Club. We all wish
him well, and, in case you missed
it, he is over the moon.

FOR THE BIRDS?

INT. ARD 257 STUDIO – EVENING
The station is broadcasting its
Friday evening sports show called
257 World of Sport. The host is
twenty-four-year-old Brendan O'Carroll.
The show is on an advert break as we
join it. Standing by is Jim Healy,
president of the Clonakilty Racing
Pigeon Club. Jim is so stereotypical;
he wears a long brown woollen coat and
a cloth cap.
  The advert break ends.

BRENDAN
Welcome back to *257 World of Sport*. Coming
up later we'll be having a look at all
this week's football fixtures that matter
in the League of Ireland, but first I am
delighted to welcome to the studio Jim
Healy. Welcome, Jim.
Jim blows into the microphone so hard that
Brendan has to remove his headphones.

BRENDAN (CONT'D)
Wow! Jim. Eh, don't do that.

JIM (*LOUDLY*)
ONE, TWO, TESTING, ONE, TWO!
I can't hear anything.

BRENDAN
No, you need to put on those headphones
on the table there, and you'll hear
everything.
Jim spots the headphones and puts them on.

BRENDAN (CONT'D)
How is that for you?
Jim gives a thumbs up.

BRENDAN (CONT'D)
Eh, you can speak now . . . just to make
sure you can hear yourself.

JIM (*TENTATIVE*)
Helloooo?

BRENDAN
That's great. OK, well, as I said, you
are welcome to *257 World of Sport*, Jim.
For those of you listening that are into
pigeons, this will interest you. Jim
is . . . . Well, Jim, why don't you tell
our audience what you are?
There is a pause for a few seconds.

JIM
I'm a carpenter.

*Brendan is now wondering if Jim is
taking the piss. Or if he is being
pranked. He looks over to the window
of the control room where the producer,
Gene Kerrigan, is sitting. Gene
shrugs.*

> BRENDAN
> No, I mean outside of your carpentry
> work . . . what you are.

> JIM
> I'm married with four children.

Brendan laughs.

> BRENDAN
> You're a funny man, Jim.

*Brendan realizes that this is going to be
tough-going.*

> Jim is the president of the Clonakilty
> Racing Pigeon Club.

> JIM (*BRIGHTENS*)
> That's right, I am, for the last five
> years.

*Brendan is delighted to at last have Jim
on topic.*

> BRENDAN
> And the club has how many members?

                    JIM
It goes up and down, but on average
around seventy. But there is a core
      membership of fifty-five.
*Things seem to be back on track. Brendan
decides to give Jim a soft question to
lead him in to describing what it's all
about.*

                  BRENDAN
Well, I have to tell you, Jim, that I
know very little about pigeon racing,
and I'm sure many listeners to the
       show are the same, so?

                    JIM
                    OK.
That's all he says. Silence.

                  BRENDAN
     Tell me about the sport.

                    JIM
Well, we basically breed and race
              pigeons.

                  BRENDAN
OK. You make it sound simple, Jim, but
   I'm sure it's more complex.

                    JIM
              Not really.

Brendan decides to lighten the interview.

BRENDAN

How long have you been racing
pigeons, Jim?

JIM

Over twenty years.

BRENDAN

Have you ever beaten one?

Brendan laughs. Jim is puzzled

JIM (*SERIOUS*)

I don't race them myself; they race each
other.

*Brendan is stunned. But thankfully Jim
elaborates.*

JIM (CONT'D)

At the clubhouse, all clocks are synced
up. Then the pigeons are taken to a
prearranged location and set off all at
the same time.When they arrive back to
their handlers, the ring is clocked and
the winner is determined by, as in any
race, the fastest bird.

*This is exactly what Brendan needs the
listeners to hear and Jim is great in his
explanation. Brendan now tries to keep
him talking about it.*

BRENDAN

But I'm sure that some members live further
from the prearranged starting point; is
there an allowance made for that?

JIM

Yes.

Brendan waits . . . Nope. That's it.

BRENDAN

Is there a training regime involved to
keep the birds . . . I suppose I want to
say 'fit'?

JIM

Yes.

*Nothing else. Remembering that when he
tried to lighten the interview before
that spurred Jim on, Brendan tries again.*

BRENDAN (*JOKINGLY*)

I can just see you cycling along with
the bird on a leash, you know,
saying 'Pick up the pace.'

Jim remains serious.

JIM

That would be illegal.

BRENDAN

What?

                            JIM
        Tethering a bird in any way would be
                illegal, never mind cruel.
Brendan gives up.

                          BRENDAN
        Indeed, I'm sure it is, and we should all
        remember that. Right then, eh, well, Jim,
        thank you for coming into the studio, and
          for anyone who wants to find out more
        about the sport who should they contact?

                            JIM
                            Me.
Silence.

                          BRENDAN
        Great! OK, I will get Jim's details from
          him, and you can call the station if
          you're interested. Here's Bonnie Tyler
                with 'It's a Heartache'.

  Those were heady days, and the pirate stations were bursting with talent like Ian Dempsey or Simon Young. When
they were eventually closed down by the government, many
of the presenters went on to work on television or 'real'
radio.

11

I have been avoiding writing about my first marriage, but not for the reasons that you think. My ex-wife Doreen hated being in the public eye. The life I chose was not the life she would have chosen. She is very private and does not like the limelight. Doreen asked me, when we separated, to promise not to talk about her in interviews or in any public form. However, it is impossible to talk about my children without mentioning that she was their mother. So the brief headlines are as follows. We met when we were fifteen years old. We became friends really, good friends. I was very fond of her family in general, but I loved her mother, Dolly.

As always happens, the lads on the football team became great friends and the wives and girlfriends became great friends. One by one the lads and girlfriends got engaged to be married. So, even though many of the team were older than us, it soon became our turn. By the time it was coming up to her eighteenth birthday I proposed, kind of. We just agreed we'd get engaged. When I told Mammy she went nuts. She actually ran out of words and picked up a poker to hit me. This only hardened my resolve.

When we both calmed down this was her reasoning: 'Doreen is a lovely girl. But if you marry her, you will ruin both your lives. Brendan, you are going places that Doreen has no intention of going. You're more like brother and sister than boyfriend and girlfriend.'

I stood my ground. 'I am getting engaged. We will be celebrating that in Doreen's house and you are welcome to come.'

Mammy just shook her head.

We got engaged on Doreen's eighteenth birthday and none of my family came.

Around this time I was working in a new resort up in the Dublin Mountains called Pat Quinn's Club. It was an exciting new idea, which included an artificial ski slope, an eighteen-hole golf course, three restaurants, a cabaret room and many, many other amenities. Unfortunately it fell victim to the fuel crisis of the 1970s, because the only way to get to the resort was to drive. Even the shipping lines were running into trouble, with the result that many of the amusements the club had promised were held up. For instance, the ski slope arrived but no skis. It was a mess for Pat Quinn, whose vision and dedication to the project nearly broke him.

Anyhow, at that time the biggest star in Ireland was a comedian named Brendan Grace. He was huge. There were three big comedians at that time: Billy Connolly in Scotland, Max Boyce in Wales and Brendan Grace in Ireland. All three had started as folk or ballad singers and branched out, in some cases by accident, into comedy. Brendan Grace got married at the resort and I was one of the waiters. The other waiters were telling Brendan about my impersonations of Hal Roach, a hero of Brendan's too, so at the wedding I got up and did a few gags as Hal and got a few laughs.

Brendan came to me later and said he was impressed; he took my phone number and told me that when he returned from his honeymoon he would call me. I thought to myself, *I will never hear from him again.* But I was wrong. Brendan offered me a job and I took it. I unloaded the van, set up the sound, I worked on scripts, I wound up cables, I did the spotlights and I loved it.

We were on the road virtually all the time. But after two years of this, relations between Doreen and me got a bit frayed. I knew that this on-the-road life and getting married was not going to work so I came off the road.

I learned so much from Brendan Grace that I never thought I would use but, believe me, none of it went to waste. Over the next few months we attended many weddings as the football team got married one by one. Always the taunt from the other guys and girls at the weddings was 'You're next, you two. Get a move on.' So, indeed, our turn came, and we got married.

12

I couldn't wait to become a father but I had to.

We were nearly two years married when Doreen became pregnant. I was now working two jobs in an effort to save enough for a deposit on a house. I was a van driver for Traynor Motors, delivering car parts, and at night I worked as the night cleaner in the Jeyes factory in Finglas where they made toilet tissue and babies' nappies. With me working so much we were seeing little of each other and we often joked that we passed each other in the corridor. That wasn't far wrong.

Then, after nine and a half months, on her final visit to the maternity-hospital doctor, a date was set for Doreen to be admitted. As it transpired, it was the same date that the football team's end-of-season function was to take place. I didn't care; I could easily miss that. When she was settled in her bed, I sat by the bedside and we chatted. 'Nothing is going to happen tonight,' she said. 'I'm tired anyway. You may as well head off to the function.' I said I would stay, but within half an hour she was asleep. She wasn't kidding; she really was tired. I waited another half-hour and then silently left.

I arrived at the function just at the tail end of it. All the wives and girlfriends wanted to know what was happening. I told them she was comfortable and sleeping. I stayed about a half-hour and headed home. The next morning I called to see how she was. A nurse answered but instead of giving me the rundown a doctor came on the phone. 'Do you intend coming in to visit your wife today?' Of course I did, I told him. 'Well, I need you to ask for me. I need to talk to you when you get here. '

I left for the hospital immediately. When I got there Doreen wasn't in the ward. I asked a nurse where she was and was told she was in the delivery room. I hurried there and was met at the door by the doctor that had been on the phone. He took me aside. 'Mr O'Carroll, your wife has a tough fight ahead of her.'

I couldn't understand what had happened. 'Why, what's wrong?'

The doctor, I'm sure, told me what was wrong, but for the life of me I cannot remember what he said. 'Can I go in?' I asked.

He advised me not to as there was a team in there and it wouldn't be helpful if I was in the way.

I called Mammy. I told her what I knew, which was very little, and she told me to stay strong for Doreen.

I went to the waiting room and, well, I waited. My brother Micko arrived about an hour later. I was never so glad to see him. I hugged him and told him I had no news.

Eventually, at about 3 a.m. the doctor found me. 'You have a son.'

I was waiting for the 'but' and it came.

'Your son has a condition called hydrocephalus and spina bifida.' The doctor may as well have been speaking in Greek; I had no idea what he was talking about. He went on. 'The baby has been taken to the Angels ward for intensive care and your wife is in a private room just two doors down.'

'Can I see her now?' I asked.

He nodded, all the while holding me firmly by the shoulders. 'She has been heavily sedated. You can see her, but you won't get a response. She'll sleep for a few hours.'

144

And she did sleep for many hours. I called Mammy. 'Mammy, what the hell is hydrocephalus and spina bifida?'

Mammy was quiet. 'Not on the phone, love. Come here for a cup of tea.'

I checked in again on Doreen and she was still asleep, so I drove to Finglas and sat with Mammy for a cup of tea.

Mammy explained what the battle my son faced was. Let me point out a couple of things here. Although I was very young, I could not wait to be a father, probably because for most of my life I didn't have one. So because of this, before the baby was even born, I had the picture in my head of the nice house with a white picket fence and the baby out back on a swing that I had made. Suddenly I had found myself in what I thought was a nightmare.

I returned to the hospital, where Doreen was still asleep.

A nurse came to me and quietly said, 'Your son is up in the Angels ward. Would you like to go up and see him?'

I don't know why but I recoiled. 'NO!' I snapped.

She left and I sat there in the quiet. I started to ask myself why I'd reacted like that. What was wrong with me? I think it was because somewhere in my mind, and I know this is crazy, I thought it was my fault. I felt guilty. Doreen was lying in a hospital bed, the baby was in intensive care, and here I was just sitting doing nothing.

I went out to the nurses' station and over to the nurse that had spoken to me. 'Excuse me, I'm really sorry for snapping. Of course I'd like to see Brendan.'

She smiled. 'You've picked his name then?'

I hadn't even realized I had said it. But, yes, I had picked his name. Long before he was born, long before I was even married, I had wanted a Brendan Junior, and when he was growing up I'd call him 'Brendy' just like Mr Reddin had called me.

The nurse walked me up to the Angels ward, where I was gowned and masked. She sat me in an office and went to get the doctor. The room it seemed was nearly all glass. I could see lots of baby incubators. I could see the nurse that had brought me there speaking to a doctor, then she went to one of the incubators and I saw her rub the side of it. On her way out she popped her head into the office. 'The paediatrician will be with you shortly. That's your son over there.' She pointed to the incubator that I had seen her at. 'You can go over if you wish?'

I shook my head and said, 'I'm fine, thanks.' Again I heard my head scream at me: *What the fuck is wrong with you? Go and see your son.*

I got up and slowly made my way to the incubator. I don't know what I expected him to look like, but it certainly wasn't what he *did* look like. He was beautiful. Big blue eyes. God love him, he looked like me. I know it sounds stupid, but I counted his fingers and I counted his toes. Ten of each. I couldn't see anything wrong with him. With the exception of a long wide plaster down his back he looked like any other baby I had ever seen, except more beautiful.

A voice from behind me said, 'Touch him, if you want.' It was the doctor.

'Can I?' I asked.

He smiled. 'Sure, Brendan is *your* son.'

I frowned. 'How did you know his name?'

He pointed to the side of the incubator. The nurse had written on a strip of plaster and stuck it on. *Baby Brendan.* I put my hand in through one of the holes of the incubator, and my son held on to my finger.

Later I sat in the glass office with the doctor. He went through the details of the battle that Brendan would have ahead of him. It seemed like he would need surgery after

146

surgery. But the game had changed for me. I was now more excited than worried. Just for a few minutes. Until I asked, 'When can we take him home, doctor?'

The doctor looked at me with a sad but understanding face. He rose and walked to me. He placed his hand on my shoulder. 'Son, you'll probably never have this baby home.' I think his use of 'son' made me want to behave all adult and grown-up.

'Of course not, I understand,' I said, but I didn't. I did not go back to Doreen's ward; I went to my car and cried. I decided I would not go to her ward until I stopped crying. I walked into her ward just under an hour later. The nurse had told me on my way in that Doreen had woken briefly while I was gone, but she was asleep again now. I sat for a long time.

She woke again briefly. 'Hey there,' I said.

She asked, 'Did you see the baby?'

'Yes, he's beautiful,' I said.

She half smiled. 'That's good.' And as she said this, she drifted off to sleep again.

I wished I could do something to change all that was happening. But I couldn't. All I could do was be an onlooker and cheerleader, and, for a week, a father.

Brendan's burial was at 7.30 a.m. in the Angels plot in Glasnevin Cemetery. There were some other tiny coffins there and just myself and the workers. As they placed the tiny coffins, I crossed myself, and the workers, seeing this, left me alone for a few minutes. God bless them.

14 September 1980, nineteen months later

It's 12.30 a.m. and I am sitting in the exact same waiting room of the same maternity hospital. I have no fingernails left. The doctors had assured us throughout this pregnancy that everything was in good shape. But that's what they had said the last time, right up to the delivery. Every time I heard a door open my heart jumped. I had elected not to be there for the birth and I think Doreen was just as glad I'd made that choice. I went out of the hospital every now and then to have a smoke. Some stupid new rule had been brought in that you couldn't smoke in a hospital any more. It was awful; I'd have a smoke, make my way back to the waiting room, hear a door open and close, and suddenly I wanted a smoke again. I sat with my head against the cool wall.

I must have dozed off because suddenly I opened my eyes and the clock on the wall was showing 4.15 a.m. There was a machine in the hall that dispensed hot drinks, so I walked down the corridor, fishing the coins out of my pocket. I'd had a coffee from this machine earlier. It was muck, so I chose hot chocolate this time. The machine dropped a plastic cup on the tray and started with a cough; it made a sound like someone gargling acid.

I heard my name. It was a midwife. She was half in and half out of the waiting room.

'I'm here,' I called. I left the chocolate still in the tray and rushed to her. 'Ah, Mr O'Carroll, congratulations, you have a daughter!' She nearly sang it. I waited. She waited for me to whoop or something, but I just stared at her. 'You have a daughter,' she repeated.

I shifted, uneasy. 'And?' I asked.

'And what?'

I rolled my eyes. 'AND . . . what is wrong with her?'

The nurse was confused. 'There's nothing wrong with her; she's a perfectly healthy baby.' I began to cry. 'Really? Seriously, a daughter and she's OK?'

148

'She is more than OK, Mr O'Carroll – she is beautiful. Your wife will be back in the ward in a few minutes. I'm just going to get her a cup of tea.' And she left.

Now I whooped! Then I ran outside for the most relaxing cigarette ever.

When I returned Doreen was in bed in the ward. As soon as she saw me she was excited. She said, 'She's OK. She's perfect.'

I did a little dance. 'I know! Can you believe it, a little girl?'

We both cried, but this time with joy.

After a cup of tea, the nurse told Doreen to get some sleep and shooed me out of the room. 'I haven't seen the baby yet,' I said.

The nurse smiled. 'Well, we'll soon fix that!'

She took me to the room where all the babies were. My daughter was right at the front. *Baby O'Carroll* was written on her cot.

I stood at that window for an hour just staring at her. She was the most beautiful thing I had ever seen. A head of black hair and sallow skin. The nurse in charge of the cots took me in eventually and let me hold her. I could hardly speak.

'Have you two picked a name yet?' the young nurse asked me.

I nodded. 'We certainly have.' I turned the baby length-ways and looked into her face. 'Fiona. Fiona O'Carroll.'

I swear to you, Fiona smiled. Maybe it was wind. Those of you who are fans of *Mrs. Brown's Boys* will know Fiona and what she looks like now. Well, let me tell you something: she hasn't changed one bit from the baby I held in my arms that night. Every time I look at her that's what I see.

Danny just *arrived* at 3 a.m. There was no hullabaloo, no drama. He just . . . arrived.

Yet again I was in the same waiting room, sipping a hot chocolate (I had learned my lesson from three years previous). Here's the weird thing. The nurse, when she came to get me, simply said, 'The baby is here, Mr O'Carroll.'

I jumped up and this time they let me into the delivery room where Doreen was lying upright in the bed holding the bundle. I leaned over and pulled the blanket down a little. Fuck, the baby was ugly! Picture Winston Churchill after five rounds with Mike Tyson. The weird thing was nobody had said whether it was a boy or a girl. 'What is it?' I asked.

Doreen said it was a boy. My immediate thought was *Thank God*, because a girl that ugly would be awful.

To give Doreen time to get some rest and for the baby to be cleaned up I left the hospital to grab a decent coffee and a cigarette. Obviously I went to Bewley's Oriental Café. I came back at about 5 a.m. Doreen was sleeping so I made my way to the baby enclosure to have another look at my new son. I couldn't see him anywhere.

A nurse came to the door and opened it a crack. 'Which baby are you looking for?'

'Mine,' I answered stupidly.

'And your name is?'

'Brendan.' (I was fucking tired.) 'Sorry, O'Carroll, baby O'Carroll.'

The nurse picked out a cot from the middle row and wheeled it to the front.

I shook my head. 'No, that's not him,' I called through the glass. But it was. He was gorgeous. I don't know what they did to him between 3 a.m. and 5 a.m., but he was just gorgeous. At that moment, as I stared at this child through the window, I swear something happened. Me and that little shit machine became joined at the heart. Thirty-nine years later, nothing has changed.

Eric came along much later, so I'll get to him later.

13

When Danny was born I didn't have a full-time job. I was getting some great work with Aer Lingus Outdoor Catering, but sometimes there would be a couple of weeks between jobs. I had a good talk with myself and the conclusion was that I had got to settle down and get a permanent job. No more trying this or trying that, just settle down. I didn't want to. You see, I believe that everybody has a talent for something. Most people are born, live and die without ever discovering what that something is. I was searching for my something, trying everything and, as Bono might say, I still hadn't found what I was looking for. So the search had to stop. It was time to settle down. See, I don't even like the word 'settle'. Nobody should have to 'settle' for something. But I had two kids now and a mortgage, so I had to 'settle' down.

I didn't know where to start. Then I remembered reading something about an ex-boss of mine from the Pot Pourri restaurant, Josef Frei, a really talented Swiss chef. He had sold the restaurant and opened a new place in the Dublin Mountains. Killakee House was a very old building just down from the Hellfire Club. The Hellfire Club was supposed to be haunted; the story goes that back in the nineteenth century the Devil appeared there one night as some satanists were carrying out a ritual of some sort. The place burst into flames and the ruins of the place are still there to this day. I called Josef's wife Eileen who ran the front of house and asked if she had any work for me. Eileen said she'd be delighted to have me back and invited me out to talk about it.

When I drove into the gravelled courtyard the place had a really creepy feel to it. It was a big T-shaped building with a bell tower at the front and it had a Transylvanian look to it. However, inside, Josef and Eileen had done a remarkable job with the place. It was a beautiful restaurant. The anteroom where the guests had their pre-dinner drinks featured a huge open fire and had a wonderfully cosy feel. The restaurant itself was a long room with a bar counter as you entered, and beautifully French polished dining tables ran the length of the room, each with a silver candelabra at the centre. At the far end was the door to the kitchen. The place was class and classy people went there – many who were classy and some who just thought they were. I could tell them apart.

I really liked working there. Josef was a brilliant chef and although he and I butted heads many times, as waiters and chefs so often do, I liked him. A lot.

The place was haunted. I'm not kidding. Here's the story, as I would tell it to our lucky guests.

'My boss decided to use the bell tower as an alternative way to access the upstairs restaurant from the reception room. The problem was that although the tower was attached to the corner of the building, for access to it you had to go outside. On the inside, that corner of the building had a kind of bulbous outcrop in the corner, which could have indicated a doorway in previous times. So, one morning the boss took a sledgehammer to the corner and he had no sooner made two or three slams than it became obvious that the bulge was hollow like an eggshell. After removing a few more stones he made a scary discovery . . . a skeleton in a foetal position. So the police were called, and it emerged that the remains were that of a boy, probably in early youth. The boy had a curvature of the spine and a congenital condition called talipes equinovarus, or club foot. The remains were about two hundred years old and once the legal areas were covered the bones were removed and received a proper burial in a local graveyard.

'People wondered about this boy and what his story was. It was an amateur historian who came up with a probable story. At that time the land was owned by a rich farming family and the fields were tended by local labourers. The owners' "big" house was down close to Tallaght village, which is about three miles away (and shows how big the farm was). The building that is now the restaurant was the home of the farm manager. The owner and his wife were celebrities of their day and when she became pregnant the whole of the Dublin elite were pleased for her. But when the baby was delivered with the conditions I spoke of earlier, at that time it would have brought shame to the family. So everyone was told that the baby didn't survive the birth (all too common back then) and the mother was given all the sympathy that went with that.

'It was decided that the farm manager would take the boy to his home and raise him there. The father visited every so often and the boy adored him. But the boy grew up a prisoner. He was never allowed outside the house, and nobody would ever see him. But one night, when the boy found an open door, he wandered out and down towards the village. When he was seen by the locals they believed he was indeed the Devil summoned up by the Hellfire Club. (Maybe this was the sighting that gave life to the legend?)'

At this point I had complete and absolute silence and rapt attention. I would tease by saying, 'Well, the story goes on, and it's not very nice, so let's leave it there, shall we? More coffee? Or maybe a liqueur? We have a lovely Dow's 66 vintage port?'

They would always protest. 'No, no, go on with the story, please.'

I would take a deep breath and slowly exhale. 'OK, well, when the boy got to the village, he frightened the locals so much that they chased him. The phrase the historian used was: "He was chased from the village by torch-wielding locals." The boy, of course, made his way back to the farm manager's house and when the locals gathered in the front yard, out there where your cars are parked, the manager came out and told the mob that whatever it was must have made its way up the mountain.

'Well, the farm owner, the boy's father, was furious about the sighting. He went that night to the farmer's house where he berated the manager and then beat the boy. The boy did not understand what he had done wrong or why the village folk were so afraid of him. He was devastated. The manager could hear the boy sobbing for a long time after the father had departed. When the sobbing stopped the farm manager's wife took the boy some food, only to find he had hanged himself. Now they had a bigger problem: what to do with the boy's remains? So he interred the boy in the wall, sealing it up with the stones that my boss took out just weeks ago.'

I don't know if the story is true or not, but as Bart O'Brien had taught me years before, 'If it's not, it should be.' The story always went over well. But, one rainy night, some guests, two couples at a table for four, turned the tables on me.

I told the story and instead of the usual response of, 'Oh, wow,' or 'Oh dear me', they simply looked at each other, astonished. One of the ladies urged her husband to speak. 'Tell him, tell the waiter.'

He brushed her off. 'No, no. There's no connection.'

But she insisted and was joined in her insistence by the other couple. So I asked, 'What? What is it?'

The man took a sip of his brandy. 'Well,' he began, 'we got a bit lost on our way here tonight.'

That did happen a lot. We weren't exactly on a busy main thoroughfare. I told him this and he went on.

'We ended up about two miles past the entrance. So I turned the car and we saw a young man walking in the rain. My wife said to offer him a lift, so I did, and he was very pleased to get out of the rain. Then we drove on, but we very quickly came upon the entrance out there, so I pulled into the yard and apologized to the lad, telling him that this was as far as we were going. The lad said, "That's OK, I live here." He got out as we did, and then he went round the back of the building.'

Now my boss only had two children and they were both girls. And, other than the restaurant, there was not a house within a mile of us.

The wife now spoke up. 'That's not all. The boy was lovely, but it wasn't until he got out of the car that we noticed he was a hunchback!'

I shuddered for a moment, but I don't believe in that shit, so I brushed it off. Although, to be honest, I was more than a little careful making my way to my car at 3 a.m. for a while. Then I simply incorporated it into my story and retold it time after time.

Funny, I never saw that foursome again. I wonder if . . .?

Nah, fuck it, forget about it.

I had been working at Killakee House for about eighteen months when I got a phone call one morning. The phone was beside my bed and it woke me so I was a bit sluggishly sleepy, saying, 'Heeellllo?'

The call was from a woman I had spoken to many times but had never met. I recognized her voice straight away. 'Hello, Betty.'

Betty and her husband, Sean Hussey, were suppliers of

fresh vegetables to most of the smaller restaurants in Dublin and the surrounding areas. I had dealt with her when I was a chef in Cleary's restaurant. She would call every day for the order for delivery the following day. Betty was super-efficient and always on top of your orders. If you asked for Brussels sprouts, she might say, 'Well, Brendan, you had sprouts on the menu on Monday, maybe turnips tomorrow?' Of course, I never realized that Betty the saleswoman was pushing the turnips. But I didn't care. One of the beauties of dealing with Sean Hussey Vegetables was that they brought potatoes ready for the pot. Peeled and cleaned. It saved so much time every day. I'm sure they cost extra, but it was worth it. In any case it wasn't my money that was paying for them.

'What can I do for you, Betty?'

She always had a brightness to her voice. She was easy to listen to. 'I don't know if you've heard or not, but we've taken over the Ashbourne House Hotel – have you heard?' I hadn't and I told her so. 'Well, we have, and I'm looking for a head waiter.'

I wasn't fully awake, so I said, 'Can I call you back?'

She then said, 'Why don't you drop up to the hotel and we can talk about it?'

The hotel was no more than fifteen minutes from my house in Finglas. 'Sure, how's twelve thirty?' I said, and she was happy with that.

Let me explain that at that time I was the president and one of the founders of the Irish Waiters' Association, so I knew many waiters that might fit the bill for Betty. As I sat at our kitchen table later, I racked my brain as to who would be the best man for the job. I wanted it to be someone really good as I liked Betty and I wanted it to work for her.

At twelve thirty I sat down with her. It was great to meet her at last and put a face to the name. She was a very attractive woman and really elegant; she actually reminded me of my mother. We chatted about this and that for a while, and I made her laugh a few times and then eventually we got down to business. She spoke of her hopes for the place and where she wanted to take it. Her plans were exciting and expensive, but I could see that she was determined to make this place just as successful as she made the vegetable business. I didn't doubt that she would for a second.

It was about twenty minutes into our talk that I began to realize that Betty didn't want me to find her a head waiter; she wanted me to BE the head waiter. I explained that I was already working in what was regarded as one of the best restaurants in Dublin and that it paid really well. She asked how much, I told her and, without batting an eyelid, she said, 'I'll pay you fifty pounds more after tax.'

After tax would mean an actual rise of over £100. Another pro was that the Ashbourne House Hotel was fifteen minutes from my home. On the best days, with traffic and before the M50, it took me an hour and a half to get to Killakee House. There were obviously some cons to the idea, though. To get this place to the standard that Betty would insist on would probably mean working a seventy- or eighty-hour week. I said yes.

That night, when the restaurant at the Killakee House quietened down, I brought Eileen out a cup of coffee and told her that I was leaving. I was entitled to give just a week's notice, but I said I would work until the following Saturday week to give her nearly two weeks to find a replacement.

'That would be great. The best of luck to you,' she said, but I knew she didn't mean it. After all, she had given me a job when I had called her. But I'm afraid that is the nature of the business.

The next day I arrived in work and Josef completely blanked

me. He was in a sulk. The odd thing was that I knew that during my time working for him there were times when we would be butting heads so much that he would have loved to fire me, and I probably would have deserved it, but now that I was leaving I was a traitor. I worked out my last days being a better waiter than I had ever been, but Josef stayed mad at me for the two weeks. From Eileen's side it wasn't that she was any less mad at me than Josef; she was just better at hiding it. I finished that Saturday night, got into my car at 3 a.m. and drove out of the entrance. We never spoke again.

One of the first things we did at the Ashbourne House was to open the function room. It was a great success. Within two years it was the top place for wedding receptions. If you were from Dublin city's Northside, or anywhere in North County Dublin, and you didn't have your wedding in the Ashbourne House, wherever you went, you were taking second best. I now addressed Betty as 'Mrs Hussey' and would do thereafter. Since starting at the hotel, she was no longer a voice on the phone pushing turnips; she was my boss.

Over the next five years I would be working and not working in the Ashbourne House three times. I think I left twice and got fired once. Each time I went back Mrs Hussey would have added more to the hotel, and it just continued to get better.

It was my final time working there that was really the important one. It was just before Christmas 1986. We were busy, really busy. Mind you, busy is the way I liked the hotel to be. Believe it or not, I felt I worked better the busier we got, and not just there but anywhere I worked. By this time Mrs Hussey had a hotel manager, Kevin. I think he felt threatened by me because he gave me the cold shoulder for a long time. I was expecting him to be aloof anyway, as most hotel managers I worked for were, but over that Christmas he changed my mind. He was brilliant! He rowed in with whatever needed doing in any department. He was brilliant at paperwork. He was brilliant at managing the cash and bills from each department and, most importantly, he was brilliant at managing people. I was really impressed. It took nearly a year but by the following Christmas we were friends. We worked really well together and at the end of a busy Saturday night, having had a wedding in the function room and an oversold night in the restaurant, Kevin and I would sit at a table in the now empty restaurant with the lights off, just a candle on the table burning, me with my coffee and Kevin with a pint of cider and we would unwind and have a laugh.

I had now bought a house in Ashbourne itself, so I lived just minutes from the hotel. Although there was one night that living minutes from the hotel didn't matter. Let me explain.

It was my day off. As it happened, the head barman Tommy was also on a day off. I liked Tommy; he was a good guy, and lived just round the corner from me. Tommy had arranged a game of golf for our day off. We were to tee off at nine thirty, so I could take Fiona and Danny to school at the *bunscoil lán gailge*, the local Irish school.

Tommy and I played eighteen holes at Deer Park Golf in Howth. We had an enjoyable round. Then we packed our clubs in Tommy's car and headed back towards Ashbourne. I say 'towards' Ashbourne here and not 'to' Ashbourne, because as we were passing the Rolestown House pub, which was on our way back to Ashbourne, in the middle of nowhere, Tommy swung the car into the car park.

'We'll have a quick one to top off the golf,' he said with a wink.

I wasn't keen, as I hadn't even had breakfast, but it was his car. I smiled and said, 'Sure.'

We knew the barman. I'm sure he had worked a few nights at the hotel when we were particularly busy. Tommy ordered a pint of Guinness and I had a vodka and Coke. We toasted and Tommy took half the pint in his first mouthful. After his second mouthful Tommy signalled the barman to set them up again.

I put my hand over my glass. 'I'm good, Tommy.'

He laughed and pointed at the Coke bottle. 'You can't leave half a Coke.' (I had only used half the Coke in my vodka.)

'Sure,' I said, and tried to quickly finish my first one as I was thinking, *I have to finish my drink before Tommy or he'll order another.* To be sure I decided to make my intentions clear. 'Tommy, I'll have this one, but after these we go, all right?'

He rolled his eyes. 'OK.'

He was disappointed but I didn't care. I was halfway through my second drink when a fresh pint and a fresh vodka and Coke arrived on the bar.

'For fuck's sake, Tommy!' I was annoyed with him now. Tommy put his arms in the air. 'It wasn't me, I swear.'

The barman pointed down the bar, where the owner's wife was sitting, reading a newspaper. 'The boss sent it.' The owners were customers at the restaurant.

Tommy raised his glass. 'Thank you,' he called down the long bar, and I did the same.

The owner's wife, myself and Tommy were the only people there. But before I even took a sip out of that drink, another pint and a vodka arrived. 'The boss said you can't leave a half bottle of Coke.'

Fuck. I was getting wobbly now. *I am definitely leaving after this one. Even if I have to call a taxi and leave Tommy here, I am going.* Next I knew, it was 8 p.m. and I am standing on the piano entertaining a now packed pub.

When I got off the piano, I said to Tommy, 'Tommy, I have to go. I'm starving.'

Tommy drained his glass and we headed for his car. I know what you are thinking about driving while drunk, but I cannot emphasize enough that it was a different time, and I hate myself now for it. Anyway, it's not an excuse but I wasn't driving. Before we got into the car Tommy said he knows where we can get some food at this hour. Ten minutes later we pulled up in the car park of the Ashbourne House. We went in – Tommy to the bar and me straight to the kitchen.

I opened the large fridge. I needed food, anything. I swear if the first thing I had come across was a candle, I would have eaten it. I got lucky – there was a whole roast chicken there. I like chicken anyway, but see that chicken? I could have made love to it. I didn't even get a knife and fork. I ripped it apart and scoffed it. It was beautiful, every bite. When I had finished there was just a pile of bones, and my face was covered in grease.

I joined Tommy in the bar and Kevin was there too. 'Look at you, you're a disgrace,' Kevin said, playfully admonishing me and handed me a vodka and Coke.

I took just two sips and started to feel queasy. 'I'm going home,' I said to nobody in particular.

Kevin took the drink from my hand as I was spilling it everywhere. 'Go,' he said, and added, 'You'd better be here on time tomorrow.' He laughed out loud.

I left out of the back door, but I had only gone a few steps when I felt my tummy begin to heave. I stopped at a drain and threw up, and threw up again and again. The next thing I remember was waking up in my bed with the curtains open and the sunlight carving out my pupils. I dressed, took two paracetamol pills and went to work. I don't know how I got through lunch, but I did. When my break came, I knew I had three hours, so I hid in a corner of the function room and slept. I woke feeling a lot better and by the night's end I was back to near normal.

I had forgotten that rough day until a customer brought it up a couple of weeks later. Not just an ordinary customer, but a local council member. Seán Conway owned the local pharmacy in Ashbourne. He was also an elected member of the county council. I thought he had acted peculiar when I brought him the lunch menu. Here it is in a script:

THE LONGEST DAY OF GOLF

EXT. ASHBOURNE, IRELAND - NIGHT

The rain is hammering down and hopping off the hood of Councillor Seán Conway's Mercedes-Benz. The wipers can barely keep up. The window is slightly steamed up as Seán has the heater down to a minimum to stop him dozing off on the long drive back from Cork. He sees a figure way ahead on the far side of the road. On the footpath. It's a man thumbing a lift. Seán glances at his watch. It is 3 a.m.

SEÁN (*ALOUD TO HIMSELF*)

Who the fuck is thumbing at this hour? *Weirdly, the man is stripped to the waist, holding his clothing over his left arm, while thumbing for a lift in the opposite direction towards Dublin. There are no cars coming, nor are there likely to be, so the man's thumbing is useless. As Seán gets closer he thinks he recognizes the*

man. Seán slows his car and at the next
junction he turns it round and drives
back.

SEÁN (*ALOUD TO HIMSELF*) (CONT'D)
I'm right. It's the head waiter from the
Ashbourne House. What the fuck?
Seán stops the car right beside the man.
The man is drenched.
Without an invitation the man opens the
passenger door, sits in the Merc and puts
on the seat belt and sits in silence.
Seán waits a moment then . . .

SEÁN (CONT'D)
Where are you going to, Brendan?
Brendan looks at Seán with disdain.

BRENDAN
Did I ask you where you were fucking
going?
Seán has seen drunks many times before.
But Brendan is drunk, drunk.
Realizing he will get no sense from
Brendan, he drives him round to his home –
two minutes from where he had been
standing. It takes Seán an hour to get
Brendan out of the car. Brendan tells
Seán that he isn't any good as a
politician, that his own mother was a
brilliant politician, and tons and tons
of bullshit like that. Eventually Brendan
gets out of the car. Seán again turns his

car to go home and drives past Brendan's home.

Brendan is pissing on a neighbour's hedge and as Seán passes he gives Seán the finger.

The thing that frightened me more than anything was that Seán had picked me up at 3 a.m. just 300 yards from the hotel. I know that I had left the hotel at midnight. I have no idea where I was and what I had done for those three hours. None. I vowed that this would never happen to me again. It never has and it never will.

Back to me and Kevin.

Our relationship was tripping along just fine. Friends in work but outside of work we didn't ever see each other. The perfect work relationship. Kevin was happy at the Ashbourne House and so was I. We had our jobs running really smoothly and we both were planning on a long stay there. I was settled. Or was I? The last task I had to do for a wedding reception was to go to the noticeboard inside the entrance and write out *Welcome Mr and Mrs Whomever*. I would then roll out the red carpet from the front door to the edge of the path, give it a sweep and we were done. I'd wait at the front door for the bride and groom to arrive so I could greet them and steer them to the flower garden for photos, while their guests were taken to the piano room for drinks. I would stand there waiting in my tuxedo and wearing a bow tie and pocket kerchief that matched the colour of the bridesmaids' dresses. I would have checked this with the happy couple in our chat a couple of days before the wedding when we went over the final details. The serviettes would match their dresses too. It sounds difficult but it wasn't. Every wedding season the bridesmaids' dress colours usually came down to three or four colours. I would light a cigarette, waiting for them to arrive, and if it was a sunny day I would see the weekenders heading off for the beach with surfboards on their roof rack. Caravans passing with families in the towing car all aglow with the thought of the fun they would have wherever they were going. I envied them. But I was 'settled'.

Paddy owned a caravan-manufacturing company. Tom owned one of the biggest bathroom and plumbing suppliers in Ireland. They were friends and I presume they did business with each other over time. They had a dream. They wanted to build a top-class pub. And they did. They had a greenfield site, and they started from scratch and built a beautiful pseudo castle; in a stroke of creative genius they named it Finglas Castle. I had been there a few times on a Sunday night that I had off. They had a kind of open-mic there then. Billy Hughes would open the night with a few classics. There would then be an open-mic and afterwards an interval, during which you collected sausage and chips from the bar. Serving the sausage and chips covered the pub for a late extension for the bar. The law required a substantial meal. Apparently sausage was substantial enough.

The place opened with a lot of ceremony. It really was a beautiful building. Nothing was cheap. The double arched doors were oak, the carpets in the cabaret room, quiet lounge and bar were top quality. Needless to say, with Tom in the business the bathrooms had top-drawer fittings and were really elegant. Outside, big granite blocks gave the place an elegance and the feel of a bygone age. Finally the up and down crenels of a castle were replicated round the whole building. All that was missing was a moat and a drawbridge. Paddy and Tom had only been open a few months before they wished they HAD a moat and drawbridge.

Let me say something here. So many people that I have met over the years who become successful in their field, like Tom and Paddy, for some reason dream of owning a pub or a restaurant. They seriously think that all they have to do is fit out a place, open the doors and the money rolls in. But it is fucking hard. Really fucking hard. I had to train to learn how to be just one part of a restaurant. These guys hadn't trained at all. Let me give you an example. In a pub, especially a local, where the owner is local and the staff are local, like Finglas Castle, during a week the owner will drop a few drinks to friends or relatives of his. The barman will also slip the odd pint or two per night to his friends. You have three barmen. All of them have friends. To save on costs you will have taken those barmen on because they are local, not because they are trained. When you heard how much a qualified barman would cost, you thought, *Fuck that, anyone with a pair of hands can pull a pint.* You think? There are seventy-two pints in the average keg. A qualified barman will get you sixty-nine to seventy out of it. Your untrained 'pair of hands' will put at least twenty pints of it down the sink. So here's the thing. Let's say a pint is £6. Your average percentage mark-up (profit) taking heat, light, background music rights, TV licence, maintenance, cleaning, barmen salary, rent or rates, insurance, and, of course, excise tax, as well as profit tax, is about fifteen per cent. That's about £1 a pint. But if your barman gives away, say, four pints a night, you have to sell twenty-four pints to break even. It's fucking hard. Then there's the stress. Managing any hospitality business is about managing people.

14

Back to Paddy and Tom.

Although I didn't know Tom at all, I did know that Paddy was one of the owners of Finglas Castle. Paddy was also a regular customer of the Ashbourne House. He was fairly quiet when he came in as a customer and usually his party would arrive, eat and leave. So I was a bit surprised when Kevin said that Paddy had approached him and asked if he and Tom could meet Kevin and me away from the hotel.

I raised my eyebrows. 'If he's looking for us to manage the Finglas Castle for him, he can fuck off!' I told Kevin.

'God, no way. I heard it's really rough?' said Kevin. Then he asked, 'But will we meet them?'

I shrugged. 'Why not? It'll be interesting to see what they want.'

Kevin wasn't kidding that he had heard it was really rough. It was. There were many problems. One of them was the name. Finglas and Ballymun are two very working-class areas and at that time both were rife with petty crime, drugs and gang crime. They were also very tribal and bitter rivals, especially when it came to gang territories. This rivalry didn't just exist in Ballymun or Finglas, Irish people are tribal by nature. In the sixties Dublin Council built an outdoor swimming bath right on the border between Finglas and adjoining Cabra. It was built there so it could be fed by the Tolka, the very river that divided Finglas from Cabra. There were riots. The thugs of both areas fought over it night after night. People, on both sides, lost an eye or were concussed or would arrive home bruised and bloody. Today that pool is filled in with cement. The point I'm making is that you cannot call a pub 'Finglas Castle' and build it in Ballymun. Both tribes believed it was *their* pub. If you think the trouble over the swimming pool was bad, try now adding alcohol to the mix. Explosive!

Anyhow, we met Tom and Paddy. They immediately got down to business. 'We want you to buy Finglas Castle from us.'

Kevin and I laughed, but they were serious. I could feel it from both men; they had had enough. They were at the end of their tether. They had reduced the opening hours of the bar from 5 p.m. to 11.30 p.m. The cabaret room and lounge were only open one day a week, Sunday. They were done with the place. I said that there was no way we could raise the money to buy the place, and Kevin agreed. They asked us to give it some thought and said they would meet us in a week. I stood to leave, and my final words were: 'There is nothing to think about; it's not a runner for us.' Kevin agreed and we left the meeting.

There was nothing to think about, but of course we did. When we were at work we would talk about it all the time. Lots of conversations that started with 'What if?'

Kevin had never set foot in Finglas Castle so he wasn't really sure of what could be done with the place. So we called Paddy and said we would go and have a look at the place. It was so sad. The place that had opened as a palace was now in virtual tatters. The carpets were filthy with the smell of urine, the bathrooms had broken sinks and urinals. The quiet lounge, which when I had visited it years before was plush and inviting, was now dirty, with much of the velvet seating in the cubicles ripped and slashed. Paddy left us to look around by ourselves.

'This is a fucking dump, Kevin,' I said.

Kevin nodded, but then he said, 'OK, we can see the problems, let's change our perspective and see what is GOOD or OK about the place.'

A good idea, I thought. So we split up and twenty minutes later we met in the bar.

Kevin had written a list. 'Well, the kitchen is small but everything in it works. The cellar is fabulous, refrigerated and well organized. Behind all the bar counters is in good shape – plenty of glasses and plenty of storage. The sound system is working, and the lighting all works. Finally all the tills work.' He put his list down.

I tried to be as positive as I could. 'OK, the bathrooms could be put back to a reasonable shape with a lick of paint and the broken stuff replaced. The alarm system works and I could get a safety officer to look over the sprinkler system, but it looks OK. There are plenty of fire extinguishers.' But as much as we tried we couldn't get our enthusiasm up.

When Paddy arrived to lock the place, I asked him, 'What's the place turning over at the moment?'

He thought for a moment. 'Between eight and nine thousand a week,' he lied.

No matter. I tried to put him on the spot. 'How much are you asking, Paddy?'

Without hesitation he said, 'Four hundred thousand.'

I shook my head. 'With an eight-thousand-a-week turnover? Not a chance.'

'Make me an offer then,' he shot back.

'No,' I said with a laugh.

Kevin and I went our merry way. Not really. We talked about it non-stop over the following week. I had to keep ignoring a voice in my head: *You would own a pub; imagine the things you and Kevin could do.* Often I would blurt out, 'Fuck off, no, I'm settled!' without realizing it and whoever was near me I'm sure thought I was mad.

One night during our after-work chat Kevin slapped his hand down on the table. 'We have to stop thinking about it. Put it out of our heads. It's simple – we don't have access to four hundred thousand pounds and that's that.'

We sipped our drinks, thinking.

'We don't, but *they* do,' I mused.

'What do you mean?'

'Kevin, they are fucking loaded. They are not waiting for four hundred thousand to improve their lives. And they want rid of that place; it's an anchor round their necks. I reckon I could put a deal together that they would accept.'

Kevin perked up. 'Really?'

We met Paddy and Tom later that week to put our offer, my deal, to them. Now, you must remember that throughout all this neither Kevin nor I had any money. Not a fucking penny.

'So what's the offer,' asked Paddy.

I didn't produce a notepad or figures; I did it off the top of my head. They waited. 'First off, we won't pay four hundred thousand. It'll be three hundred and fifty at best.'

Paddy stood. 'Right, well, that's the end of that then,' he snapped.

Tom put his hand on Paddy's arm. 'Hold on, hear them out,' he said quietly. 'Go on, three hundred and fifty, you're saying, go on,' Tom urged.

I continued. 'We agree the price now, and we'll buy it in two years' time.'

Paddy nearly burst a blood vessel. 'Ah, you've lost your fucking mind. We are not running this place for two years, waiting for you two to buy it. Seriously, no. No way.'

I raised my hand. 'I'm not finished,' I said.

Tom never took his eyes off me. 'Go ahead then, go on,' he said again.

'In the meantime, we'll lease the place for six thousand a month.'

Tom looked at Paddy with a hopeful look.

'But,' I added.

Paddy now stood again. 'I knew there would be a fucking "but".'

Tom just raised his hand to Paddy this time, and I went on.

'After two years, when we buy it, the rent we've paid over the two years, which will be one hundred and forty-four thousand pounds, gets deducted from the three hundred and fifty and we pay the balance.' I sat back. 'That's it. That's the offer.'

Paddy was exasperated. 'You give us a hundred and forty-four thousand pounds and after two years we give it back to you? Are you fucking mad, or do you think me and Tom are fucking stupid?'

I made the argument. 'It depends on how you look at it,' I said. 'You don't give us back anything. You keep the one hundred and forty-four thousand *and* we will give you another two hundred and six, but, more importantly, you never have to worry about that place again.'

During all this Tom barely spoke. Not so Paddy. 'No fucking way. That won't work for us.'

Tom then spoke. 'Well, lads, thank you for your offer. Paddy and I will have a chat about it, and we'll be in touch.'

Over the next two weeks we heard nothing. We weren't buying the no-news-is-good-news thing. They weren't taking our offer.

Cleverly they called Kevin, who called me straight away. 'They want to know if we would do it over one year.'

I was pleased. They had obviously accepted that £350K was all they would get. I also believed that they had met other potential buyers and had got nowhere. 'Tell them no. The offer is the offer, that's that.'

Kevin called them and told them. Again they said they would get back to us.

This time it was Tom that called me. I think he meant it to be a short call because he simply said, 'OK. Our lawyers will draw up the lease/buy papers.'

'That would be great,' I said, 'but there are a couple of other things.'

Tom laughed. 'Of course there are.' Now I laughed. 'What are the other things?' he asked.

'I want any broken toilets to be replaced, including new seats.' I knew this would be a yes as he had all the stuff that was needed.

'Go on.'

'All the carpets need to be completely shampooed and dried. The dance floor needs to be sanded and varnished.'

Silence. 'Is that all?' he asked sarcastically.

'No.'

He waited.

'We want the first month rent-free and the second month at fifty per cent.'

Tom said nothing at first. I suspect that Paddy was beside him listening to this and going red in the face with anger. When Tom spoke it was to say, 'OK, I'll get our lawyers to draw up the papers.'

I called Kevin and told him. He couldn't believe it. I couldn't fucking believe it. We were buying a pub!

'So,' Kevin asked, 'what's next?'

I knew what was next. 'Next, Kevin, we close the place and change the fucking name.'

Five weeks later the *Abbot's* Castle opened under new management.

It was agreed that our 'month' would start the day we opened. The carpets were cleaned; the painting was done. I had a mate that was an upholsterer and he had replaced the ripped or torn panels in the quiet lounge. We had a great security team, all ex-police. For the first couple of weeks I also did the door with them. I knew the bogey types. I knew them on sight. As they would approach, the security guys would look at me and I would either nod or shake my head. Don't get me wrong, we had many dodgy characters as customers – I knew them too – but they were ones that would never cause any trouble, especially when with their wives or family.

With personal guarantees Kevin and I had got a flexi-loan of £10,000 with a three-year term from a bank in town. The way the loan worked was like a credit advance. If we had paid back half of it after one year, we could use it again as long as after the three years we cleared it. That £10,000 was the total of our cash. The two boys had overstated the turnover of the place (shock!); the most they had turned over in the previous six months was £4,000. We opened in October 1986. Six weeks later we had our best turnover so far: £25,000 in one DAY. A Saturday night it was, and we were thrilled. The following week we cleared the £10,000 loan, but we knew it was there for three years if we needed it.

I didn't know it at the time but one of the most important moves we made, not just for the Castle but also for my future, came out of a visit from an old friend, Brendan Harrington.

Brendan Harrington grew up on Casement Park, back-to-back to our street. As kids we both played in the street leagues, which was a soccer tournament held every year. For this tournament Casement Grove, Casement Park, Casement Drive and Casement Road joined together as Casement United. Brendan, or 'Harrow' which was his nickname, was a cracking goalkeeper. We were both chosen for the Dublin community games team for West Finglas Tenants' Association, or WEFTA. Then, when we got older, our paths crossed again, twice. First when he played goalkeeper for Saints United and I played up front. Then, when I was a van driver for Traynor Motors, he worked in the stores room. We had not long been open when Harrow called me at the Castle and asked to come and see me for a chat. I was delighted to hear from him. What he wanted to see me about was a band that he played with, a ballad group called Tinkers Fancy. He suggested that if we booked them for Sunday mornings that they would fill the place. I hadn't heard of the band, although I did know that Harrow played with one. I agreed to try them out for a fee of £50 and 'a couple of pints'.

Harrow wasn't kidding. They packed the place every Sunday morning. They were really good too; by the show's end they would have the place rocking. The band leader was Gerry Browne. Gerry was to play a big role in my life, but that's for later. For now the band were great and the tills were ringing. I knew of Gerry; I had even played football against him. He, like myself, came from a big family and grew up no more than ten minutes from Casement Grove, but we had never met. The fee went up to £150 and 'a lot of pints', but they were well worth it as for weeks they packed the cabaret room every Sunday morning.

The cabaret room was packed every Sunday night too. And we turned the lounge into a nightclub, which would be packed and hopping until 2 a.m. every Friday and Saturday night. We had the place ticking over nicely. Soon I was approached by more bands. They heard that we were putting on live music during the week and asked for a try-out. Some worked OK, some bombed. None of them were as popular as Tinkers Fancy.

I had a very strange experience during this time that was associated with one band in particular. They were a four-piece rock band named Face to Face. They didn't pull a crowd; in fact, they couldn't pull your sister off a soldier, but I thought they were brilliant. They wrote their own stuff and some of it was amazing. When I discovered that they didn't have a manager I offered to manage them. So, along with running the Castle, I spent any spare time I had trying to get Face to Face 'away', in other words get them a deal. Following the rising success of U2 and other bands, the UK labels were horny for Irish rock groups. I had a friend in London, actually a friend who I'd met through my sister Éilish, who was living in London then. Bruce White was deeply involved in the recording industry. His was a reggae label, but he had contacts with many other labels, and Bruce set up an appointment for me to meet an A & R guy from EMI named Nick Briskie. The date was set, and I bought an APEX flight (google it) with Aer Lingus. However, the day before I was to fly over, the meeting was shifted to the following day. But with the ticket I had I couldn't change the date. So I found myself in London with nothing to do.

I called Bruce from Heathrow when I arrived. He wanted to meet for dinner that night with his beautiful wife, Sue. I took out my wallet, as I had a phone card, and as I took it out a business card popped out of my wallet and fell to the floor. I had the phone wedged between my shoulder and ear, and my wallet in one hand and the card in the other, so I just put my foot on the card on the ground. When I finished the call I picked it up. It was a business card from my boss in the Ashbourne House, Mrs Hussey. I turned it over and there was a phone number written on the back. It was a London number with the name 'Doris' written under it. I recognized that it was Mrs Hussey's handwriting but couldn't for the life of me remember why I had this card or whose number was on the back. I got a coffee and sat in the airport and had a smoke looking at it. Then it struck me. Mrs Hussey had given me this woman's phone number to pass on to my sister Éilish. It was the number of a spiritualist and she had given it to me as Éilish was into that kind of shit.

I sat sipping my coffee and the thought crossed my mind that I had never been to anything like a spiritualist or fortune-teller. I knew it was all bullshit, but I had nothing to do all day and the experience might open my mind. So I called Doris. She sounded weirdly surprised to get my call. She said that she had been booked solid but had just had two cancellations (she didn't see them coming) and said that if I could get there soon, she could 'do' me. As it happens her home was quite close to the airport, so I went to the taxi stand and got into a taxi and gave the driver the address. Here's the script of this encounter:

THE SPIRITUALIST

EXT. HEATHROW AIRPORT, LONDON - MORNING
The taxi stand is busy but there are plenty of cabs. When Brendan, a handsome young man of athletic build (fuck off), gets to the top of the line a black London cab pulls up. Brendan jumps in and gives the driver the address he wants to go to.

DRIVER
Are you sure you want to go there?
Brendan is puzzled.

177

BRENDAN
I'm sure. Why?

DRIVER
It's a rough area, mate, but, hey, it's
your fiver.
The cab takes off.

**EXT. RED-BRICK HOUSE IN ROUGH AREA,
LONDON - LATER**
The cab pulls up outside 120.

DRIVER
Here we are, mate!
*Brendan fishes out a five-pound note. He
hands it to the driver through the small
hatch.*

BRENDAN
Will you wait? I'll make it worth your
while.

DRIVER
Nope.
*Brendan exits the cab and it drives
quickly away. Brendan makes his way
up the short path to the front door
that would be improved by a decent
coat of paint. Before he can knock the
door is opened by a sixty-ish woman.
White-haired and pleasant-looking. She
smiles.*

DORIS

Ah, you must be the man on the phone?
I'm Doris.

BRENDAN

Yes, hello, Doris. Eh, Brendan.
He extends his hand and Doris takes it
and holds on to it.

DORIS

Come in. If you are only off a flight, I
bet you would love a cup of tea?

BRENDAN

Actually, yes, I would.
They both exit the hallway to the kitchen.

INT. DORIS'S KITCHEN – MOMENTS LATER

DORIS

It's amazing that you should call on the
day I get two cancellations. I never get
them you know, never.

BRENDAN

Well, I was supposed to have a meeting . . .
Doris holds up her hand.

DORIS

Brendan, don't tell me anything. I don't
want it to come up and then you might
think it's a scam.

Brendan doesn't tell her anything,
especially that he already thinks it's
a scam.
The tea is finished.

                 DORIS (CONT'D)
Right, well, shall we go into the front
       room? That's where I work.
They exit to the front room.

INT. DORIS'S FRONT ROOM - MOMENTS LATER
Brendan is sitting in one of two
armchairs in the room. There is no other
furniture. A small hearth has a fire
burning in it. Brendan looks about the
room. To his surprise the walls are
decorated with religious pictures and one
or two crosses. Brendan is now surprised
that he is surprised. *Why shouldn't she*
have these? he thinks.

                 DORIS
      Are you comfortable?

                 BRENDAN
Yes, very. Can I ask you something?

                 DORIS
         What's that?

                 BRENDAN
I know many people who have been to fortu-
things like this. They go in, are there

for an hour, and when they come out they
tell you everything in five minutes.

DORIS
OK. And?

BRENDAN
Well, do you mind if I take some notes? I
don't want to forget anything.
Brendan says this as he takes out a
notebook and pen. He holds it up as if he
is expecting Doris to examine it.

DORIS
Of course. You do whatever you need
to do. You know, someone recorded
a session once, and when they
got home and played the tape,
it was blank.

BRENDAN (*NOT BUYING IT*)
They forgot to press record and play at
the same time.

DORIS (*SEEING THE SARCASM*)
If you say so. I don't know about that
stuff. Are you ready?

BRENDAN
I am.

DORIS
OK. Well, firstly I want to read your aura.

                        BRENDAN
                        My aura?

                         DORIS
Yes. Everyone has an aura and reading the
         colours can tell me so much.

                        BRENDAN
                 Oh, right. Go ahead.
*Doris closes her eyes and now begins to
use both her hands as if outlining
Brendan's form.*

  *Brendan now decides that he will not help
Doris, but he will not lie to her either.
If she says, 'There's an "e" in your
mother's name,' he will say, 'Is there?'
But if she says, 'Your mother's name is
Maureen,' he will say, 'Yes, it is.'*

  *Doris opens her eyes. Her eyes widen
immediately.*

                         DORIS
               Oh my! Oh, dearie me.

                        BRENDAN
                  What? What is it?

                         DORIS
Your aura . . . it's only got one colour.
              It's just golden.

                        BRENDAN
               Is that good or bad?

DORIS
I don't know. I've never seen it before.

BRENDAN (THOUGHTS)
Fuck sake. Trust me to get a fuckin'
beginner.

DORIS
Brendan, there are spirits lining up and
dropping golden keys in your lap.
Whatever is coming to you in your future,
you really deserve it.
Brendan is writing.

BRENDAN
Nice.
Doris suddenly looks across the room and
speaks harshly.

DORIS
Go away. This has nothing to do with you.
Back to Brendan.

DORIS (CONT'D)
Your mother is on the other side.

BRENDAN
Is she here now?

DORIS
No, but I can see her in God's garden.
Your father is walking behind her. Oh,
she's the boss.

Doris giggles. Brendan writes.

> BRENDAN (THOUGHTS)
> *The wife is the 'boss' in ninety per cent of Irish homes. Good guess.*

> DORIS
> She used to bake brown bread.

> BRENDAN
> She did.

> BRENDAN (CONT'D) (THOUGHTS)
> *Every Irish mother bakes brown bread. This is a load of bollocks.*

Again Doris speaks to this mystery spirit.

> DORIS
> Please stop. (*Points at Brendan.*) This gentleman . . . has . . .

She pauses.

> DORIS (CONT'D)
> OK, I'll ask Brendan.

She now looks back to Brendan.

> DORIS (CONT'D)
> This spirit's name is Chalky White. Do you know him, or did you know him?

BRENDAN
No and NO.
Doris is now back to the spirit.

DORIS
Now, he does not know you so please leave.
(*Pause.*) He's gone.
Brendan is starting to lose interest. Doris
closes her eyes. Brendan yawns. It was an
early start this morning.
 Doris opens her eyes.

DORIS (CONT'D)
I have a child in the spirit world.
I think he's yours.
The hair stands up on Brendan's neck.
He tries not to show it.

DORIS (CONT'D)
Can I bring him across?

BRENDAN (*QUIETLY*)
Sure.
Doris now smiles and giggles.

DORIS
Oh my Lord, he's yours all right. He is
the spitting image of you. Did you know
that children continue to grow in the
spirit world?

                    BRENDAN
                No, I didn't.

                    DORIS
          He says he's nearly ten now.
In one week's time Brendan's son, who has
passed, would have been ten years old.
Brendan is trying not to show any emotion.

                DORIS (CONT'D)
      He says to tell you not to worry. He is
    exactly where he is meant to be, and he
                  is happy.
Doris now closes her eyes again. Brendan's
gaze is fixed on her. She opens her eyes.

                    DORIS
        I see a studio. A microphone?

                   BRENDAN
      Ah, well, I'm here in London for a
            meeting about a band.
Brendan has broken his rule about NOT
helping her. Doris shakes her head.

                    DORIS
      No. This is you at the microphone. In a
                   studio.

                   BRENDAN
      No. You're wrong there. I have a pub.

My grandad O'Carroll.

Hardy, the M16 agent sent to assassinate my grandad and, in the process, shot his nine-year-old son, my father.

My dad the day before he was shot.

Michael McHugh, the man who carried my nine-year-old wounded father to the hospital, and would years later become my other grandad.

MICK
PETER

My grandad and the three sons that the MI6 agents really wanted.

My mum, Maureen O'Carroll, leaving the Four Courts. You can barely see it but I'm in this photo too. (She's pregnant.)

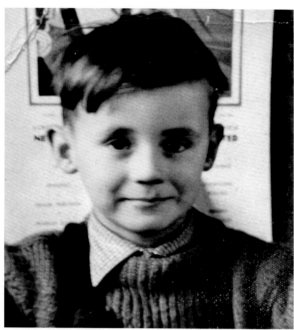

My first and only school photo. I was four years old. Yet again wearing an Éilish cast-off PINK jumper.

Me and Daddy. You can tell by my face that the shorts I was forced to wear were my sister's cast-offs.

Me and Mammy on my tenth birthday fulfilling my promise to make her laugh every day.

The family in our garden in Finglas. That's me at the front with Mammy's hand on my shoulder.

Colm, Donal and me with the actual van from *The Van*.

The waiter.

My grandad's shop in Manor Street today. My Daddy's family used to live above it – now it's a 'SeKsi' nail bar.

Presenting *257 World of Sport* on ARD radio.

Me with Gay Byrne. This is a heartfelt kiss! This man was a kingmaker. He made me a prince!

Me and my darling sister Fiona.

Fiona at the 'Women in Politics' exhibition, next to my mother's portrait.

My Dearest sister Fiona,

I am not going to get into the thank-you's, because that's your forte and I cannot compete with you in that arena.

Instead I ask you to please accept the enclosed poem, and know that when you are feeling in anyway below par, that someone who loves you very much is thinking about you.

FIONN AIGE.
Irish, meaning "fair faced"

As a child I remember only your happy eyes.
You are all that is good in any of us.
You are all that I would wish others to see in me.
How you skip a generation,
nurture my children, as you nurtured a little blonde boy,
so long ago, who needed it more than you will ever know.
You are a wonder.
You are joy itself.
You are courage.
You are compassion.
You are tenderness.
You shine on all of us, and yet allow us to shine too.
To you "happy eyes" I send the softest kiss, from a little blonde boy.

Have a wonderful journey, and may you never change.

With all my love.
Your brother, Brendan.

My poem for Fiona.

Me on the set of *Mrs. Brown's Boys*. That's Jenny in the foreground with her back to us.

The cast of *Mrs. Brown's Boys*. From left: Bugsy, Jenny, Mike, Me, Gary, Rory, Fiona, Paddy, Amanda and Jamie, Pepsi, Danny and Éilish.

Jenny with her husband, who wears a bra and women's clothes for a living.

The woman who has bought my home for me, educated my children and bought their homes for them too. Agnes Loretta Brown.

Doris starts wagging her finger.

                    DORIS
        Shush, shush, write this down . . .
Brendan has his pen ready.

                DORIS (CONT'D)
              OK. Glasgow.

                    BRENDAN
                    What?

                    DORIS
        Write it down. Glasgow. Glasgow will
            change your life, remember that.
Brendan is writing it down.
The rogue spirit is back. Doris again
addresses him.

                DORIS (CONT'D)
            Please go away. Please.
She pauses as if the spirit is talking to
her. She now addresses Brendan.

                DORIS (CONT'D)
        He wants you to write down a message. He
            says that you will deliver it.

                    BRENDAN
        No way. Absolutely not. I am a lot of
        things, but I am not going to be a dead
                man's fucking postman.

Doris bows her head.

DORIS

Brendan, please just write it down so I
can get rid of Chalky. Please.

Brendan gives in.

BRENDAN

OK, but I'm not promising anybody or
anything.

DORIS

That's OK. Here's the message: Of course
I love you, and I have always been proud
of you.

*The 'reading' goes on for another twenty
minutes but there is nothing of
importance. Brendan thinks it is just
padding. Doris calls a local cab and
watches as Brendan and the cab drive off
to London City.*

INT. NICO'S RESTAURANT, LONDON - NIGHT
Brendan is sitting at the restaurant
table alone. He is early and Bruce and
Sue have not arrived yet. Brendan is
only there fifteen minutes but he's
already on his second double vodka. The
menu is in front of him, but Brendan
pays it no heed. He sits looking out to
space, thinking, remembering his morning
experience with Doris. His dream state

is interrupted by the arrival of his
hosts.

                    BRUCE
            You were here early.
Brendan stands, hugs Bruce and then
kisses Sue on both cheeks. The manager is
taking Bruce and Sue's coats.

                    BRENDAN
    Excuse me, could I get a double vodka,
                    please?
The manager nods.
  Bruce points at the glass in Brendan's
hand.

                    BRUCE
              What's that?
Brendan realizes he has a drink and in
one gulp knocks it back.

                    BRENDAN
                Oh, right.
The waiter arrives with menus for Bruce
and Sue, and a vodka for Brendan.
  Without thinking Brendan takes it and
knocks it straight back and hands the
glass to the waiter.

              BRENDAN (CONT'D)
            Same again, please.

BRUCE

Would you like a drink while you're
waiting on that?

Brendan realizes how he is behaving.

BRENDAN

I'm so sorry. You know, I had the
weirdest experience today.

*Between the ordering of the food, the
serving and the eating of the meal
Brendan recounts the morning's events
with Doris. Now they are on coffee.*

BRENDAN (CONT'D)

So then the spirt comes back and wants me
to take a message.

BRUCE

Fuck that, mate, no farking way. I 'ope
you tells 'er ta fuck off.

BRENDAN

No. I took the message.

SUE

So what is it? What's the message?

*Brendan fishes in his pocket and takes
out the message.*

BRENDAN

Here it is. 'Of course I love you, and I
have always been proud of you.' From

Chalky. That's it. I don't know what the
fuck to do with it.

*Bruce has gone silent now. Sue is looking
at Bruce with a sad face. She gently puts
her hand on his. Bruce stares at Brendan.*

                    BRENDAN (CONT'D)
              What? What is it?

                    BRUCE
         Are you farking windin' me up?

                    BRENDAN
         I don't know what you mean.

                    BRUCE
            Chalky? Farking Chalky?

                    BRENDAN
                Yes. So?

                    BRUCE
              What's my name?

                    BRENDAN
                Bruce.

                    BRUCE
              Bruce what?

                    BRENDAN
              Bruce White.

That's right, and Chalky White was my dad.
Bruce tells Brendan about a family story
that made Bruce and his dad fall out,
which ends with Bruce at his father's
bedside as his dad lay unconscious, and
Bruce telling him, 'Don't you die without
telling me you love me and that you're
proud of me.'

Bruce passed away just a few years ago. He was so kind to me. Such a wonderful friend, and he gave me such knowledge of our business that I could never have repaid him. I loved him. I hope that he and Chalky are strolling together through God's garden. If you bump into my mother, Bruce, give her a message. Tell her I'm OK.

Back to the Castle. A voice in my head was saying, *See, I told you that taking the risk was worth it.* But as much as I thought we had 'made it', the voice was wrong. I could not have predicted in my wildest dreams what was round the corner.

15

It began with a not insignificant but not uncommon incident. Sundays at the Abbot's Castle became our busiest day. The bar would be packed right from opening time, and in the cabaret room we would have either a ballad session or maybe a novelty act in the morning, then we closed from two till five o'clock. In the evening the cabaret room would be sold out, the nightclub packed, and, again, the bar full to the brim. During the break we would clear the tills and reset them for the evening session. Rather than keep any cash in our homes we used our bank's night safe every night.

I had had an incident previously when an attempt was made to mug me with the night-safe bag. It was 2 a.m., and I had pulled up not just outside the bank but as close to the night safe as I could. I checked all around me before leaving the car. All clear. The bank had a portico entrance, with the night safe on one side of it. As I approached the night safe, I don't know where he came from but a guy with a balaclava stepped in front of me. He was holding a syringe. 'Gimme the bag. Don't fuck with me.'

I have no idea how it entered my head, but I tossed the bag up on to the roof of the portico and said to him, 'There you go, pal. I worked my fucking arse off for that. If you want it, you're going to have to work for it.' Then I walked back to the car. He was puzzled at first then he took off running. It was the fire service that later helped me retrieve the bag.

Anyway, because of this, we decided that on Sundays

especially we would make two night-safe visits. One at tea-time and one later in the early hours. On the Sunday in question Kevin took the night-safe bag for the teatime run. It held about £12,000. He had been gone about an hour when he phoned me. He was upset.

'Kevin, are you all right?' I asked, worried.

'The night-safe bag is gone. It's gone. I'm so fucking sorry. It's gone.'

Obviously my first thought was that he had been mugged and my concern was for his well-being. But he hadn't been mugged. Here's what he said had happened. When he got to the bank there had been a few dodgy-looking characters knocking around, so he didn't go near it. Instead, he went to another pub in Finglas village to wait it out. He then left the pub and drove to the bank but when he got there realized he had left the bag of money in the pub. He went back to ask if anybody had handed it in. Needless to say, they hadn't.

I assured him that as long as he was OK the money didn't matter. It did, but it didn't if you know what I mean. It did strike me that the pub he had gone to was no more than five minutes from the Castle. Why didn't he come back to the Castle? But it was a fleeting thought, nothing more.

A couple of weeks passed, and it was a Tuesday, my day off. Kevin took Mondays off. I was asleep when I got a call from one of the staff to say that the staff were all there, but Kevin hadn't arrived to open up. I dressed and phoned Kevin. No answer. So I drove to the Castle and opened up. I then drove to Kevin's apartment to check he was OK. I got no answer. I got into the apartment (don't ask) and it was spotlessly clean. The bed hadn't been slept in. I was puzzled but relieved that I hadn't found him unconscious after a stroke or something. I drove back to the Castle and worked the day. There was nothing from him that day, or the next, or the next. Then, amazingly, on the Friday Kevin arrived at work.

He was full of beans. 'Good morning,' he greeted me.

'Hi there,' I said, as I waited for an explanation.

None came. 'Do you want a coffee? I'll make us a coffee,' he said, and went off to the kitchen.

I was baffled. I followed him to the kitchen. 'Kevin, where have you been?'

He looked genuinely puzzled. 'What do you mean, where was I? I was on me day off.'

Now I was the one that was puzzled. 'Kevin, that was Monday. Your day off was Monday.'

He was now stirring the coffee. Then he asked me, 'Why? What day is today?'

'It's Friday, Kevin, fucking Friday! You've been missing for three days.'

Then it got really bizarre. 'Oh, is it?' he asked. He spoke so matter-of-factly that I couldn't take it in. 'I must have been sick then. Well, I'm here now, that's all that matters.' He walked past me, handing me a coffee.

I went after him. 'Kevin, wait a minute. What do you mean, you must have been sick?'

He shrugged. 'You know the way it is; you get a fever or something and you lose track of time.'

I wasn't happy. 'No. No, Kevin. You lose track of time; you don't lose track of three fucking days. I was here on my own for three days, worried sick.'

Kevin put his hand on my shoulder. 'I'll tell you what, you take the next three days off and we're even.'

I pushed his hand off. 'That's not the point.'

He smiled, then asked me, 'Then what is the point?'

I was exasperated. 'You were missing for three fucking days.'

He shrugged again. 'I told you: I was sick.' He went into the office and that was the last he would say about it.

I was disturbed about this for a week. But he went back to work, and he was his usual fantastic self and eventually I let it go. Until Berlin.

The next time Kevin went missing was a few months later. It was just two days this time. I got a call from the police in Berlin asking if I knew Kevin. He had been found blacked out in a train station in Berlin. I booked him a flight home and met him at the airport.

We sat and spoke. 'OK, the first thing you should know about me is that I have personal problems that I don't want to talk about.'

I had worked side by side with Kevin for years and had anybody but Kevin himself told me that Kevin had ANY problems I would have defended him to the hilt. I was shocked, and now I felt sorry for him. 'Kevin, I'm so sorry but what do we do now?'

Kevin had the solution. 'I've booked myself into rehab and I promise you, Brendan, this will never happen again.'

Kevin returned to the Castle from his 'holiday' four weeks later. He was truly back. He was fantastic at his work, and if anything he was even better than before. He continued to be so for the next few months.

During that time what I hadn't told Kevin was that my sister Fiona and her fiancé Larry were due to be married in Toronto. I had bought the flight tickets but didn't tell him. I so wanted to be there to share in Fiona's happiness, but I was terrified of leaving Kevin to run the place alone. So although I had the tickets I really wasn't sure whether to go or not. I waited until the night before I was supposed to go, when he and I went to dinner at a local restaurant.

'Kevin, my sister Fiona is getting married this week in Toronto.'

'Yes, I know.'

It threw me. 'How did you know?'

'Brendan, you can't keep a secret in the Castle. All the staff know.'

He was right, I suppose. 'I was going to go to the wedding, but I'm afraid to leave you alone, afraid of what might happen.'

He took a sip from his soup. 'I don't blame you,' he said ever so casually.

We sat in silence for a few minutes, then Kevin finished his soup and put his spoon down. 'Let me tell you something. I don't blame you for feeling the way you do, but here's the thing. If you do go, it would be the biggest vote of confidence anyone has ever given me. I won't let you down.'

I smiled at him. 'I have the tickets.'

He smiled too. 'For when?'

'Tomorrow. And I'm going to go.'

We shook on it and Kevin was so pleased. The next day I went off to Toronto and celebrated for ten days with my beautiful sister Fiona.

I should NEVER have gone.

The trip to Toronto was fantastic. Fiona and Larry were married two days after we arrived. It was a super wedding, and they had the reception back at their home. It was a glorious sunny day, so drinks were had on the lovely wooden deck at the back of the house. Many of the family were there. It was a Canadian wedding, so it wrapped up, for the Canadians, at seven in the evening. However, we carried on. As a family we all decided that we should give the happy couple at least a few days alone, so we should make ourselves scarce.

I had no idea where to go until my eldest sister, Maureen,

said she had never seen the Statue of Liberty and I suggested that I would drive her to New York and on the way take her to Niagara Falls. So we set off on an adventure. I love driving, especially in America, so it was a joy to me. We spent the first day at Niagara Falls, and then I drove to Syracuse where we spent the second night. Then next day we entered beautiful Manhattan. We didn't stop there, not even for a coffee. We literally went to Battery Park, parked the car, got a ferry to Liberty Island, climbed the Statue of Liberty and then headed back, staying that night again in Syracuse. The next day I drove non-stop to Toronto, passing through Niagara Falls and not stopping. It was a great three days and I really enjoyed the time with Maureen and her husband Reg. They lived in Sussex, and I hadn't seen either of them for quite a while.

The flight home was pleasant enough and, as wonderful a time as I had had, it was nice to be home. When I got home I called the Castle. I got no answer, so I called Kevin's number. No answer. I feared what I believed was the worst, but it was even worse than I could imagine. Kevin was gone. But so was every bit of stock from the Castle. Our bank accounts had been cleared out.

When I called in to our bar manager's house he seemed surprised to see me. 'He had a truck pull up in the early hours of the morning and clean the place out three days after you left,' he told me. 'I didn't know where to contact you.' Then he said, with a hint of guilt in his voice, 'To be honest, Brendan, I thought you were a part of it.'

Even as I am typing this I want to throw up.

The Abbot's Castle bank accounts were not just cleared out; he had even bit into our overdraft. Remember that £10,000 flexi-loan? The one we had paid back within two months? He had topped it up by another £10,000 and took that too. Paddy and Tom repossessed the place and there was a total of £96,000 in debts that I then became responsible for. For the first time in my life I owed more than I owned. I had also been self-employed, so I didn't even qualify for social welfare. I spent the next few months in and out of court as company after company went for judgements against me. Those months were the most terrifying of my life. I would have darker times in the future, but what was supposed to be a nice rags-to-riches story had instead become a rags-to-not-even-rags story.

I went looking for Kevin everywhere. I thank God that I did not find him because I don't know what I would have done. I had lost my senses; I had lost all my prospects and any chance of ever having success. That was my shot and I had missed. Eventually I stopped looking for him. I don't know where he went or what he did. But I'd like to see him today. If I bumped into Kevin today, I would run at him, throw my arms round him and kiss him on both cheeks. Because wherever you are, Kevin, you doing what you did sent me on my greatest adventure ever, a journey I had never expected to take that would send me to amazing places. It would change my life completely. It was a journey that would introduce me to two of the most amazing people I have ever met.

Myself – and Mrs. Brown.

The real adventure was about to begin. Thank you, Kevin.

16

Keep in mind that earlier I talked about Tinkers Fancy and how good they were. Well, when they would take a break I would get up and tell a few gags. So when things went belly up with the Castle I tried everywhere to get work. There was no way Mrs Hussey would take me back at the Ashbourne House, but I did get some smaller events from the Aer Lingus Outdoor Catering. But, on the whole, things were bleak. I did get a little help from the 'relieving' officer of the social welfare, but once again it was St Vincent de Paul that saved my bacon. They gave me some help with electricity bills, heating and even new shoes for Fiona and Danny for going back to school. They were great, but I was at a loss for where to get some work, well-paid work. For as well as trying to keep a roof over my head I was £96,000 in debt.

I saw an advert in the wanted column in the newspaper that read: *Do you want to earn £1,000 a week?* I thought, *Fuck yeh!* It was an ad for an insurance company. So I called the number and got an interview. The interview went pretty well, and the interviewer said he thought I might be good for the job but he would get back to me in a few weeks. The first week passed with no call. Then sitting in my kitchen, nursing a cup of tea, I had an idea. Comedy. For years my friends had been telling me that I should be on the stage. But you needed to meet my friends to know that you couldn't trust those bastards. But it struck me that maybe I could. Maybe I could get one or two gigs a week. It would be cash in hand and could be a well-paid nixer, even if I got the insurance thing. So I called a friend.

You may remember me mentioning John Sweeney. He was training in the Green Isle as a barman while I was there as a waiter. Well, he was now not only qualified but managing a bar in Dublin called the Rathmines Inn. It was probably the most popular bar in the area; it was situated right in the middle of flatland. The entire area was rented apartments or flats, so the clientele were young, mostly from outside Dublin, and had a few bob to spend. When John answered the phone, he sounded really delighted to hear from me.

I wasted no time. 'John, I need you to give me a gig!'

He was silent for a moment, then he asked, 'Doing what?' He was serious.

'Comedy,' was all I answered.

So he began to fob me off at first. 'Brendan, I could have Glen Miller in the corner here and we'd be packed anyway.'

I didn't exactly beg, but I was close. 'Come on, John, there must be some night you can give me?'

He thought about it for a moment. 'Tuesday. Tuesday nights are the quiet nights. But it will have to be free admission. I'll get one of the breweries to cough up a few bob for you, but you're only talking about seventy-five pounds.'

I didn't hesitate. 'I'll take it.'

Then John came back with: 'And it can't just be you telling jokes. Do a game show or something.'

'Eh, yeh, sure, I'll come up with something,' I lied.

He gave me Tuesday 9 October as the date, said he'd book me for three weeks and review it then.

I hung up and thought, *A game show? What the fuck will I do?* My mind went back to when I had worked in the Ashbourne House. Mrs Hussey was very good with charity fundraising and at one event in the function room I did a mock game of the huge TV hit Cilla Black's *Blind Date*. I remembered it being a bit of fun so I told John that this is what I would do, and he was happy.

The Rathmines Inn had no sound system so I had to rent this; it would cost £15 for the night. Still, I'm thinking, *It leaves me sixty pounds, not bad.*

Two things happened in the gap between my call to John and the performance date. First off, I got a call to tell me I had got the insurance job. I had to start their training course on Monday 22 October and I would be booked into a hotel for two weeks down in Athlone. That gave me a lift.

The second thing, not so much. John Sweeney called me to confirm the gig and asked, 'What time will your band start?'

Band? What fucking band? I told John I wasn't planning on having a band.

'You have to have somebody warm up for you; you can't just get up and start talking shite!' John exclaimed.

I was tempted to tell him that I wasn't planning on talking shite, but I was too busy trying to think of what the fuck I could do for a band. I called Gerry Browne from Tinkers Fancy and asked him if himself and one of the lads from the band would do a warm-up as a duo? He agreed but it would be £20 each. But they had their own sound equipment that I could then use for my comedy, so they would cost £40 but I would save £15. I'd still come out with £35. I made the deal with him. I didn't know that he'd been trying to get Tinkers Fancy into the Rathmines Inn for a long time and that he saw this as a possible 'in'.

So arrived the 9 October. I got to the gig far too early at 6 p.m. The gig was due to start at 8 p.m. I had a coffee at the bar and John asked me if I was nervous. I smiled and calmly said, 'Nope.' Because I wasn't nervous; I was fucking terrified.

Gerry and 'Dicey', a guy with an amazing voice, arrived and went about setting up their gear. They joined me at the bar and ordered a couple of pints. I stared at the, for the moment, empty stage. The two guitars in their stands. The microphones sitting snugly in their mic stands and I thought, *What the fuck am I doing here?*

Gerry interrupted my thoughts. 'So how does this work? This *Blind Date* thing?'

'I haven't the foggiest idea.'

He smiled. 'Making it up as you go along?'

I just nodded.

'Fair play, you're a brave man.' He smiled and toasted my 'bravery'.

I went to the stage and placed four stools across the front of the platform. One for the guy and three for his prospective dates. There was no prize, no glory; I didn't even care if they never went on a date. I looked at my watch. Seven thirty. About forty people had wandered in – the place held 650 so it was to all extents empty. The watch ticked on and at 8 p.m. Gerry and Dicey got on the stage and began playing and singing. This at least got the crowd, which had been spread out around the huge room, to gather towards the stage. Gerry and Dicey were fantastic. The crowd really warmed to them. As I had prearranged with him, Gerry announced that a waitress would be going around the room giving out tickets and that if Brendan called out your name you were invited up on to the stage to play *Blind Date*. They did a few more numbers and then at 8.45 Gerry put his guitar down and said to the audience, 'OK, boys and girls, you have a very funny man coming up on stage to play the game and give you all a few laughs.'

I was thirty-five years old and for the first time in my life I heard 'Ladies and gentlemen . . . Brendan O'Carroll.'

It had begun.

17

As I made my way to the small stage in the Rathmines Inn, nobody clapped; they just waited in silence. I climbed on to the stage and took the mic and began my performance.

'So, how are we all doing tonight then, eh?'

Silence.

'This reminds me of where I was last night . . . a funeral.' There was one titter but, in general, silence. I chickened out. 'OK, let's play the game.' I looked over at John Sweeney who was behind the bar. He had his head down, I figured with embarrassment.

To my great surprise the first ticket I picked out, for the guy, the man actually came up on stage straight away. I had been sure the men would be reluctant. He sat on the stool and I blindfolded him. Then I called out three more tickets and again was surprised when all three women bounded up to the stage.

I sat them on their stools and asked their names and where they were from. Two of the women were from an affluent part of Dublin and were quite prim and proper, but the third was a townie like myself. A real 'Dub'.

The first question asked by the first-ever guy I had on *Blind Date* was, 'What is the first thing you look for in a man?' I turned to the audience and gave a little chortle. 'Well, that's an interesting first question. What do you look for in a man?' Again silence. In fact, if there was possibly anything more silent than silence, that's what it was.

I was now feeling beads of sweat pop out on my forehead, but I moved on and I asked the question to prim woman one.

She thought for a moment. 'Eyes,' she answered. 'The first thing I notice in a man are the eyes. You can tell a lot about a man from his eye contact.'

I'm thinking, *The question is what do you look FOR, not what do you look at, yeh dozy cunt.* But obviously I didn't say any of that. I heard a female voice in the audience. 'Too true, love, you're right.' So I moved on to prim woman number two.

She had had time to think, so she was ready with her answer. 'Deportment,' she snapped out.

I was flummoxed. 'Deportment?' I was hoping she would expand and she did.

'Oh yes, the way a man carries himself can tell you whether he's confident, or maybe shy, or even if he is a thug!'

I was on a downward spiral. I silently prayed, *Oh God, please make me funny.*

I went to woman number three with little hope in my heart. She too was ready with her answer. 'I don't care . . . as long as he has a big cock.'

The other two women were shocked, and I didn't know what to say, but the forty people in the audience roared with laughter. I mean it, they screamed for a good twenty seconds. I looked over at John, expecting a disapproving look but, no, he was bent double laughing.

I can't remember the other two questions but I know that I couldn't wait to get to woman number three each time for her answer. Neither could the audience. The guy picked her, to the delight of the crowd, and I actually saw them having a drink after the show. Once the game part was over I told a few gags and Gerry and Dicey joined me on stage where we finished with 'Sweet Caroline' and, of course, the national anthem, which was the norm at the end of every gig back then.

As I left the stage and made my way to the bar, John was

walking swiftly past me towards the stage. He took the mic and announced, 'Don't forget: Brendan will be back again next Tuesday with *Blind Date*.'

I was chuffed and when John got back to the bar he slapped me on the back. 'You were great up there. What'll you have?'

I wasn't great; *she* had been great, woman number three. But I was getting the credit. I went home that night with my £35 and a lot to ponder.

I sat up into the early hours thinking about what had transpired. What was it that had made her funny? It wasn't her saying 'cock'; cock on its own wasn't funny. It was the context in which she said it. I thought and thought about it. Then it dawned on me. I had been so fixated on the 'cock' part of her answer that I had discounted the rest of the sentence. She had started it with 'I DON'T CARE'. That was it. She really didn't care. She was just being herself and she didn't care whether anybody liked it or not. Yet the guy had picked her. She was authentic. She was being herself and she didn't care. *Fuck!* I thought, *The freedom of that.*

I decided there and then that this was the route I wanted to go, not just with my comedy but with the rest of my life. I realized that all my life so far I had been performing, pretending to be what I thought someone else would like me to be. I could even remember when it had started. Twenty years previously, in the hotel I worked in then, there were a good twenty other commis waiters all aged between fourteen and sixteen. After six months of working there I had no friends. I would look at myself in the mirror and think, *I'm a good guy. Why have I no mates?* Then I came upon the answer.

We would all be in the canteen for, say, breakfast and one of the lads might say something like, 'Did you see there was a big chunk of cheese out of the moon last night?' I felt obliged to inform him and the others that the moon was actually mostly porous rock, although scientists felt that there may be some trace elements that could indicate that our moon, rather than being a satellite that just wandered into our orbit and gravity field, may actually have broken away from our own planet, Earth, and over time become the moon it is today. By the time I had finished educating him, I would be sitting at the table alone. I had too much to say for myself. So I decided that when something like this happened again, I would look puzzled, put on a performance, and say, 'Oh, I thought it was made of ice cream?' This would first get a laugh and then I would let him explain to ME why it couldn't be ice cream as it would melt. I tried it and it worked! Within weeks I had lots of pals.

But, and here's the dangerous thing, it's an easy way out; it becomes habit. Soon you're performing all the time, playing dumb or at least dumber than the person you are trying to make a friend of, or to keep a boss happy, or even in your relationships. Before you know it, twenty years have passed, and you have no idea who the fuck you are. Who you really are! Who you could be if you could have the courage to be like woman number three and just not fucking care. To have the courage to just be yourself, to follow your instinct and see where it takes you, to not try to please everybody. *Wow*, I thought, *FREEDOM*.

John Sweeney that night was being as nice and supportive as he could be, but he was wrong. I hadn't been 'great' up there, but I resolved that I was going to be. If not great, at least I would be me, and if I sank or swam it wouldn't be because I hadn't given all I had, and, believe me, I mean all, even what I had kept hidden for over twenty years. While I had thought my life had come to a dead end after the failure of the Castle, I now had two great opportunities in front of me. A chance to go on stage and let loose, plus a new job selling insurance. Things were looking up! I couldn't wait for the next Tuesday.

Funnily enough it came just seven days later. Here was my plan. Comics of that time were very self-regulated. None ever said 'fuck' or any cuss words. Yet when I spoke to my mates in the football club I did swear – not deliberately; it was the way I spoke. It was the way most people spoke. At that time some of the pubs in Dublin would set aside Sunday mornings for what they called 'stag' mornings. A comic would get on stage and tell 'dirty' jokes. The place would be rocking with laughter. I was of the firm belief that women would enjoy those jokes just as much as men did and that there was no need for a 'stag' morning. I was going to get on that stage and shoot from the hip. The gags would come out whatever way they came out. I would tell them as if I were telling them to my brother Micháel.

To my surprise, this week there were about 150 in the audience. Gerry and Dicey were brilliant yet again, and the time soon arrived for me to get going. I hadn't told John Sweeney or Gerry my intention. I went on stage and, after politely saying hello, I told the audience that my mother was very sensitive about the language she used so that when we were kids my father, if he wanted to keep something private, would spell out the words. Like he would say to my mother, 'Maureen, do you want to go up S.T.A.I.R.S. for a fuck?' The audience howled. After two or three more of these I noticed a few people leaving, but I carried on. This was me, baring my balls, and I didn't fucking care!

Blind Date was just the same; instead of pandering to the contestants, I took the piss in a friendly way and without either insulting or belittling them. It was a great night. I came off the stage and I wasn't sure what John's reaction would be, but more than the previous week I knew I had been GREAT up there.

John waved me to part of the bar that was quiet. 'I want to talk to you.'

Oops, I thought, *here we go*.

We settled at the end of the bar counter. 'We're going to have to charge for this show.'

I had not been expecting this. 'What?'

He leaned in to me as if it were a secret. 'First off, it's too good a show for free, and, secondly, once people pay in they're making a choice to be here, so there's no complaints.'

I was thrown a little off guard. 'Were there complaints?'

'A few, but I handled it. I'm going to charge a pound in from next week. Whatever comes in at the door is yours, less the cost of the cashier.' He held out his hand.

'The door plus the seventy-five pounds,' I said before I put out my hand.

John smiled. 'You're on.'

And we shook on it. It was great but I worried now that what I had done that night might deter those who were in the audience from coming back. But before I was to find out, I was starting my training the following Monday for my new job.

The hotel where I was to stay and where my training would begin was grubby – not dirty just a little unkempt. I arrived at eight thirty on the Monday morning, checked in and, as instructed by my recruiter, was in the training room at 9.25 a.m. sharp for a 9.30 a.m. start. There were eight other candidates in the room, and we all sat on one side of a twelve-foot table. I said good morning to each of them and shook hands.

At exactly nine thirty our trainer made his entrance. He burst in through the double doors and at the top of his voice shouted, 'GOOD MORNING!'

We were all of us startled.

He smiled and ordered us to all stand up, so we did. Then he began to march on the spot and started singing at the top of his voice. *'It's a long way to Tipperary, it's a long way to go!* Come on, join in.'

We did, quietly and shyly at first, but between verses he would shout, 'Louder, come on.'

Before the end of the song we were all singing heartily and smiling. He had broken down any barriers that had existed before he had walked into that room.

He went to a large white pad on a stand, took up a marker and wrote *JOE* on the page, underlining it. 'That's me. I am Joe, and over the next two weeks I will be teaching you lucky people . . .'

He didn't finish the sentence; instead he turned and ripped the page with his name on off the pad and wrote *THE SYS-TEM* on the new clean page. 'The System.' He puffed out his chest as he said this.

I'll bet you are just dying to know what the system is. Well, I will tell you. Just turn the page.

18

The system is an American-devised way of selling insurance. It is a tried-and-tested principle that is based on this: if you can learn the sales talk word for word, and, when giving a prospective customer a demonstration of the product, repeat the sales talk word for word, then for every five times you deliver it you will positively sell once.

But it must be word for word. They even had a joke built into it that you had to do. 'We pay you if your leg is broken. We pay you if your arm is broken. Heck, we even pay you if your heart is broken.' Here you would fake a laugh, then: 'Seriously, though . . .' And on you go with your sales talk.

But here are a couple of things you need to know. The accident policy that we were to sell cost only £30 for six months' cover, and if you were in any accident that required hospitalization, we would pay you £250 for every week you were in there. Although the sales talk was really good, I'm convinced that you would only get paid if the accident you were involved in was if you were cycling a unicycle on top of a train that was hit by an aircraft. But, and this is a big but and the second thing I want to tell you, although your commission on a £30 policy was £15 (the company made more on the renewal) in order to make a decent £300 a week, never mind the promised £1,000, you had to sell twenty policies. Well, if you are using the system and selling one for every five you demonstrate, then you have to make a hundred calls a week, or twenty a day. These are cold door-to-door calls. Ask anyone who has sold door-to-door and they will tell you it is soul-destroying. The hardest call of any salesman's day is the first one. Just getting up the moxie to get out of the car and knock at that first door is really tough. This is where the good part comes in. To give you that moxie the company, parallel to the sales training, gave you a PMA course. Positive Mental Attitude.

There are a couple of books you can get if you feel you need some PMA. The one that our course was based on was *Success Through a Positive Mental Attitude* by Napoleon Hill and W. Clement Stone. It was superb! I learned about things like positive speech. A good example of this is if you are visiting any Disney Park. The custodians there never use negative speech. If you ask, 'What time does the park close?', because 'close' is a negative word, they might answer: 'The park is *open* until nine thirty.' It's a small thing but really effective. Another one is the three-yes principle. If you can get someone to say yes three times in a row, on the fourth question you will make the sale.

For example:

'You love your children, don't you?'

'YES.'

'You want the best for them?'

'YES.'

'If you were injured in an accident, you'd want them to be looked after?'

'YES.'

'Ah, then you can see how this policy makes sense?'

'YES.'

Sign here and gimme the cheque!

There are lots of examples and I highly recommend having a look at some of them even if only for entertainment.

So Joe began the training course. I buckled down and worked really hard for those first two days. It was during lunch on the second day, the Tuesday, that Joe suggested that we all meet down in the bar at 8 p.m. and he would answer any questions we had about that day's work.

'I won't be there,' I said, not expecting it to matter.

'What do you mean, you won't be there?' Joe snapped at me.

'I have to go to . . . work.' I didn't want to explain in front of everyone that I had a show to do at the Rathmines Inn.

Joe took me aside and basically told me that if I left the hotel without a good reason he would have to end my participation in the training programme. 'What's so important?' he asked.

Away from the others I could now tell him. It turned out that Joe was a bit of a frustrated actor himself and he wished me well but said not to tell anyone.

The traffic when I reached the outskirts of the city was dreadful. I made it to the Rathmines Inn with about thirty minutes to spare. When I went into the place I got the shock of my life. It was packed. Really stuffed. The cashier handed me £600 from the door and John gave me £75. It was a bonanza. The gig too went incredibly well. They laughed and heckled, which I loved, and the *Blind Date* contestants were hilarious. Even as we ended with 'Sweet Caroline' the windows of the pub rattled with the cheers. It was a miracle.

I drove back to Athlone that night with my head full of ideas and buzzing. It would have been easy to say 'Fuck selling insurance' and pack it in. But I just knew that I wanted to finish the course and see what happened. I did finish it and went on the road selling the following week. In that first week I broke the first week in the field sales record. At each morning meeting the sales manager would announce the sales and everyone would clap. Then he would say, 'How did you do it, Brendan?' and you HAD to answer 'I used the system,' and the manager would look at the other reps and, nodding his head, he'd slowly say, 'He used the system.'

I left the job after a few weeks. As it turned out, some of the family of John Douglas, the manager, were street traders and I knew most of them. We got on famously and are still great friends today. At the time John asked me why I had stayed even for the few weeks I had, and I told him two reasons that he repeats to this day to anyone who will listen: the PMA, and that someday I would write a comedy play about this. And I did.

Read on, and later in the book I'll tell you about THAT saga. But for now it's back to the Rathmines Inn.

I was over two months into Tuesday nights doing *Blind Date*. It was starting to dawn on me that comedy could be a viable full-time business for me, so I began to look around at possible venues.

There were very few. Gerry invited me to do a gig in a local football club with his band Tinkers Fancy, so I tried it out – no game show, just pure stand-up. It went OK, just OK. My most enduring memory of that gig was after the show we were in the football changing room and that Gerry's cousin, who sometimes hauled gear for Tinkers Fancy, walked in. 'Great gig,' he said aloud, then pointed at me and added, 'but that little prick has to go.'

I looked at him with a frown.

He was sympathetic. 'Sorry, pal, you're just not funny.'

His name was Dermot O'Neill, or, as we call him, Bugsy. He has worked with me for over thirty years now and you might know him as Grandad in the TV series.

19

Although that football club gig had not been great, as the Tuesday-night gigs in the Rathmines Inn became even more popular, my name began to spread as a comic around Dublin. My next two gigs came from a couple of venue owners that had seen me in the Rathmines Inn. One of them was from Fat Sam's nightclub in Waterford. As the club had a full-time DJ I didn't need Gerry and Dicey, so I would just arrive with my suit cover, do the *Blind Date* gig and I was out of there. A handy couple of quid, and no pressure.

My most vivid memory of Fat Sam's was that it was the youngest crowd I had ever performed in front of. The joke in Waterford at the time was 'What has sixty legs and two pubic hairs?' The answer being: 'The front row of *Blind Date* at Fat Sam's.' Still they were a happy crowd and I loved Waterford, so it was a joy to go there and make them laugh, which I did every Monday for over six months. However, many of the places that I had a look at didn't do live entertainment and weren't geared for it. So I sat down and drew up a plan. If the venues didn't have a stage, lighting or a sound system what could I do? Well, the only answer was to bring the whole lot with me. I researched the cost of setting this up. The lights, sound system, a portable stage and, last but certainly not least, a van to carry them in. It was a lot – an awful lot. I didn't have the money for it. There was no point in going to a bank for finance because if you put my name into a bank's computer at that time it would start smoking and probably burst into flames.

I had discussed this with Gerry and said to him that I could see the day when I would earn £1,000 a week. Gerry also thought that comedy was the right route for me; he wasn't sure if it was for him, though. As well as having the band, Gerry's main income came from his milk round. He had built it up over the years and he had a big round and did very well with it. I kept looking for more gigs but not doing *Blind Date*. I had put together a stand-up show that would run for forty-five minutes. Top and tail that with music from Gerry and Dicey and you had a whole show. I called it the Outrageous Comedy Show, or the OCS, to differentiate it from the *Blind Date* thing. So a gig would be either *Blind Date* or an OCS.

Tinkers Fancy themselves were gigging away. They had a residency on Sunday nights in a pub in Mary Street that would be packed every week and they played the odd gig locally in the Northway House, which was literally just over Gerry's back garden wall. I can't remember where it came from but Tinkers Fancy were asked to do a few gigs across the water in the UK. Just two or three. Gerry suggested trying out the Outrageous Comedy Show as being Tinkers Fancy plus me, and I agreed.

I had neither a van nor any sound gear of my own, but I knew someone who did. He was the biggest comedy pull in Ireland at that time. His name was Paul Malone. Paul was not just a funny guy; he was a very clever writer. In fact, one parody he wrote called 'Baggot Street Bridge' was a hilarious song about a guy trying to negotiate with a Dublin prostitute. Paul would sing it at parties, but he never did it on stage – he felt it was too raunchy for his set. I dived on it, added a few pauses in it, threw in a few gags and it became the most requested song every Tuesday at the Rathmines Inn.

I had known Paul before I even dreamed of stepping on

to a stage. He and his sidekick, Tony Mellon, had even gigged for me in the Castle. I had heard that Paul was taking a break, so I approached him to ask if he would loan me his van and gear for the UK trip. He very kindly said yes, provided I used and paid his roadie to man the equipment and do the sound. I was delighted to agree to that. I needed someone who knew their way around the gear. The roadie was a guy named Padraig or Patrick Shields. He was a big, tall, really handsome kid with jet-black hair. He did a brilliant impersonation of Elvis. There was an advert on TV at that time for Pepsi where a cool *Grease*-looking guy slid up to some girls and in an Elvis kind of voice sang, '*Well, you can tell by what I'm drinking that I'm really kind of smooth, oh yeah!*' Padraig would imitate this to a tee, so I started calling him Pepsi and that's what he's known as today.

The UK trip was a disaster. We played three venues: the Sugar Loaf in Luton, the Glasgow Celtic Supporters Club in Luton and a pub on the Seven Sisters Road in Leytonstone. Tinkers Fancy simply rocked the three venues. But with the exception of the Celtic Supporters club, where I got maybe a few laughs, I bombed. Big time.

I remember the ferry ride back to Dublin as we were just pulling out of Holyhead. It was dark and I was broke. After paying Pepsi's wage and paying for petrol and accommodation, I had lost money and I was very down. I was out on the deck, having a smoke. It was windy and a bit rough as the big ferry left the tide barrier, which I don't mind, and Pepsi came out for a smoke too. He is a man of few words. We stood there smoking, holding on to the rail.

'Pepsi, I'm sorry the trip wasn't more successful. I had hoped it might click over there. No chance.'

Pepsi shrugged. He tossed the butt of his roll-up overboard, turned to go back inside and, as he walked, said,

'Maybe so, but you're still the funniest little fucker I've ever seen.'

Without giving me a chance to reply he went back inside. I stood on the deck for a couple more cigarettes and even though the trip had been awful I made a big decision. *I'm going into this full-time and full tilt. I am going to give it every ounce of time, energy and whatever talent I can muster.* That trip may have been a disaster, but I knew I mustn't look back. I wasn't going that direction; I was going forward.

I went to the rail and flicked my butt into the dark sea. I looked over at the distant shore. The lights on land were fading away. Over the crash of the waves against the hull I shouted to those fading lights. 'I'll be fucking back!'

20

It was shortly after I returned from that disastrous trip to England that I made an approach to Gerry Browne. He knew the plan I had drawn up, and he had worked on many of the gigs with me. We had done enough OCS gigs for him to decide if the OCS had any potential as a full-time venture. I had been to my bank and run the idea past the manager, explaining that I needed £30,000 to purchase what I needed to launch myself as a full-time comedian.

He laughed at first. 'You? In a band?'

I couldn't get it through to him. 'The band is just for the show. I'll be the comedian,' I tried to explain.

'Comedian? But are you funny?' was the stupid question he asked.

'I must be, or I wouldn't be drawing crowds to the Rathmines Inn every Tuesday night,' I answered.

He looked over the business plan I had made up – actually 'made up' because if you read through it I was only short of including a week at the London Palladium in the list of gigs I would be doing according to the cashflow section. But he was surprisingly sympathetic. He wrapped up our meeting with this: 'That business is notoriously fickle, Brendan. Who knows what will happen. Maybe you WILL make a success of it, but the truth is that very few bands succeed.'

I said 'comedian' through clenched teeth.

'Even less of them!' he countered. I had almost given up hope of getting any good out of the meeting when he said, 'The only way I could sanction that amount of money would be as a personal loan, but with your record I would need a solid guarantor.' He handed me back my plan and I left the bank with a glimmer of hope.

Guarantor. Where would I get a solid guarantor?

Gerry Browne had his milkman's account in the same bank. The next Tuesday night before we went on stage I had asked Gerry to get to the Rathmines Inn early as I wanted to have a chat with him. When he arrived early I ordered myself a coffee and a Guinness for Gerry, and I told him of my meeting with the bank manager and how it had gone. He knew the guy, so he said he could have told me not to bother.

'I don't know what you should do,' Gerry said, and he took a gulp of his creamy pint of Guinness.

'What if we became partners?' I asked, as if I had just thought of that there and then, even though I had been thinking about asking him since I had left the bank.

Gerry nearly choked on his mouthful of Guinness. 'Partners?' He genuinely had not seen that coming.

'Yes,' I enthused, 'you go guarantor on the loan, and we split the profit down the middle?'

He didn't say no. But what he did say gave me little or no hope. 'Myself and the lads are talking about the band going full-time.'

I wasn't expecting that. 'Oh?'

Gerry went on. 'Yeh, we've been talking about it for a long time now and we think it might be time to give it a go.'

I nodded. 'Well, there you go. Great minds think alike, I suppose.'

Gerry drained the last of his pint. 'I'll think about what you said, and I'll make a decision when we get back from England.'

I frowned. 'You're going to England again?' He got a bit embarrassed. 'Eh, yeh, the places we played on that last trip asked us to come back –' pause – 'without the comedian.' He shrugged.

'No problem,' I told him. 'I understand.' But I was devastated.

Tinkers Fancy left for England on a Wednesday. The trip was just up to Saturday, and they would be back on the Sunday morning. That Sunday night they were booked to play a gig in a pub in the village where I lived. I went to the show that night to see them play and they were brilliant. Yet again they had the place rocking with a mixture of ballads and even some pop hits. Really great stuff. Gerry himself had a beautiful deep singing voice that would mesmerize you. He even sang a couple of songs he had written himself and the audience loved them too. As the night went on and the crowd cheered more and more I could see my partnership plans go up in smoke. If Tinkers Fancy decided to go full-time, there was no doubt in my mind that they would become huge. But something strange happened after the gig. I went into the kitchen of the pub, where they had changed, and nobody was speaking to anybody. The lads were estranged. To this day I don't know what happened on the short trip across the Irish Sea to split these long-time mates up, but for sure something had. I went home puzzled.

The next day Gerry called me and said, 'Let's give it a go.'

Stage two of my journey was about to begin.

Almost immediately Dicey stopped doing the Rathmines Inn with Gerry, so we needed someone to replace him. I suggested a guy I had met when he played keyboards for Face to Face. Colin Goodall. What a talent. He had an amazing singing voice and he could replicate any big pop hit of the time. He was a self-taught musician on guitar and keyboards, both of which he mastered. Gerry and Colin began rehearsing together and their very different voices complemented each other. Within a week they had a set that although still a bit loose sounded great. The audience in the Rathmines Inn loved the 'new' sound. The Rathmines Inn had now added a Sunday-morning gig to our diary, and we always managed to pick up a third gig every week. So with three gigs we were making the bank payments, covering our costs and earning enough to keep us going.

Although Gerry had pledged himself to our project he kept his milk round for the time being, just in case. Colin also had a full-time job in a music store in town and it was through him we bought the sound equipment we needed – top of the range, by the way. As for a crew, we didn't have one. I drove the van, and Gerry and I loaded and unloaded it, put up speakers and set up the stage lights. Colin felt we needed a bass player and had a guy in mind – Willie Demange – and Gerry agreed. He was a good guy and a fine bass player. Bugsy, Gerry's cousin, was still helping with lumping the gear for free, but we needed someone to control the sound. At first Gerry or Colin would do it on the stage, but for the comedy I wasn't happy. I wanted the audience to hear me even if I whispered; I wanted them to hear every inflection of my voice. So we agreed that we would take one on. I had just the guy in mind . . .

I hadn't seen Pepsi Shields since that trip to the UK. I had his phone number and called him. I offered him the job at the same money he was on with Paul but promised that, as things got better, it would increase.

'Whatever way the show goes, you'll go,' I told him.

'What if the show goes on its arse?' he was quick to ask.

I didn't dress it up. 'Then so will you!'

He was very polite on the phone and thanked me, but turned the job down.

You know, you never know what changes people's minds,

though. I have never had any interest in even asking them. For instance, I truly do not know what happened on that Tinkers Fancy trip across the water that changed Gerry's mind, and I had no interest in finding out. I'm the same when someone leaves the show. If they go, they go – unless they tell me themselves what is making their decision for them I wouldn't ever ask. I just move on.

Pepsi called me within a few weeks and said, 'If it's still available, I'll take the job.' He joined us a week later in the Rathmines Inn.

That was 1991. Today you may know him as Mark Brown, Mrs. Brown's eldest son.

The whole show was now looking and sounding so much more professional. The quality of Gerry and the boys had picked up so much that I now had to up my game. I suppose it was only natural then that, as word spread, more gigs were coming in. Not just in Dublin either. By the end of 1990 we had performed in Galway, Cork, Wexford, Dundalk, Sligo and Limerick. But our mainstay was Dublin. Now that we had the whole kit and caboodle – stage, lights, sound, etc. – we could gig anywhere. If it were a pub, we would clear a spot, erect everything and suddenly the place became a new venue.

We were cracking along when we got bad news. The Rathmines Inn had been sold and was closing for a few months. The new owners, we were told, had plans for the place and those plans didn't include live music or comedy. This was potentially a huge setback as the Sunday mornings and Tuesday nights in the Rathmines Inn were our staple. Without them we were dependent on whatever odd gig might come in. A quick scan around the area led us to the Barge. Although it was only a mile from the Rathmines Inn it had a very different audience. During the day the pub did a really brisk lunch trade, as it was flanked on its south side by office buildings. In the evenings it became the local bar for the blocks of council flats that flanked its north side. It was also right on the Grand Canal, hence the name. But, more importantly, that canal divided the council flats from the more upmarket private flats. The Barge was owned by the McCabe family, and they all worked in it. The owners of the pub well knew about our success in the Rathmines Inn and readily offered us a Sunday morning and a Tuesday night. They had no stage, so we did the gig with us half in and half out of the kitchen area. I loved that gig from the very first time we performed there.

It was also a great training ground. When you gig in a place every Sunday morning and Tuesday night, you have to keep the show fresh. Now there were some gag routines or songs that we did almost every show, as they were requested, kind of my greatest hits vibe, but, on the whole, I needed to come up with 'something' every week, twice a week, because that audience was very critical and could be vicious when they wanted to be, so I had to be vicious right back.

I recall that in the middle of a piece about trying to find the G-spot, a young woman in the audience, timed perfectly, shouted up at the stage, 'If you were my husband, I'd kill yeh.'

This got a laugh, so I had to win them back, which I did with: 'Missus, if I were your husband, I'd fuckin' kill meself.'

There was a bigger laugh, the biggest from the woman herself.

Word soon spread that if you went to 'that' show, don't even go to the bathroom or 'he'll savage you'.

The gigs continued to come in. I was now manning the phone myself, calling places all over the country and selling the show. This might just work. Life was looking up.

It was Henry W. Longfellow that coined the phrase 'Into each life some rain must fall'. He didn't have a quote for the fucking monsoon that was about to hit me. I'm only now starting to get back on my feet. Give me a fucking BREAK.

22

1990 had ended with the show now well established in Dublin and gaining a little ground in the surrounding counties. We had a great Christmas and the new year looked bright. That first week in January I had an appointment to meet someone in the lobby of the Burlington Hotel. I was there a little early, and he arrived on time but looked a tiny bit uncomfortable. Let me explain what we were doing there by taking you back to April 1990.

I was having a breakfast of a mug of tea and a cigarette as I was playing back the messages on my answering machine. The house was quiet as the kids were at school and Doreen, I think, had gone to her mother's. I had been away a lot over the previous few months and things at home were getting more than a little tense. So she was keeping herself busy *out* of the house, and I was staying overnight at as many gigs as I could. I didn't know it then, but our marriage was in trouble.

We were taking a break after that night's gig in the Jolly Beggarman in Donnycarney; it was Easter the following week, all the kids were off school, and many people would be taking holidays. We knew the gigs would have been quiet anyway so we thought we might as well have a couple of weeks to have a rest ourselves. I skipped the first few messages as I recognized the voices and knew they were just requests for a callback. I listed them as I listened.

On came a voice I didn't recognize. It was a man that wanted to book me, he said, for the Wexford Inn in Wexford Street in Dublin. This was a big venue. I called him back. His name was Rory Cowan, he said, and he wanted to book the show for 4 June. I flipped through the diary. I came to 4 June and saw it was a bank holiday.

'Are you sure that's the date you want?'

He replied, 'That's the only available date they will give me.'

I'm sure it was, and I knew exactly why. The Wexford Inn was a favourite venue with the 'country' crowd. Let me explain. Back then, before decentralization, all the government and civil services, all the main hospitals, were based in Dublin. But the civil servants, nurses and government aides came from counties all over Ireland, from Donegal to Cork, and Kerry to Drogheda. Many of them went home at weekends, but on a bank holiday weekend they ALL went home. The roads out of Dublin would be jammed on the Friday evening and that would be repeated on the Monday night coming into Dublin. That is why the Wexford Inn was available to Rory on 4 June because their clientele would have deserted them.

I told Rory this and he surprised me by saying he knew that was the case, but he still wanted to book the show. Being a big-risk venue that night I wanted a guarantee of £400 and he said that this wasn't a problem, so I penned in the booking and thought no more about it.

That evening we played the Jolly Beggarman to a great audience and afterwards, as we sat having a drink, Colin our keyboard player announced that he and Willie were leaving the show. They were going it alone, they said. The irony of this was that I had just a few weeks before taken my nephew on as a roadie and he too was leaving to manage the two boys on their venture. Gerry and I bade them goodbye and thanked God we had a few weeks to find and rehearse replacements.

When we went back on the road the replacements changed every couple of gigs. In fact, I think we went through about thirty or forty musicians during that time. It wasn't *that* big a deal. Gerry carried the musical end of the show, so the others were there just to accompany him. I also wanted to wait as there were two guys I really wanted to join us: two of the most talented musicians in the country. I knew if we could get them on board the sky was the limit for the show. One was guitarist Eric Sharpe. What a musician. He could make his guitar talk. I saw him once do a random spot where he took the guitar from the resident guitarist, who was left-handed; Eric simply played the thing upside down. He was remarkable. Problem was Eric was playing with the band Jump the Gun, who had represented Ireland in the Eurovision just three years previously where they finished in a respectable eighth place. The other was Gerry Simpson. Gerry was an amazing piano player and music arranger. Gerry's beginnings in the business were with his brother's band The Spider Simpson Band. Spider, a charismatic and hugely popular star, was also regarded as one of the nicest guys in the business. Tragically, following a dreadful car collision, Spider went into a coma that would last for many years. Awful for Gerry and his family. I had approached Gerry in Drogheda when he came to our show in his home town. He actually laughed at the idea, but I persisted. The problem was Gerry was the musical director of the Don Baker Band. I cannot adequately describe how big a star Don Baker was at that time. His blues albums are available online. So here we were then. Eric said he would think about it. Gerry Simpson said fuck off.

Eventually Eric Sharpe took the job. I never asked him why; I was just glad to have him. But it took me many visits to Gerry Simpson's home to find his trigger (everyone has a trigger). I tried arriving with a gift. I tried flattery – didn't work. I even tried begging. Nope. It was on one of my

228

multiple visits that I cottoned on. Money. Everybody likes money. But Gerry really liked money. We struck a price and Gerry joined us within a week.

Obviously we paid Eric the same. On our first meeting with the four of us I actually offered the two boys a piece of the action, but they had been stung before, they said. They wanted to play, sing, get their money per gig and go home. Gerry Browne began rehearsing with both of them. After a day or two I noticed something. Gerry Simpson (who we eventually called Simmo to separate the two Gerrys) was used to being the musical director and was calling the shots at rehearsals. I think Gerry Browne was a bit star-struck at first. As soon as I pointed this out to Gerry, he made his presence felt. Gerry handled the money in our partnership and he who pays the piper. Well, you know.

They struck a fantastic working balance, and the new set was amazing. After shows many people would say to me, 'I would come to see that band alone.' I'd smile. I knew what they meant, so it didn't bother me. Plus, I wanted the show to be brilliant – not just the comedy (although the comedy was amazing). We hit the road just four weeks after the other two boys had left, bigger and better. (Simmo had three keyboards on stage, to the great chagrin of Pepsi and Bugsy, who by the way had sold his window-cleaning business and was now full-time with the OCS.) We were now touring non-stop and killing it! It couldn't get any better.

Then there was that gig on 4 June, the bank holiday one.

Pepsi and Bugsy arrived at the Wexford Inn in the late afternoon. They set up the room with our sound and lights, then went for a 'coffee' (I put that in quotations because 'coffee' usually meant 'pint'). They returned to the gig for the doors opening as the safety of the gear and the audience was their responsibility. The doors opened at seven for an eight thirty start.

When I arrived at the Wexford Inn, just after eight, Bugsy met me downstairs at the door. 'This is a fucking lolly!' he said. It was rhyming slang – 'lollypop' meant a 'flop'.

'Why, how many are in?' I asked him.

'Twenty-five so far,' he said and rolled his eyes.

I went to the dressing rooms. The boys were depressed.

'Did you see that empty room?' one of them asked.

I shrugged, then I hung up my suit cover and began to strip off to get dressed for the gig.

'You are not seriously going to gig in front of twenty-five punters?' Simmo asked.

Gerry chimed in. 'Brenny, maybe he's right. Maybe we should pull the gig?'

I held out my arms. 'Lads, we're here now. It's not the fault of those twenty-five that they're the only ones here. Let's do the show and chalk it down to experience?'

We started to change.

'Yer man is a wanker,' Simmo said about the Rory fella that had booked us, but I wasn't so sure.

By the time we went on stage there were forty-two people. I know because I could count them. But we did the show and they loved it and so did we. We took the piss out of each other and out of the audience and it was fun.

Afterwards I went to Rory. He was ready for me. He stretched out his hand, which held £400 in twenty-pound notes. It had been £4 in and forty-two attended so he had taken £168 at the door. 'Here you go, four hundred.' He smiled as he said this.

I took him to one side. 'How much did you take on the door?' I asked.

'It doesn't matter; a guarantee is a guarantee,' Rory insisted, and proffered the money again.

'How much?' I insisted.

'A hundred and fifty-five,' he quietly said. So at least two people had got in for free.

I nodded and thought for a minute.

Rory again insisted, 'A guarantee is a guarantee. Take it. I'm hoping to book you for another gig.' He was such a lovely, honest man.

I had an idea. 'Give me a hundred and fifty; that's all I need to pay the band for tonight. And, yes, I will do another gig for you and for another four-hundred-pound guarantee. Contact the Bottom of the Hill pub in Finglas and make a booking there. If you do well, then we can talk about the balance of tonight's fee.' He agreed. He gave me £150 and bought the band a drink too.

I knew what I was doing. Gerry and I were both from Finglas. We had never played the OCS in Finglas. I knew the pub would give Rory the date and that it would be stuffed. They did and it was. Rory took in £2,600 that night and paid the guarantee and the £250 from the Wexford Inn gig.

Gerry was a bit annoyed. 'We could have done that ourselves. We didn't need him.'

I calmed him down. 'It's just one gig, Gerry, just to give him a break.'

Gerry relented. 'OK.' Then he smiled. 'But no more cheapos, yeh little bollix.'

There were no more. But I had a very good reason for doing what I did. And that is why I was now sitting across a coffee table in the Burlington Hotel from one Rory Cowan.

Although the Wexford Inn gig was the disaster I had

expected it to be, it didn't lack for promotion. From the day I put it in my diary to the day of the gig, everywhere I looked on the entertainment pages of either the newspapers or magazines it was mentioned or promoted. I didn't know who this guy was, but I was sure of something – he had done this before, professionally. So I opened with that. Here is the script of the meeting.

RORY COWAN

INT. HOTEL LOBBY - AFTERNOON
The two men sitting waiting for their coffee to arrive in the plush lobby of the hotel are Brendan, a comedian, and Rory, a promotor, who had booked Brendan for two venues a couple of months previously. One on which he had lost money and the other on which he had made a substantial profit.

BRENDAN
Thanks for coming, Rory.

RORY
No problem. I'm just wondering what this
is about.
The coffee arrives. Brendan pours for
both of them and when Brendan has sugared
and stirred his he takes a sip.

BRENDAN
It's about the two gigs we just
did for you.

RORY

Well, the first was my fault, and the
second I know what you were doing. Yous
had never played Finglas. You knew that
place would be stuffed. So if you're
looking for a thanks for that, well
then . . . thanks, I suppose.
Brendan laughs at Rory's frankness.

BRENDAN

Well, it's about that, but it's
more about you.

RORY

OK. Well, look, thanks for doing the
gig. But anything else is none of
your business, so let's end it there,
all right?

BRENDAN

I'm looking to hire you.

RORY

Oh. What do you want to know?
*Again Brendan laughs. Rory has a wicked
sense of humour, but Brendan likes it. He
likes Rory.*

BRENDAN

So, I've been following your promotion
of those two gigs. It was incredible.
Have you done press and PR in
Ireland before?

RORY
Yes.

BRENDAN
For what clients?

RORY
Shirley Bassey, Elton John, Paul
McCartney, a few more.
Brendan doesn't speak for a few minutes.
He actually can't speak.
Rory breaks the silence.

RORY (CONT'D)
I worked for EMI Records and that's how I
got to do what I did.

BRENDAN
And why did you stop?

RORY
They were offering a really
good voluntary redundancy package,
so I thought, Fuck it! I'm
taking that.
Brendan sips on his coffee.

BRENDAN
Wow.

RORY
I blew the lot.

BRENDAN
What the fuck? On what?
Rory thinks for a moment.

RORY
That's personal, but all you need to
know is that it wasn't alcohol,
drugs or gambling.
Brendan nods.

BRENDAN
That's fair enough.

RORY
So what do you want done?

BRENDAN
If I knew that, I wouldn't need you. The
question is, what can you do?

RORY
If I take the job, and I'm not saying yes,
you'll be mentioned every day for the next
year somewhere. In a magazine, on radio
or in a newspaper article. Every day.

BRENDAN
That's a big prediction!

RORY
It's not a prediction. It's what
I do. I mean, did.

BRENDAN

So how are things for you now?

RORY

I'm three months behind in me mortgage,
close to having my electricity cut, I've
no heating. But otherwise I'm grand,
thanks.
*Rory bursts into laughter. So does
Brendan.*

BRENDAN

Look, I'm offering three hundred and
fifty a week, and I'll tell you that will
leave me earning the same.

RORY

Not for long. I'll change that. I'm
interested.

BRENDAN

Last question.

RORY

Go ahead.

BRENDAN

Are you gay?
*Brendan knows he is, but wants to see his
reaction.*

RORY

Which answer gets me the job?

Brendan howls laughing. He stretches out his hand.

                    BRENDAN
              Welcome to the team.
Rory shakes his hand.

                     RORY
         I'll get started right away.

Rory took the job and, as promised, my name was mentioned somewhere in some publication or on radio every day for the following twelve months. But he did something much more important than that. He didn't know it would be as monumental as it was, and to be honest neither did I. It began with a very simple radio interview.

23

I was a bit nervous and distracted as I drove, and I lost my concentration for a moment, and it was the loud horn of the truck that shook me back to reality. I was driving my Toyota Corolla and had wandered over the middle broken line. Luckily the truck wasn't coming towards me; it was behind me. I acknowledged the trucker's warning with a wave out of the window. He flashed his lights to either return my wave or tell me I was an asshole. I'm going to go with the first.

I was nervous because Rory had set up a radio interview on Gareth O'Callaghan's show on RTÉ 2FM. It had a big listenership, and he was a very clever presenter. I didn't know what was expected of me in the interview but I needed to be funny. This was my first radio interview and even though I knew it was recorded and could be edited I still didn't want to put a foot wrong.

Rory had said he would meet me there. That was good. I was always relaxed when he was with me. He knew the business and wasn't afraid to interrupt any interview with 'Excuse me, Brendan's not answering that.'

I lit another cigarette and turned on the radio. RTÉ Radio One news was on. In the bulletin the reporter spoke about that day being the twelfth birthday of Louise Joy Brown, the very first 'test-tube' baby, which we now call IVF. It crossed my mind how amazing it was. How so many people's lives had changed in the twelve years since she was born.

At the radio centre Rory was waiting for me in the reception, then we went down to the small studio and joined

Gareth. He was very friendly and welcoming. So here was the item. As Gareth had done with many C-list celebrities before, he had cut some clips out of magazines that he thought were either funny or quirky. We sat each side of his control desk.

I glanced over at the snippets. They were not very funny or quirky. I must have displayed this in either my body language or maybe I sighed, I don't know, but whatever it was Gareth picked up on it.

'Don't like them?' he asked.

'Hey, I'll read whatever you want me to read, Gareth, but these aren't really that funny.'

He smiled at me across the desk. 'Do you think you could be funnier than those?'

Now I smiled. 'I know I can,' I said, and I gave him a wink.

He pressed record and said, 'Off you go so.'

Off I went. I can't remember what I did off the cuff, but I do remember saying I wanted to speak on behalf of the DNA, the National Dyslexic Association. Then in another voice I made a statement on behalf of the Irish Diarrhoea Community. 'There is not enough attention paid to – pause – 'excuse me, please,' and I ran out of the studio. Gareth laughed heartily.

When we had finished the recording Gareth asked me if I'd like to join him for a coffee in the upstairs coffee shop. We went up ahead of him while he was wrapping up. On the stairs Rory said to me, 'This is odd; he never has a coffee with the guests.'

I shrugged in reply.

Well, the coffee was good and we chatted for quite a while. Towards the end Gareth told Rory that he was looking for something quirky for his afternoon show, something funny that had continuity to it.

'That's funny, Gareth, because at the moment I'm writing a five-minute soap opera for radio,' I lied.

'Are you?' Gareth asked, surprised.

'Are you?' Rory said, even more so.

I just answered, 'Yeh.'

Gareth sat a bit more upright in his chair. 'What's it about?' he asked.

This was followed by Rory saying, 'Yeh, what IS it about?'

So I waffled. 'It's about a Dublin city trader and her grown-up kids that she really treats like infants.'

Gareth's eyes widened. 'What's the format?'

I didn't really know what he meant so I took a guess. 'It's five minutes a day, five days a week.'

Gareth now became excited. 'I'd love to see it,' he said.

'So would fuckin' I,' Rory mumbled under his breath.

'I'll record some of it and get it to you,' I said, getting ready to make my exit before I was found out.

'What's it called?' Gareth asked.

I know my partner Gerry would have loved to think that I called it after him, but all that went through my head was Louise Brown, the test-tube baby, and I said, '*Mrs. Brown's Boys.*'

Gareth and I shook hands and he said to get it to him as soon as I could.

So over the following weekend I sat at my word processor and wrote the first ten five-minute episodes. Then I needed to record them. I think it was Charlie McCabe of the Barge that recommended a studio close by. I called the owner and booked the studio for the following Monday for the recording and the next day, Tuesday, for the edit. I couldn't afford actors, so I asked the boys of the band to play the roles, well, just say the words. I had an actress in mind to voice Mrs. Brown but I got word that she had a kidney infection so I decided that, as the studio was booked, I would read her lines and when she was well I would dub her voice in.

We recorded all ten episodes and it was unexpectedly fun, really fun. We laughed at the scripts, we laughed at our fuck-ups, we laughed at some of the voices each of the lads were doing. I did Mrs. Brown's lines and to give it a bit of a lift I did a voice I often used in stand-up if I was imitating an older Dublin woman. We recorded them all in about an hour and we had a coffee together before we headed off to our gig.

The next morning I went into Alan's studio as arranged for the edit. When I arrived Alan told me to get myself a coffee as Jonathan was still digitizing the tapes. Jonathan McEvoy was the edit engineer. I got a coffee for myself and joined him. As soon as I walked into the booth, Jonathan turned to me, smiling. 'These are very funny, really funny.'

I thanked him, but he then asked a question that made me smile. 'Who's the actress playing Mrs. Brown?'

I realized he was serious, and I laughed. 'Jonathan, that's me.'

He was aghast. 'You are kidding me?'

I explained that I would be overdubbing the lines with an actress.

'No way, Brendan, you have to keep that voice. It's – it's Mrs. Brown. That's the widow who I really believe is head of that family.'

I was flattered but really unsure. We sat together, adding music and sound effects, and the episodes really came alive. Later, when I had finished the edit and played the episodes for the boys in the OCS, they too felt that the voice I had done for Mrs. Brown was the one to keep. I went with popular opinion and sent the tapes to Gareth O'Callaghan.

He called me to say that he had listened to them and he loved them. He wanted to run them from the following Monday and see what kind of reaction the show got. I was really excited, but disappointment was to come. I now had a mobile phone with an 083 number and on the Friday, as we were driving to a gig, Gareth called.

He couldn't run the shows. His producer Ian Demsey had blocked them. I asked why and Gareth said the producer had pointed out that it's because Mrs. Brown said 'bum'. As petty as it was – it was 'bum'! – he couldn't air that at four thirty in the afternoon. So that was that.

In the meantime, things were not improving at home. The more public my name became, the more nervous Doreen got, as she loathed the spotlight, whereas I loved it. The gigs were coming in more than ever before and we were close to paying off the personal loan in the bank. Being on the road was not without its mishaps and sometimes I reflect on those days and wonder how I managed to keep going.

I remember one night really well. The gig was in Ennis town, a good three hours' drive from Dublin. The odd thing was that I had got a call from the owner the night before, telling me he had heard a rumour that we weren't coming down to do the gig.

I was baffled. 'I don't know where you got that from, but we are coming down for sure,' I told the relieved owner.

We left Dublin in plenty of time and, although it was cold and raining, the mood in the van was good. This was the van we had bought with the bank loan. It had had three previous owners, but it was a joy to drive, and I loved driving it. It was a high-top Renault van. We had sectioned two thirds of it off to hold the gear in the very back of the van and forward of the partition we had bolted in some second-hand aeroplane seats we had picked up at a scrapyard near the airport.

We got through Limerick without too much traffic and hit a long stretch of straight road. The van was purring along when there was a loud bang and the van rolled into the hard shoulder with a dead engine. I had AA cover but did not yet have a mobile phone. However, there was a house across the road from where we stopped. It was up on a hill, so I ran up the hill in the rain, fishing in my pocket for my address book.

I knocked on the door and to my surprise a priest answered, however he opened the door no more than an inch. 'What do you want?' he asked.

'Father, I'm sorry to knock, but we are a band on the road to Ennis and our van has just clapped out over there.' I then pointed at the van. 'Could I possibly use your phone to call the AA?'

He closed the door without speaking, then he opened it again, this time three inches, and he passed me a wireless phone through the gap. Once I took the phone he closed the door again.

I called the AA and they told me to sit tight and that they would get a local mechanic to come to us. I then called the owner and told him what had happened.

He was furious. 'I should have known the rumour was true, yeh bastard.'

I tried to calm him down. 'Look, we're just waiting for the AA, and then we'll be on our way.'

He hung up unconvinced.

When the local mechanic arrived with a tow truck he said, 'I'm going to tow you to my garage and I'll look at it there.'

I told him of the pickle we were in and how we HAD to get to the gig.

He was really nice. 'I'll tell you what, let's get this to the garage and if it's not fixable, I have a van there you can use.' What a lovely man.

Our van was indeed unfixable; it needed a part from Dublin and it wouldn't be there before tomorrow. Before I could even ask he was away. 'I'll get the other van.' What a lovely, lovely, man.

As he rounded the front of the garage with the van, I swear I had seen something like it on *The Beverly Hillbillies*. It was smaller than ours, so we just took the bare necessities we would need to do the gig and packed them in the other van. It also didn't have a second cab, so three of the lads sat in the front and the other three had to lie on top of the gear in the back. I closed them in and started the van. I hadn't even put it in gear when the boys in the back were banging on the bulkhead.

I went round and opened it up. It was Sharpie that slid out. 'For fuck sake, it's refrigerated.'

I called the guy over. 'Can you turn off the refrigeration on this?'

He laughed. 'Bejaysus, if I could do that, it wouldn't be in here for repair.'

I looked at the boys and shrugged. We got every coat we had and the boys put them on before climbing back on top of the gear. I used the garage phone to call the owner and tell him we had got a replacement van and were just a couple of hours away. Then I drove.

The van was a banger, a heap of shit, but it was all we had, and it was getting us out of a hole. We got as far as a village called Sixmilebridge, when – BANG – the van stopped. I couldn't fucking believe it.

I walked to a pub about two miles away that had a phone. I called the mechanic first and told him that the van had stopped and asked whether he had a replacement.

'Ah, for fuck sake, do you think I'm made of vans?' was his answer.

I called the owner. 'We've broken down again.'

He was furious. 'Do you take me for an idiot?' he screamed down the phone. 'The place is packed here and you were never coming here, were you? Well, I'll tell you now, you will never gig here again.'

I have to be honest, I wouldn't have believed me either, and we never did gig there again.

We were towed back to the garage. We had enough to get a B & B for the band and Gerry and I slept in the van. Next day Gerry had his brother come and collect him and the lads. I hung around until the van was fixed and drove it home, broke and dispirited. Yet I got up the next day and went to a gig and wowed them.

There were so many days like that, but sometimes there was a day that was waiting to surprise you. For me it started with an announcement over breakfast that we were going to have another child. Danny, our youngest, was nine years old, so this was wholly unexpected. There was something else Doreen had to tell me. She had been for a mammogram and she had been called back for more tests. So obviously the feelings were mixed. I tried to comfort her, saying they were probably related. Doreen was scared and upset, but I had to go to work. I felt terrible leaving her, but I had convinced myself that it was an anomaly caused by her pregnancy.

As we were driving down to a gig in Wexford, I got a call from Gareth O'Callaghan. It had been a long time since he had decided not to run *Mrs. Brown's Boys* on his radio show. He called to tell me that his producer was going on two weeks' holiday and that he had been told to produce the show himself. This meant that he had decided for the next two weeks what would run on the show, and he was running the soap. I should have been delighted, I should have whooped all the way to Wexford, but the earlier surprises had taken the wind out of my sails.

I called Doreen to see how she was. She didn't sound as worried as she had that morning. This was good; I could now concentrate on the gig. All was right with the world.

24

I can't explain it and I'm certain I am not unique in this, but once a doctor says the word 'cancer' you don't hear anything else after that. The word seems to swim around in your head like in an echo chamber at first. Then it drops down to your stomach where it becomes a gymnast.

I looked over at an ashen-faced Doreen, her lip trembling.

We left the doctor's office in the Mater Hospital and went just outside, where we stood at the railings and in sync lit up our cigarettes. No, I didn't see the irony. All I can tell you is that for the first hour or so your brain becomes guacamole.

Doreen took a drag of her cigarette. 'I'm going to die,' she said.

I was dazed and in another world. 'I know,' I answered. Probably the worst reply I could ever give to anything, ever.

When we got home our family doctor was waiting for us. The hospital had sent him the diagnosis and he wanted to check that Doreen was OK mentally. They sat in the front room together while I made tea. The doctor told us what the doctor in the hospital I'm sure had said, which we didn't hear. The treatment would include eight doses of chemotherapy. He explained that it would be a tough time but that we could get through it.

Doreen cried and even the doctor cried. I didn't. I don't know why not. Some sort of survival instinct kicked in instead. I hadn't thought about the pregnancy, but when I asked the doctor his voice was sad.

'I think the treatment will take care of that.'

My mind raced and I dug deep into my PMA reserves. *Every neggie can be turned into a possie.* 'No!' I said aloud. 'We'll be having that baby and the treatment will work. The proof of that will be the baby.'

The doctor looked at me sympathetically. 'Let's hope for the best then,' he said before he left.

I don't know what kind of husband I had been up to then but for the next few months I became husband of the year. I attended every hospital visit, and there were two teams: one in the Mater Hospital for the cancer and one in the Rotunda Maternity Hospital for the baby. The regime was Thursday to the Mater for chemo, Monday to the Rotunda for a special injection, then back the next day to the Rotunda for a scan. At every scan I prayed that the baby would hold on. I assured everyone, especially Doreen, that everything would work out OK. I told both Fiona and Danny; I told them because I knew that all along the way we would have little victories, like after every scan, and I wanted them to share in those victories. Then I would go to my gig and be funny.

But on the way home from the gig I would pull up somewhere dark and I'd climb a fence and walk to the middle of a field, or once it was a beach. There, where nobody could see me, I would first cry. I would fill my lungs and I would scream as loud as I possibly could. Now that I think of it I literally would howl at the moon. Then I would get home, sleep and start the whole thing all over again.

But this story has a happy ending. Thankfully, following the treatment, the doctors in the Mater were sure that they had got the cancer, though they wouldn't know for sure for a few years; but Doreen was first put on a yearly visit, a really great sign. Eric arrived at one twenty on 5 May 1992 and although he was born at just twenty-five weeks, weighing a mere 2lb 13 oz, he was as healthy as a pup. The only thing wrong with him was that he was the image of his father. He was kept in the hospital for over two months. I would drop in there after every gig; the nurses allowed me to. They also would allow me to feed him. It only took seconds as he was fed by syringe, but I loved doing it.

His name came from my favourite people. Naming a baby is hard as whatever name someone suggests for your baby you can remember someone from your childhood that had that name that you hated! Eric's was easy. My favourite people were Erics. Eric Sykes, Eric Clapton, Eric Idle, Eric Sharpe and especially Eric Morecambe. I can now add Eric O'Carroll to that list of my favourite Erics.

Wait, no! Not add him TO the list; he goes straight to the top. Always!

25

Gareth O'Callaghan was a man of his word. He ran *Mrs. Brown's Boys* that first week that he produced the show. The 'bum' piece was in the second episode on the Tuesday and I wondered if there would be a third broadcast on the Wednesday. I listened in and at half past four the intro music started and we were on.

As it was running, I got a phone call at home from the head of 2FM, Bill O'Donovan. He wanted me to come in and see him. I thought, *Here's trouble, this can't be good.*

As it turned out, it wasn't trouble, but it wasn't exactly what I expected either.

'I love the show. The audience loves the show,' Bill O'Donovan said to me.

I was sitting at his desk in what I thought was a small office for someone running something as successful as 2FM. I smiled at him. 'Thank you, Mr O'Donovan.'

He smiled back. 'Bill, it's Bill. Now, I want to commission the show, but here's the thing.'

Ah, I thought, *there's a BUT*. I waited for what the but was.

He went on. 'This is a music station; it's not RTÉ Radio One, so I don't have a budget for drama.' He stopped.

I realized that I was supposed to ask a question here. 'So, eh, what does that mean?'

Bill leaned forward, putting his hands flat on his desk. 'I want it, but I can't pay for it.' He then slapped out a drumbeat with his hands and finished with: 'There you have it.'

I was now trying to figure this out. *He wants it but can't pay for it? He wants it for free?*

'With all due respect, Mr . . . Bill, I can get lots of fucking gigs like that, if I work for free.'

I wasn't being cheeky. Truth be told, I wasn't looking to be paid much, but I did want something to cover costs. Plus, I had something in mind that I'd not been sure I would get, but the conversation we were having was increasing my chances of getting it.

'I think I have a solution,' Bill said, and waited.

Again I realized I was supposed to ask a question. 'What's the solution?' I asked, hoping that this was the right question.

'I don't have a drama budget –' he paused here for effect – 'but I do have a T-shirt budget.' He leaned back and smiled.

I am now totally fucking confused. It showed on my face.

Bill leaned forward again, and as if revealing the solution to world poverty, announced more than said, 'I'll pay you in T-shirts!' There was another drumbeat and he sat back.

When I spoke I did so slowly, not because I was confused but because I was trying to get what he had said to register in my brain as I was speaking. 'You will pay me in T-shirts?'

He smiled, thinking I understood. 'Exactly,' he said.

I couldn't even pretend that I understood. 'I'm sorry, Bill, I am really not with you here.'

He leaned forward again. 'I'll get T-shirts done reading –' he now moved his finger across his chest – '*Mrs. Brown's Boys on 2FM*, with the 2FM logo. I'll give you two hundred shirts a week and you can sell them at your gigs and keep the dosh.' He now held his arms wide as if it were a done deal.

Mentally I'm calculating 200 @ £5 a shirt is £1,000, if they sell at all. The studio costs £800. *Hmm, I don't know.*

Then Bill added, 'And you can record it here in one of our studios at no cost.'

I smiled. 'That sounds all right.'

He stood. 'Great,' he said and put his hand out.

I didn't shake on it, not yet. 'There's just one more thing,' I said. It was time to ask for the only thing I'd really come in to get.

'What's that?'

'I'd like at the end of each episode for Gareth to say "*Mrs. Brown's Boys* is a Brendan O'Carroll production, and you can see Brendan tonight in . . ." and put in wherever we are that night, or whenever the next gig is.'

He didn't hesitate. 'If that's all right with Gareth, it's good with me.'

We shook. I already knew it would be all right with Gareth. He was always generous with his praise for the show and for me. I left there very happy. *Mrs. Brown's Boys* was now officially a 2FM show, and the addition of the 'Brendan O'Carroll production' would retain all the rights for me.

I swear to you when I say this, I had no idea whatsoever when *Mrs. Brown's Boys* started running on 2FM of the impact that five-minute piece was having nationwide. I wasn't aware that at 4.30 p.m. hairdressers would switch off their dryers for the five minutes, that taxis would pull in and take a five-minute break, that prisoners would ask for it to be put on the loudspeakers in the exercise yard, that newspapers would halt the printing presses for the five minutes. I truly had no idea. Sure, I could see that we were getting more punters at the gigs and that the T-shirts were selling, but I saw that as just germane to the individual gigs, not that *Mrs. Brown's Boys* was reaching across the entire country.

I suppose it really hit home when Rory pulled off one of his masterstrokes. He got me a booking on *The Late Late*

Show. How big was this? Huge, that's how big. The interview was booked for 'some time' in either late January or February 1993. This was only October 1992, so I was to have nearly five months to think about it, no, worry about it. The motto of *The Late Late Show* is 'It started on *The Late Late Show*', and for good reason. U2, Bob Geldof, Sinéad O'Connor, The Corrs and so many more were all introduced to the wider public on that show. Gay Byrne, the long-time host, was a national icon, a national treasure and the show itself a national institution. One quote was that there was no sex in Ireland before *The Late Late Show*. It is the longest-running talk show in the world and celebrated its sixtieth year in 2022.

So why would I worry about it? Because I have seen people go on *The Late Late* and bomb or overplay their hand. In some cases this led to the end of their performing life, or their business, or their political career. You can shine on *The Late Late*, but you could also be 'found out'. It's live, so there is no taking back what you say, no explaining, nothing. You are balls out to the world. A tightrope that you walked while Gay Byrne was setting it on fire. He pulled no punches and his integrity was impeccable and he expected the same from you. Be authentic or fuck off. Every time I would think about it I would throw up. Seriously, if someone mentioned *The Late Late*, I would have to find a bathroom.

We were busy, really busy, and by the year's end exhausted. Gerry suggested we take a holiday in early January so we all did, and I mean all – there were sixteen of us. Some in couples, the rest just either Gerry's friends or brothers; we set off for Gerry's favourite destination, Playa del Inglés, for a week in Greenfield Apartments. I hated every minute of it. I had never been on an adult group holiday before. The group were fine, funny and friendly, but the place was a kip.

The routine was the same every day. A late breakfast, say

2 p.m., then lie by the pool until about 4 p.m., then sleep until 8 p.m. Then it was over to the Hawaiian bar for happy hour two-for-one and a steak. From there to the Shamrock Bar, singing and dancing until 3 a.m., bed and repeat tomorrow.

The gang really were having a ball. I wasn't. I got very drunk one night and came out of the Shamrock Bar. There was a Mercedes taxi outside. I got in and said, 'Greenfield Apartments, *por favor.*'

The apartments were no more than 200 yards away. The driver hadn't even got the car out of second gear when he pulled up.

I reached into my pocket and took out a fistful of notes; there must have been £100 in my hand.

In perfect English he said, 'This is far too much.'

I gave him a drunken wink and slapped his shoulder. 'Keep the change, buddy – Paddy is in town!'

That taxi followed me home every night after that. He would shout out of the window at me, 'Hey, Paddy, need a taxi?'

Rory and I stuck together during that trip and indeed we had a good laugh ourselves, unless he reminded me that *The Late Late Show* was getting near, then I would excuse myself and go somewhere quiet to throw up yet again.

On our return from the 'holiday' we got a date for *The Late Late*: 5 February. We were cutting it close as we were to leave for some New York gigs on 7 February. We had some gigs in the run-up to *The Late Late* and, in fact, played McKeon's in Stoneybatter, which was across the street from my grand-father's old shop and the place where he had been assassinated, though I didn't think about it at the time. Then D-Day arrived.

I had never met Gay Byrne. So on the night of the show, I thought that if I got a chance before we went on air I would introduce myself. I tried but it just didn't happen. The first attempt was when I was just coming in to the long corridor where the dressing rooms were. He was walking towards me. In my head I rehearsed, *'Hello, Gay' – no, don't be too familiar, more formal. 'Hello, Mr Byrne, I'm a guest on your show tonight.' Is that weird me telling him who his guest is? Maybe just say 'Hi, Gay'?*

As we passed each other I froze up and all that came out was the weirdest word. 'Gnuk'. *Seriously, Brendan, fucking 'gnuk'? What the fuck does that even mean?*

I had blown my chance, but I was to get another. It was the same corridor, but this time in reverse as I was coming from make-up and he was coming from reception. I was ready this time. *'Hello, Mr Byrne, I'm Brendan O'Carroll. I'm really looking forward to being on the show tonight. Let's do it.'*

I got within twenty feet of him, and then he turned into a dressing room and closed the door. I stood at the door and my closed hand hovered for a good ten seconds, ready to knock on the door. Then . . . I chickened out and went to my own dressing room.

For days I had rehearsed my answers in the mirror. If he asks me this, I'll answer that, and so on. I was watching the show on the screen in the green room as I waited to go on. It was very lacklustre. During the advert breaks Gay even chastised the audience, telling them to react more and get involved. I perked up; I could really shine here tonight.

I went to the bathroom and in the mirror, instead of going over the possible questions again, I said to my reflection, 'Go back to your first night and woman number three. Blank out your thoughts, go on and just be yourself. Be authentic.' Already I felt better and much more relaxed.

Soon the floor manager came and got me, and I walked to the back of the studio where a mic was clipped to my shirt and the pack stuck to my waistband. Then I was guided to the steps I would climb to walk on to the set when Gay intro-duced me. Gay was just finishing with a guest and there was to be an ad break, then me.

The floor manager approached me with one hand cover-ing the mic on his headset. 'Brendan, I know you were told the interview would be six minutes, but Gay has cut a guest short, so it'll be nine minutes. That OK?'

I gave him a thumbs up. I was ready. Having watched the show for many years I knew how Gay brought his guests on. He'd do a spiel about the guest, then say their name and they would walk on. Then they would pause and Gay would indi-cate with his left arm for them to sit and then he would also sit. I wasn't sure how far Gay would let me go, so I decided to find out once I'd walked on to the set. I should tell you at this point that the word 'mickey' in the context I was about to use it is a childish way of saying penis.

The ad break over, the cameras lit on Gay and his intro-duction went something like this: 'You may not have seen my next guest, but you will probably know of him as the writer and star of Radio 2FM's *Mrs. Brown's Boys*.' I heard an agree-able murmur come from the audience at that. I couldn't believe how calm and assured I felt. I was so fucking ready. 'Ladies and gentlemen, will you welcome, please, Brendan O'Carroll?'

There was applause even before I had walked on to the set. I paused and Gay did the thing with his arm, but I stayed put. He then moved towards me, hand outstretched, I pre-sume to pull me towards the guest seat. I took his hand and, as he gently pulled, I pulled back as I wanted to be away from the desk mic.

Gay looked up into my face, and I said, 'Hiya, Gay, how's your mickey?'

An audible bark of laughter came from Gay, and I knew I

was OK. I could go for it, and I did. The nine-minute interview went on for thirty-five minutes, during which I had Gay bent in half laughing several times. The audience loved it, and even as I was doing it I knew I was knocking it out of the park. At the end Gay brilliantly said, 'Brendan will be coming to a venue near you soon, but be warned – compared to his live show he has been like an altar boy here tonight.'

I was to then go across to where Gerry and the boys from the OCS were waiting as we were going to sing our popular song 'Hey, Paddy'. I was so relaxed by then that during the song I actually forgot the words, so I mumbled something. Thankfully the song itself is so fast and loud that unless you knew it you wouldn't notice I had fucked up.

In the green room after the show I at last got to speak to Mr Byrne. I went up to him, extended my hand and said, 'Mr Byrne, I just want to say thank you for the opportunity.'

He took my hand and smiled at me. 'Son, I think we launched a star tonight – don't waste it.'

I have been on *The Late Late Show* so many times now that I have lost count. But every time with Gay was a treat for me. He was the perfect straight man for a comic. We became friends and I got to love him. I also got to show him that I didn't waste it. Thank you so much, Gay. So much.

Gay passed away on 4 November 2019, just before the pandemic. I knew he had been unwell for some time. A week before he passed he called me. He wanted me to assure him that I was taking care of myself. And that, ladies and gentlemen, is Gay Byrne.

26

What followed the *Late Late Show* performance was like an explosion. It seemed the very next day everybody in Ireland knew my name. The show was also repeated on Channel 4 on the following Monday and that garnered great interest from the UK too. I had met so many artists that had had a *Late Late Show* appearance and had the attitude of 'I've made it!', so when I woke up the day after, and I could hear the phone downstairs ringing non-stop, my overwhelming feeling was not that I had made it but that NOW it starts.

Two days after, we flew to the USA to fulfil gigs that we had taken bookings for in New York and Boston long before. I wrote about the flight in another chapter, and the trip itself was fabulous fun; it was our first time at the Fitzpatrick Hotel on Lexington Avenue. I could write an entire book on Fitzpatrick's, so for now all I will say is that Paddy Fitzpatrick and his wonderful wife, Nora, were very welcoming, eventually.

One huge downer was that during the trip Pepsi came to me and told me he was leaving. He said that the success he believed was coming for the show was far too much for him and that we would need someone better on sound. It made me sad that he felt that way; in other words, the more successful we were getting, the less he was enjoying it. The USA trip was to be his final farewell, he said, although I convinced him to hang on until we had finished at the Tivoli in Dublin.

In the weeks running up to *The Late Late Show* Rory had suggested we take on a promoter. I had told Rory that I wanted to finish doing the show in pubs and move up a notch to small theatres. He agreed and recommended Pat Egan Promotions. I knew of Pat Egan; he was the promoter who handled all the Irish bookings for Billy Connolly. Rory set up a meet. Pat came across as an elderly rock and roller, wearing jeans and a black T-shirt and either a charcoal or black linen jacket all the time. Still, I was delighted when Pat agreed to take us on; he sounded like he knew what he was doing.

One of the first bookings he made was for the Tivoli Theatre. He booked it for four nights to begin three weeks after *The Late Late Show* appearance. When we had arrived in New York and settled into Fitzpatrick's, I called Pat to see how sales were.

He was elated; the four nights were already sold out, so he had extended it to ten nights, and they were already fifty per cent sold.

I would tell anybody working in this business that the difference between £50 a night and £500 a night is just a millimetre. Never give up – it could be tomorrow that 'it' happens for you. From walking on to the stage at the Rathmines Inn in 1990 to *The Late Late Show* just three years later is virtually overnight by any standard, but you have to believe me that for those three years I had worked my arse off. And surrounded myself with the right people.

So here's what I mean by 'now it starts!' I wanted to do so much more. I had my sights set very high. I had personal targets I had set in my own mind and all my achievements so far were stepping stones to those targets. It might sound like an overnight success story but you must define success. Success is very personal. To me it was doing what you were doing because you wanted to do it, and to have a solid feeling of happiness. By that measure success was a long way off for me yet.

When we returned to Ireland from America we played the show to a sit-down audience in the Tivoli Theatre for a total of fourteen nights, all of which were sold out. It was amazing. Playing in a theatre was completely different; your timing has to change, as does the dynamic of the comedy. You are no longer competing with the clink of glasses or the ding-ding of the tills behind the bar, the shouting of drink orders and the constant banging of the toilet doors. In a theatre the audience are all sitting facing you, and there is silence except for the laughter I was bringing from the audience like a conductor with an orchestra. The audience expected a two-hour show with an interval, which I was only too happy to give them. It was magnificent.

Magnificent up to the end of the last performance when Pat Egan informed me that Rory had finished by 'mutual agreement'. I was baffled and so sad about that. Then later, as we were all having a drink together, Simmo and Sharpie announced that they were quitting the band. I was dumbfounded, but I didn't ask why and they didn't say why. The Rory thing bothered me more than anything. I was to find out much later what Pat's idea of mutual agreement was.

That night, and that news aside, I revelled being in the Super Trouper spotlight in that theatre.

I was just an eleven-year-old when Mammy took me to a theatre for the first time. It was the Gate Theatre on Dublin's Parnell Street, the theatre where Orson Welles honed his art. I think it was during the Dublin Theatre Festival. It was a play called, again I think, *A Two-Foot-Six-Inch World Above the Ground*. It was about a boys' school and all the children's parts were played by adults. It was brilliant. I sat there in the dark, having recently been told that I would never be a pilot, and marvelled at what was taking place in front of me. The darkness gave the illusion that these wonderful actors were doing this show just for me. I remember thinking, *Wow, imagine if you ever got a chance to do that!* And now here I was. If Mammy could see me now.

The Tivoli was followed by the Everyman Theatre in Cork, the National Opera House in Wexford, Waterford Town Hall Theatre, the Siamsa Theatre in Tralee, the Millennium Forum Theatre in Derry and even a theatre in Belfast. Simmo and Sharpie had been replaced by Doc O'Connor and David Molloy, who very quickly picked up the nickname 'Molly'. Both were really talented: Doc on keyboard/piano and Molly was a superb guitarist. The new band meant a new sound, but once they had settled in it was a great sound. The only constant throughout all the years since we had started was the comedy, Gerry's fabulous voice and, of course, Bugsy, who was always there.

All those theatre gigs were sold out and we were flying! In between those we also did gigs for the Swarbrigg brothers. Tommy and Jimmy were from Mullingar in Westmeath, and had been a really successful singer/songwriter pair, who had twice represented Ireland at the Eurovision Song Contest with songs they had penned themselves – 'That's What Friends Are For' and 'It's Nice to Be in Love Again' – once as The Swarbriggs and the second time with two female singers, calling themselves The Swarbriggs Plus Two. They were two really great guys. We dealt mostly with Tommy, who I loved being around. He was gregarious and full of energy; he had a childlike demeanour too, as if everything was a surprise to him. With the Swarbriggs as promoters we did mostly town halls, or nightclubs in the smaller towns around the country. They kept us busy, filling any date we had available.

The continuous bookings meant being away so much that I could really feel the strain on my marriage. But we both soldiered on, more now like two friends, ignoring any tensions.

Doreen did drop hints that she was unhappy, but I either didn't see them or ignored them. We had New Year's Eve together in the company of Gerry and his fiancée Colette as guests of Pat Egan, though it ended early as we had a gig in Cork the next day.

1994 looked like being a good year, for me if not my marriage. We planned a holiday for the summer, but that too went by the wayside, thanks to a man neither Doreen nor I had ever met.

His name was Alan McLoughlin.

27

The night of 17 November 1993 was full of soccer drama across Europe. It was the final night of the qualifiers for World Cup '94, which was to be held in the USA for the very first time. Apart from the cup holders, Germany, the only European teams to have qualified at that time were Norway, Russia, Sweden and Greece. The likes of Spain, Holland, England and even the European champions Denmark were fighting for their qualification lives. Italy, who had never missed a World Cup since 1938, needed to beat Portugal to qualify and left it to the final five minutes before Roberto Baggio scored the goal that would get them there. Had VAR existed back then, I am convinced the goal would have been ruled offside.

In San Marino, England needed to win seven–nil to qualify. They were easily capable of that, but shit hit the fan when San Marino scored only their third goal in international football just nine seconds after the kick-off – the fastest goal in World Cup history. England got the seven goals they needed, but that historic (for San Marino) goal left England out of the finals. But the *only* two games that mattered to me and virtually every Irish person anywhere in the world were Spain against Denmark in Seville and the Republic of Ireland against Northern Ireland in Belfast. It was a complicated group (which of Ireland's groups are ever not? I ask myself). As the group stood, Denmark were top with eighteen points, and Spain and the Republic were joint second with seventeen points each. So Spain and the Republic knew they had to win, but in Spain's case a draw would do them as they had scored more goals. A draw was enough for Denmark, a draw *might* be enough for the Republic, as long as Spain beat Denmark. It would come down then to goals scored. As I said, it was a complicated group.

Excitement was high all over Ireland, but that was soon quashed when we heard over the radio that Spain's goalkeeper Zubizarreta had been sent off after just ten minutes. Spain were now down to ten men and we needed them to win. The heads of the very few Republic supporters that had gone to the game, following a government plea not to travel, were bowed in the stand. Our game was nil–all at the half. It had been a lacklustre first half and the writing seemed to be on the wall, but our hearts lifted when news reached us that Spain had taken the lead in the sixty-third minute. Cheering and dancing ensued, but for only eight minutes. In the seventy-first minute Northern Ireland's Jimmy Quinn smashed a cracking volley into the Republic's net. Never mind a win, even our draw seemed a long way away. But then there was Alan McLoughlin. Five minutes after Quinn's goal, the Republic got a free kick about thirty yards out. It was a mediocre effort, but it was badly cleared by the Northern Irish defence. Alan McLoughlin took it down beautifully on his chest and whacked it into the corner of the net. We cheered, we cried and we danced again. Spain finished top of the group and, on more goals scored, the Republic of Ireland were going to America! Yippee!

So what has all that to do with me? Read on.

28

I had no idea that 1994 was to be probably the most important year yet for me and my future. So much was going to happen and so much was going to change.

Myself, Gerry and the band were gigging all over Ireland and packed them in, selling out nearly every venue. I was enjoying myself so much and we were making good money. We were due another trip to the US with gigs from Boston to New York in the January, and between our then manager Pat Egan and Tommy Swarbrigg we had a tour waiting for us when we got back. A week of theatres in Dublin, Belfast, Cork, Killarney, Derry, Limerick, Waterford, Wexford, Wicklow, Sligo and Dundalk. Plus, a plethora of venues for Tommy Swarbrigg.

But the year held a couple of surprises. The first came on my return from the States with a phone call from RTÉ. Not, as I would have expected, from the light entertainment department, but from the news and sports department. It was a nice woman who asked me when I would be free to come to RTÉ to meet the head of sport? We agreed a time and date and I asked what it was in connection with.

She simply said, 'I'll leave that to Mr O'Connor to tell you.'

I arrived at RTÉ the following week and was met by a wonderfully enthusiastic head of sport, Tim O'Connor. So why was I there, I asked.

Tim explained that the World Cup in the USA was a huge thing for Ireland and that during the finals RTÉ would be covering as much as was possible, not just the games but trying to capture the atmosphere and reflect the fun and colour of the event in its programming. He had a fantastic team heading out there, but he wanted someone to do some colour pieces over the length of the event – in other words, as long as Ireland were still in the competition. 'I think you might be the person I'm looking for,' said Tim, and went on to tell me what he needed. 'I want you to travel out with the team on their flight; you'll be there for a minimum of five weeks. I need you to go to the training ground with the team, maybe do some side commentary at the games and even hang out in the changing room, when Jack Charlton lets you, of course.'

I sat with my heart thumping, nodding my head. It really was one of those moments where when he said, 'Now let's talk about money,' I was thinking, *I hope he doesn't charge me too much for this*. It was a dream gig. A dream and a half gig. But me being me I had to just nudge it a bit. 'Tim, that sounds great. I just have one small problem with it.'

He sat up. 'And what would that be?'

I coughed. 'Erm, I promised my son Danny that whenever the World Cup was to be held in an English-speaking country, that I would take him.'

Tim sat back; he wasn't happy about this.

'I don't mean for the entire thing, just for a couple of weeks, maybe three.'

Tim gave me a sideways look. 'RTÉ . . .' he began, 'will not pay a penny towards you taking your son out there.' He tapped the desk with his finger on virtually every word.

'Of course not. I wouldn't expect that. I'll pay for him, of course. But he would share my room while he's there.'

Tim gave it some thought. 'OK, but if I think it's interfering with your work, I'm bringing you straight back.'

I nodded. 'That's fair enough.' I stood and Tim shook my hand.

'Welcome to the team.'

He smiled as he said this, and I really did feel welcome.

29

The announcement that I was now going to the World Cup didn't go down well at home, except with Danny. When I look back now, for the life of me I cannot remember why I didn't also include my daughter Fiona. She would have been thirteen then and she loved soccer. In fact, for one of her earlier birthdays she asked me to take her and some friends to a Bohemian FC match at Dalymount Park. I regret that now. For Ireland's first few games at home under Jack Charlton it was me and Fiona sitting in a virtually empty east stand at Landsdowne Road. I have no idea why I didn't take her, and although she has never said anything to me about my lack of thought, I'm sure it must have rankled with her. Sorry, Fiona. I am so sorry.

Gerry and I were still gigging like crazy in the run-up to the World Cup. At this point I now had a PA, Warren Donoghue. Warren hailed from Australia where he had played rugby league. He was built like a brick shithouse, and he was a funny guy, with great instincts, and a handsome bastard too. I think Gerry was a bit pissed off with me when I chose Warren to travel to the World Cup with me and not him. But I needed someone who would take the pressure off me, look after luggage and check schedules, and to hang out with Danny when he came out to join me and I had to work, so I would know that Danny was safe. I wouldn't ask Gerry to do any of that. Warren would follow me out on a separate flight. I shadow-booked him a room in every hotel I was to stay in and booked him matching flights that I would be taking. Remember, I was on the players' chartered aircraft.

When we finished our last gig before I was to depart for America, Gerry and I parted with a very stilted 'good luck'. I was so excited; I felt like a kid again. A few days later I packed for America and because the flight was an early-morning one I left the house quietly at 5 a.m. to head to the airport. There were no goodbyes, which I hate anyway. At the airport there were lots of excited fans trying to get a glimpse of the team. They would be unlucky as the team had been taken to a private departure place for press conferences and where they could have private farewells with their families. I checked in and, before I knew it, we were rolling down the runway and lifting into the blue Irish sky on our way, I hoped, to conquer the world.

It was a lovely flight. Unlike today there was no direct flight from Dublin to Orlando, Florida, where the team would be based and play two of their three group matches. So we were to fly into JFK in New York and from there board a plane that had been chartered for the rest of their flights, starting with this one from JFK to Orlando. Being an aeroplane buff I was hoping for a 737.

The Aer Lingus plane we were on was a brand-new Airbus and it was beautiful. The pilot announced that it was the aircraft's maiden flight to New York. When we landed it was really smooth but then there was a sudden jerk. The pilot came on: 'That was the automatic brake. I won't be using that again.' We all laughed.

We didn't taxi to the terminal, instead we parked out on the apron and a bus took us directly to our next plane. I was disappointed. It was a Boeing 727. I didn't even think they were still flying. It was very old-fashioned inside, but comfortable enough once you got seated. The FAI had not broken the bank for this aircraft for sure.

Less than two and a half hours later we landed in Orlando. I stepped off the plane and could barely breathe. It was sweltering hot. I had never been to Florida before, and it was not even on my bucket list. I remember during my Castle days that Gerry and Colette had decided to give emigrating a go, but he was back in a couple of months saying, 'Not for me.' The first thing that struck me, apart from the heat, was how clean it was. The place was spotless and the greenery manicured to within an inch of its life.

RTÉ had arranged a car rental for me, and, let me tell you, if you are ever going to Orlando, you NEED it. Not just to get around but because even walking a few hundred yards had you perspiring profusely. Driving out of the airport, flanked by palm trees and with the sun just going down, was just delightful. Driving in America didn't faze me. I had driven all around the east coast for gigs. If you can drive in New York, you can drive anywhere.

RTÉ couldn't get us rooms in the team hotel for the first two nights, so we stayed in a motel across the road. It was a nice place; it had a pool with the rooms surrounding it. Two nights later we checked into the Hilton where the team were staying and the strangest thing happened. As it transpired, our producer was Michael O'Carroll, and we are not related in any way at all. Michael was checking in with one receptionist and I was beside him, checking in with another. They asked our names and nearly in concert we said, 'O'Carroll'.

One of the receptionists smiled and said, 'Ah, so you're here for the family reunion?'

Michael and I looked at each other, puzzled. I answered. 'No, we're with Irish television – here for the World Cup.' I could tell by her face that she had no idea what the World Cup was, so I added, 'Soccer.'

'Oh, of course.' Nope, she didn't know.

But now I was intrigued. 'What's this family reunion you were asking us about?'

She smiled. 'Your kin are here.' She could see by my expression that I had no clue what she meant. 'The O'Carroll family reunion is taking place here tomorrow night. They've all checked in.'

I looked at Michael. He shrugged. They have *all*? 'How many are there?' I asked.

She looked at her computer. 'Over fifty.' I was really interested now.

You see, I'm very proud of my family history. I was aware that a distant relative of mine, Charles O'Carroll, had emigrated to what was then the colony of Maryland in 1659. Once there he had dropped the 'O' and become known as Charles Carroll the Settler. His son, Charles Carroll of Annapolis, was the father of Charles Carroll of Carrollton, or Carroll town. This Charles was the youngest signatory of the Declaration of Independence, and the only Catholic signatory. (See, more trivia.)

Anyway, back to the Hilton Hotel reception desk. I asked if I could be put in touch with the organizer and the receptionist handed me a phone and within a minute a lovely woman's voice came on the line. I told her my name and told her Michael was also an O'Carroll and she was delighted that we were here 'from the old country', as she put it. She invited us to a mass they would be having at seven that evening, followed by a meet and greet at eight thirty. I passed on the mass but said we would make the eight-thirty reception.

It was bizarre. Michael and I were the only two white people at the meet and greet. We were welcomed with open arms, I might add, and by the end of the evening I really did feel like family. One of the organizers, a college professor, explained to me that as people were freed from the horrors of slavery they had no surnames. So they took on the surnames of the families that they had been enslaved to. I felt awful. I think I even apologized, but the professor with a wave of his hand expunged any guilt I may have felt.

'That was then, this is now,' he said with a smile.

I had a wonderful night with my new extended family.

30

Two days later I met up with Ireland's most beloved striker, Niall Quinn. He and I would be working together for RTÉ. Here's a funny aside: a local newspaper in Ireland ran a competition with a nice prize. The question was *Which tall Irish centre forward will be partnering Brendan O'Carroll at the World Cup?* An easy question that got even easier when you read down the page. *Send your answers to the Niall Quinn competition at this address.* Anyhow, we had a drink together down at Church Street Station, the central point for entertainment at that time in Orlando, and Niall suggested that we go up to the offices at the Orange Bowl, the designated stadium for Ireland's two games in Florida, and get our credentials. So up we went. The press office there was fairly quiet when we arrived so we were seen quickly, Niall at Cubicle 1, me at Cubicle 5. Niall had his done and dusted within minutes while the guy doing mine was still clicking his mouse and frowning at the screen. Here's the script of what happened:

```
WORLD CUP, ORLANDO


INT. WORLD CUP ACCREDITATION OFFICES,
ORLANDO - DAY
Brendan O'Carroll and Niall Quinn arrive
at the World Cup Accreditation Offices.
The offices are spacious. There are maybe
fifteen cubicles set out in an L-shape
around the room. The office is not busy.
```

NIALL

Looks like we picked a good time.

Both Niall and Brendan are to be contributors for RTÉ during the upcoming World Cup. To have access to the press rooms and commentary boxes of the various stadiums in which the Republic of Ireland are playing, they need to pick up their accreditation. They will have both been registered by the TV station, so it is a simple case of presenting your passport and picking up your tag.

BRENDAN

You take number one and I'll take number five?

NIALL

Sure.

They go to the respective cubicles. At Cubicle 1 Niall hands over his passport.

NIALL (CONT'D)

Quinn, Niall Quinn.

The clerk looks at the passport and glances at Niall to match the photo, then turns to his computer.

BRENDAN (*AT CUBICLE 5*)

O'Carroll, Brendan O'Carroll.

*He slides over the passport. The clerk
checks the photo for a match, then turns
to his computer and types.*

*Back at Cubicle 1, the clerk has been
away to the tag printer and as we join
has just returned.*

CLERK

Just sign here, Mr Quinn.

*Niall signs and slides the form back to
the clerk.*

*The clerk hands him the tag, now with a
World Cup lanyard attached.*

CLERK (CONT'D)

OK, you are good to go. Enjoy the soccer
tournament.

NIALL

Thanks.

He stands and reads over the tag.

*At Cubicle 5, the clerk taps on the
computer keys. He looks at Brendan and
frowns. He taps some more. He stops and
with a finger to his lips he studies
Brendan.*

CLERK

Hmmm.

BRENDAN

What? What's that?

CLERK
I, erm, well, it's . . . Just
hold on a moment.
*The clerk leaves, taking Brendan's
passport with him. Brendan watches as the
clerk makes his way down to the very last
cubicle and, handing the passport to
another man, they both now stare at
Brendan.*

*Brendan looks over at Niall. Niall
mouths, 'What?' Brendan shrugs. The clerk
is now on his way back. He sits.*

CLERK (CONT'D)
This is your passport, right?

BRENDAN
Of course. Look at the picture.
He does. Again.

CLERK
If you make your way down to the
very end booth, I'll hand this over
to my supervisor.

BRENDAN
What seems to be the problem?

CLERK
I'll leave that to him to explain.
*Brendan heads for the end cubicle,
passing Niall on the way.*

NIALL
What's up?

BRENDAN
I haven't a clue.
At the end cubicle, Brendan sits.

SUPERVISOR
Mr O'Carroll, you say?

BRENDAN
Not just 'I say', that is my name.

SUPERVISOR
I see. OK, let's see what
we have here.
*He now begins to tap away on his
computer. The clerk who has first looked
after Brendan stands a little distance
back. Brendan can't see the screen but
when the supervisor stops typing he
leans back.*

SUPERVISOR (CONT'D)
Hmmm.
The clerk now steps forward.

CLERK
See? That's what came up for me too.

BRENDAN
What? What came up?

SUPERVISOR

It's . . . eh, technical.

Brendan is racking his brain. What can be wrong? He has never overstayed his visa. He got a parking ticket in Boston two years ago, which he paid. He got a speeding ticket in New York a few weeks ago, but he paid that too. What?

The supervisor leans forward.

SUPERVISOR (CONT'D)

I'm afraid you'll need to talk to my boss.

BRENDAN

About what?

The supervisor takes a look at his computer screen again.

SUPERVISOR

Well, I'm not quite sure, that's why you will need to speak with my boss.

BRENDAN

OK. Let's do it.

SUPERVISOR

I'm afraid he's out of the office right now, but he'll be here in less than an hour. Can you wait?

BRENDAN

I'd rather come back. I'll come back in, say, an hour?

Brendan holds his hand out for his
passport.

> SUPERVISOR
> An hour would be good.
> (*Holds up the passport.*) And I'll
> hold on to this until then.

Brendan smiles.

> BRENDAN
> No you won't. I'm not leaving here
> without that passport.

> SUPERVISOR
> Then I guess you'll be
> waiting here then.

> BRENDAN
> What's your boss's name?

> SUPERVISOR
> That would be . . . Roy Rogers.

> BRENDAN
> I'm serious.

> SUPERVISOR
> So am I.

**EXT. WORLD CUP ACCREDITATION OFFICES,
ORLANDO – CONTINUOUS**
Brendan has stepped outside to have a
smoke. Niall is waiting.

BRENDAN

I'll drop you back and come back here.

NIALL

Why, what's going on?

BRENDAN

They won't tell me.

They get into the car and it drives away.

**INT. WORLD CUP ACCREDITATION OFFICES,
ORLANDO - LATER**

Brendan has returned and been shown into
an office where he waits alone for Roy
Rogers. Mr Rogers enters the room. He
holds Brendan's passport.

ROY ROGERS

Hello, Mr O'Carroll.

BRENDAN

Hello, Mr Rogers.

Rogers sits at his terminal.

ROY ROGERS

Right, let's see what we have here.

*Rogers opens the passport and begins to
type in the information from it. He sits
back as the machine does its thing. When
it stops buzzing Rogers leans in to the
screen.*

Well, well.

BRENDAN
So, what is the problem?

ROY ROGERS
The problem is that you, Mr O'Carroll,
are dead.
*With one finger he turns the screen round
to Brendan.*
*On the screen is a perfect replica of
Brendan's tag including a colour
photograph. But across the entire thing,
set at an angle, is a box with a word in
'stamp' style*: DECEASED.

BRENDAN
So what do I do now?

ROY ROGERS
Call a funeral director, I guess.
Brendan laughs at this, as does Roy.
Brendan holds his arms out wide.

BRENDAN
Well, you can see that I am obviously NOT
dead.
*Roy turns the computer screen back to
himself.*

ROY ROGERS
If my computer says you're dead, sir, you
are dead.
Roy slides the passport back to Brendan.

INT. HILTON HOTEL ROOM - LATER

Brendan is on the phone to Tim O'Connor, head of sport.

TIM

Dead?

BRENDAN

That's what he said.

TIM

But you are not dead?

BRENDAN

I am, according to Roy Rogers.

TIM

Roy fucking Rogers? Brendan, is this a joke?

BRENDAN

No, it's not a joke. That's his name.
There is silence for a few moments as Tim is thinking.

TIM

Dead? How the - Oh, fuck!

BRENDAN

What, Tim, what is it?

TIM

I know what the problem is. You see, I had to submit my list for security before

I had decided I was going to send you out. I wanted to hold the place, so I put my secretary's name in. Then, once you took the job, I sent word to them that she had died, and you were her replacement. They must have mixed it up. *Tim assures Brendan that he will clear it up and to give it a couple of days.*

INT. WORLD CUP ACCREDITATION OFFICES – TWO DAYS LATER
Brendan is shown directly into Roy Roger's office.

> ROY ROGERS
> Well, if it ain't Lazarus!

He howls at his own joke. Brendan extends his hand.

> BRENDAN
> I guess I'm the man they couldn't hang!

Now they both laugh. Brendan is handed his press tag.

Niall and I got on famously. He is such a gentle giant and, as I have often remarked, when we stood beside each other we were a cameraman's nightmare. Mind you, there was one occasion when I really put one over on our camera crew. We were heading out to cover a rodeo that was about an hour away. The cameraman insisted on driving the van while the sound man rode shotgun. Niall and I sat in the back. As it happened, I had driven the exact same model of van on our last trip to America. It was spacious and could carry all the gear from gig to gig. It also had a nice little touch that I hadn't seen before. It was possible to control the radio from the back seats as well as the front. So I winked at Niall. 'Watch this,' I said, the prankster in me coming to the fore.

I leaned forward between the two seats and said to the two boys. 'Oh, very nice. This has the voice-activated radio.' Then I sat back.

It took about a minute. 'What do you mean?' asked the sound man.

'Well, the radio will change station or change volume using your voice. Have you not tried it?' I asked.

Immediately the driver turned on the radio. The sound man then took over. He leaned towards the radio and said, 'Change.'

Of course nothing happened.

I spoke up. 'No, no. It's usually a number. Did they not give you the number when you picked up the van?' I now put my hand on the back-seat controller. 'Let me try.' So I called out 'THREE'. Nothing. Then I called out 'SEVEN', and as I did I pressed the advance button on the rear controller and, of course, the radio changed station.

The two boys were amazed. They now tried it, the sound-man first.

'Seven.'

I pressed the button and the station changed.

They both laughed now with excitement. They actually shouted 'seven' at the thing about ten times in a row. Niall was now bursting with silent laughter.

'How do you change the volume?' the driver asked.

'Well, it's double the change number to lower it and three times the number to raise it.'

Without delay the driver called out 'Fourteen' and I lowered the volume, and straight after the sound man called out 'Twenty-one' and I turned the volume up.

They changed the station and put the volume up and down all the way to and from the rodeo. Niall Quinn was in tears laughing.

When we got back to our hotel, Niall and I had a good laugh about it. But we forgot to tell the two lads that it was a prank. George Hamilton had the crew the next day. When he returned he came to see us. 'What did you do to the two boys yesterday? They've spent the day shouting numbers at the radio. They've now decided it's broken and they want to exchange the van.'

When we told George he laughed like a kid, as did we. But don't worry – I got to the lads before they went to change the van and told them. In fairness to them they took it well.

The football hadn't even started yet and I was already having a ball. The training ground was a drive away. I went there every day. I did the odd piece to camera if anything odd came up. I was sure that as soon as we started playing things would get busier. I like busy.

Niall was unlucky not to be on that team panel. He had an injury to his knee that had needed surgery. Most players' careers would have ended with the injury he had, a cruciate ligament, but not Niall's. He hadn't recovered in time for the panel selection, but he worked on that knee every day. He had taken to training with the team and, I'll be honest, when I watched him train I would have picked him. As we got closer to our first match, which was to be against Italy in Giants Stadium in New York, I expected it to get busier, but it didn't.

The flight to New York came just in time. I was buzzing on the flight. Firstly a friend, John Courtney, the Umbro agent in Ireland, was bringing Danny over with him. We had agreed to meet at Fitzpatrick's Hotel that night. But before that I had a gig in Gaelic Park on Broadway. Niall came with me to the gig, where I had arranged to meet up with Eamonn Coghlan too. I did the gig to about 8,000 Irish fans. When I introduced Eamonn on stage the crowd went nuts, and, needless to say, when Niall walked on they lost their shit altogether. The gig was a nice little payer, giving me a few dollars to get me through the trip. Now to head to Fitzpatrick's and get my hands on Danny.

Niall, myself and Eamonn hailed a cab and we cruised through the streets of Manhattan. I just knew the place would be hopping when we arrived. A singsong would be going on and general good fun mayhem would be the order of the evening. I went in through the bar door and it was packed but in complete silence. *What the hell is going on?* I thought.

Danny ran to me when he saw me, calling 'Daddy, Daddy!' and a few people shushed him.

'What the hell is going on?' I asked a guy nearby.

He shushed me and just pointed.

The date was 17 June 1994. The guy beside me was pointing at the television mounted on the wall, and around me everybody, and I mean everybody, was staring at it in silence. It was a helicopter shot of about twenty police cars following a white Ford Bronco. I looked back at the guy, a visitor from Ireland. 'What's going on?' I asked again.

'It's O. J. Simpson; he topped his bird.' He said this without any emotion whatsoever.

I took Danny outside and we hugged for a long time, then we went for a McDonald's. I hoped the police would get their man, but, to be honest, I didn't really care. I'd got my boy, and that would do me. Tomorrow we would take on Italy in our opening game. We were told in press pieces that the Irish fans would be outnumbered by the Italians three to one in Giants Stadium, as New York/New Jersey was very Italian. Danny and I cuddled up in our beds and slept knowing that when we woke we had a wonderful day ahead of us.

What a day we had. First of all, you could not see an Italian flag anywhere in the stadium. The singing of 'Low Lie the Fields of Athenry' could, I'm sure, be heard in Boston. Paul McGrath was amazing and when, in the twelfth minute, Ray Houghton scored the crowd went into raptures. When the final whistle went, we screamed and we cried. I interviewed some ecstatic fans outside the stadium and we all hugged and I had many a kiss from faces covered in stubble, and that was just the girls (boom-boom). The streets of New York belonged to the Irish that night. There was not one spot of trouble and, as usual, the Irish fans made us proud.

After the game I took Danny back to Fitzer's where we celebrated and early enough departed. Warren made to come with us, but I told him to hang on and enjoy the celebration. We got a cab back to the team hotel and went to bed, but not before packing for our flight back to Orlando.

Danny was so excited about getting to Orlando. Needless to say, that was because of Disney World. I knew that I would be taking Danny so the week before he came over I decided to visit and kind of suss it out. You know, see what was there, so I could maximize Danny's visit. Now, I must tell you that as a kid I was Superman mad. I had lots of DC comics. The inside back page of these comics had adverts for things like Daisy BB guns or X-ray specs, which always showed a silhouette of a woman in a nightdress. There were also glasses that you could wear to see behind you. But the bottom half of the page would be taken up with an advert for Disney World. I would drool over the exciting things they said they had there, but honestly, I was a kid from Finglas with the arse out of me trousers. For me Disney World may as well have been on another planet. I never believed that I would see it. The amusement arcade in Bray was the closest I would get.

So I went. To suss it out for Danny. I parked, got the tram across to the lake and the riverboat across to the Magic Kingdom. I paid and went in. If you ever get there, you'll see, just as you enter, a small square – I think they call it the Town Square. There you will find a wooden bench. I walked to the bench and looked up Main Street, USA. The shops varied from clothing stores to cafes, candy stores, ice-cream stores and, right at the end of the street, stands a stunningly beautiful pink castle. I was thirty-eight years old. I had dreamed about this place since I was a gosson (young boy). I slowly sat down on the bench and for the next few minutes I cried. I was in Disney World where Mickey Mouse lives.

I spent the entire day there. I didn't go on any rides; I wanted Danny to be with me for that. I just walked and walked, amazed at the place. Then when it got dark it was lit up in brilliant colours. It was like being inside a giant Christmas tree. I was still there when all the lights dimmed and over the castle the most amazing fireworks display was going on exactly in sequence to the music. I couldn't wait to bring Danny.

The day after we got back to Florida from New York, we went. Danny spent the whole day with his eyes wide open, and he was so excited that he cried. Needless to say, so did I – again. We had our Disney day and we loved it.

For the two weeks before Danny arrived my work in Orlando had been three minutes every second day and I'd been getting bored. I couldn't think of anything productive to do. Then I remembered something from that first stand-up show in the Tivoli Theatre.

The actor Gabriel Byrne had come to the show one night. After the show he came backstage and was so complimentary. 'You're a great storyteller,' he said.

At first I was unsure what he meant.

'Your timing makes each story pop and interesting,' he explained.

I thanked him shyly.

'You should write a screenplay,' he urged me.

'Oh, I will, I will,' I said without thinking.

We went on to chat about the merits of Irish humour, in particular that of Dublin, as we were both Dubliners. In the conversation, he mentioned 'screenplay' about a half-dozen times. Eventually I had to surrender. 'Gabriel, what the fuck is a screenplay? Is it a script?'

He laughed because I think he suspected I didn't know. 'Look, why don't you come up to my hotel tomorrow? I have a couple of screenplays that I've read that I won't be doing, but you can have a look and get an idea of what it's about. Also, there's a book by Syd Field, a brilliant screenplay teacher, I'll send that to you too.'

The next day I had coffee with Gabriel in the lobby of the Westbury Hotel and, as promised, he gave me those screenplays. I can't remember what we chatted about because all I was thinking was, *I hope somebody I know sees me having coffee with Gabriel Byrne.*

True to his word, Gabriel sent me the Syd Field book *Screenplay.* I loved it and still do. I read it when I'm feeling under any pressure. That and David Mamet's books are a staple for any aspiring writer. The point I am getting to is this: one of the recommendations Syd Field makes is that you should have a backstory of the main character that is separate to your screenplay. Drama is about taking your central character, or as we in Dublin would call him 'The Chap', from A to Z in your story, but to create the drama you need to put impossible obstacles in his way for him to overcome. The backstory, although you will not use it in the screenplay, means that you know him so well it will help you decide on how he will overcome these obstacles. Simple. Well, not really. It doesn't have to be long, say, twenty pages or so. It's fun and it's hard at the same time.

So, as I was sitting in the hotel in Orlando, I thought to myself, *Why not try doing that in the off time I have here?* I went across to the mall near the hotel, and bought a yellow legal pad (I write everything on a yellow legal pad) and a couple of fast pens. When I got back I ordered a large pot of coffee and tried to decide where to begin. Blank. I didn't have a screenplay in mind, so how could I have a central character? The *Mrs. Brown's Boys* radio series was going well on radio, so it dawned on me that maybe I could write a backstory for Agnes Brown? It was just as an exercise and to fill the boring gaps in between my real work.

Where to start? Well, Agnes was born in the thirties, an era that I knew nothing about. *Hmm. Think, where to start?* I decided I would write about her life in the seventies. OK, good! But again, where did I fucking start? I know. She is a widow that has reared her children alone; I'll start the backstory the day she becomes a widow. I poured another coffee from the pot and began writing. You could still smoke in the bar of the hotel back then, so there I sat: coffee, a fag and a pen and pad. My favourite and most relaxing position to this day.

Niall came to me in the bar. 'Hey, we have a briefing from Michael to go to.'

I looked up at him. 'That's not until eight o'clock.'

He checked his watch. 'I know. It's five past eight now!' He headed for the lift.

290

I couldn't believe it. I had been writing since two o'clock. Six hours. There were receipts on the table for six pots of coffee. I had got completely lost in the writing. I had been aiming for twenty pages. I missed by a long way; I had written seventy pages and I wasn't even near coming to an end. I tucked the pad under my arm and headed for the briefing.

As Danny had yet to arrive, I was free every day I had off. So, I wrote every day that I had off for the first two weeks, sitting in the bar at the same table. Those seventy pages went to a hundred, then two hundred and on and on. Then I tucked the pad in my case and headed to New York to meet up with Danny.

When Danny and I got back to Orlando we were very busy for the first few days, what with visiting Disney, Universal Studios and me working. I had one night where I ran into a little dilemma. I had been offered an after-dinner speech gig by one of the large Irish companies that had brought their clients over for the games. I needed Warren to come with me but it was a late gig so Danny couldn't come and I had no babysitter. My friend came to the rescue.

Ronnie Whelan, Liverpool and Republic of Ireland legend, is from Finglas, as am I, in case you missed it. In fact, we had both attended Patrician College in Finglas, albeit some years apart. His dad, Ronnie senior, was a friend of my older brother Finbar; I think they had both at some stage played for St Patrick's Athletic, and I had played with various teams with three of Ronnie's cousins, the McMullan brothers. Ron is the most decent of guys. He's a dreadful prankster, but never in an offensive or harmful manner.

I told Ronnie about my dilemma, and he said he would mind Danny for the evening. I was thrilled. I did the gig and returned and was knocking on Ron's door about midnight.

Ronnie opened the door. I could see that there was now a roll-up bed between Ronnie's bed and his roommate John Aldridge's bed. Danny was sound asleep in it. 'I'll just carry him down to our room,' I whispered to Ron.

'He fast asleep. Leave him there and I'll drop him down to you in the morning,' was Ron's answer.

I wasn't sure but then I realized that Danny, a Liverpool FC fan at this stage, would be waking up with two Liverpool legends beside him, so I left him.

By the time I got up next day, Danny had gone off training with the team. I'm not sure Danny fully grasped then how amazing a time he was having. He does now.

31

With Danny gone training I took my notebook and carried on writing what was supposed to be Agnes Brown's backstory. It was getting longer and longer. Soon I wondered if I had a book here, so I called Pat Egan and told him.

He wasn't pleased. 'What are you doing writing a book? You're just setting yourself up to be knocked down!'

This negativity was not unusual for Pat. I spent two holidays with him in Barbados where he would join me every blazing sunny day at the breakfast table with the announcement 'It's going to rain.' He is also the only person I know who could say the following: 'I got the photographs back of the Barbados trip. It's only when I went through them that I realized I had a good time.' Anyway, Pat did follow up my phone call with one of his own to Michael O'Brien, owner of the O'Brien Press.

When Pat called me back he said, 'Michael O'Brien wants the book.'

I was a bit flummoxed. 'Wait a minute, he hasn't even seen the manuscript yet!'

'I know, but he said if it's about Mrs. Brown off the radio, then he wants it.'

I finished the book before Ireland went out of the competition in the last sixteen to Holland, and on our return to Ireland I typed up the manuscript and sent it to the O'Brien Press. Michael made a few changes, expanding this and shortening that, but ninety-nine per cent of it was exactly the way I wrote it.

The Mammy, as I titled it, was released that November, and far from it being 'knocked down', it stayed at number one in the *Irish Times* bestseller list for eighteen weeks. Boy, was I pleased.

The success of *The Mammy* and the fact that we were still packing them in at the live gigs garnered a lot of interest from the media. As the end of the year approached every interviewer wanted to know what our plan was for 1995. Well, obviously we planned to keep gigging, but then I added a little something else that seemed to put the cat among the pigeons, not just with the media but with the world of the dramatic arts and most importantly with myself and Gerry.

As I mentioned earlier, my first time in a theatre had been during the Dublin Theatre Festival. I hadn't told anyone before, but my *real* ambition was to be a playwright. Writing stories that would come to life on a stage. To write plays that would hold the attention of an audience, to be able to move people. To write plays that would make my mother laugh. So doing an interview for a national Sunday newspaper, I divulged this. The interviewer asked, 'Well, Brendan, you have had success on the radio, in stand-up comedy and now with *The Mammy*. So then what's next?'

The word dropped from my lips without any connection to my brain. 'A play.'

He was surprised by that answer. I was fucking surprised by the answer!

Then it was the interviewer that made the next part happen. 'A play? That would be interesting. Would you write something for the Dublin Theatre Festival?'

'Yes, exactly. For the Dublin Theatre Festival,' I replied. My inner voice was screaming. *What the fuck are you saying, Brendan? You don't even know if you CAN write a fucking play.*

Dublin Theatre Festival? It would be polite to at least wait until you're invited. We had parted company with Pat Egan on my return from the World Cup in 1994, but I could imagine his reaction if we hadn't.

The paper ran the story. Gerry wasn't pleased. The band weren't pleased. It seemed that nobody liked the idea. Except the Dublin Theatre Festival. I got a lovely letter from Tony O'Dalaigh, the brilliant head of the festival. *Welcome to the festival*, it said. It seemed he was OK with it. What was wrong with everybody else?

Gerry, as I say, was not pleased. I got it. Gerry is a singer-songwriter and entertainer; he had no interest in drama. I tried to assure him that we were not moving away from what we do; this was just a slight diversion. I also told him that he would be in the play. 'I can't act,' was his reply. He was dead wrong, but that comes later.

I had a meeting a few days after that with Tony Byrne, the owner of the Tivoli Theatre, as I wanted to book the theatre during the festival. Tony was very enthusiastic for the play and offered to jointly produce it. I was delighted. This meant he would put in half the money it would take to get to opening night or, as he termed it, 'turn the key', and we would split the income. He estimated it would cost about £76,000 to 'turn the key', so we would keep a couple of weeks in our OCS gigs free in case the play was a success and we could run on. I agreed and went back to my day job of stand-up comedian. For now, myself, Gerry and the OCS just carried on gigging into 1995. It was a busy year and, thank you, God, we were packing them in with my new comedy show *How's Your Snowballs?*

On one occasion, when returning home from ten days of one-nights, my secretary (yes, I now had a secretary) told me that a man named Stephen Frears had called. I hadn't the foggiest idea who he was, so I phoned Tommy Swarbrigg and asked if he did.

'Jesus, yes, he's a brilliant film director. He got an Oscar for *My Beautiful Launderette*.' I called the number he had left, and he was lovely. He said he was interested in talking to me about a role in the movie he was currently making of Roddy Doyle's *The Van* and he asked me to meet him in a Dublin hotel.

I agreed. I had read ALL Roddy Doyle's books. Why? Because he was writing about 'us' Dubliners. No dressing it up; he wrote about us exactly as we are. To me he was and still is a fucking genius. I arrived early at the hotel and when I saw Stephen Frears I got very excited – not for him, but because with him was Roddy Doyle.

I tried to stay cool. I tried to relax. But it was difficult because every time Roddy spoke I wanted to shout at him 'I LOVE YOU'. But I am sure that would have been inappropriate. Stephen went through the dates and what he would expect of me and I nodded in the right places, I think.

Roddy then capped it off with: 'What we're looking for is a character that's a bit of a rogue, funny, and you like him, but you know he'd smash your face in if he wanted to. He could be a thief? But definitely a scumbag. I think you're the man.' (I'm nearly sure that this was a compliment.)

I got the job. I was over the moon. The shooting was around the gigs we had in the diary, so nothing had to be changed. But again, when I told Gerry, I felt that we had taken yet another step away from each other.

Around the same time a friend of both mine and Gerry's was professional boxer Stephen Collins. Gerry, Steve and I and our wives drank every Sunday night together. During one of those nights Stephen got a call on his cell phone. He stepped outside to take it. When he came back in he was smiling from ear to ear. He had just been told he was getting a shot at the world middleweight title against Chris Eubank.

It was what he deserved. Stephen had plied his trade in the USA, where he was known as the Celtic Warrior, and he had a huge following there and at home in Ireland. The date was set and we didn't see Stephen again until after the fight, which he would subsequently win, becoming world champion. His defence of this win would later spur me on, just when I needed it.

The OCS gigged on right up to the night before I was due on set for the first time for *The Van*. When we finished that gig there were no 'good lucks' or anything. Gerry headed off to meet Colette for a drink and I went home.

Arriving on the set for the first time was so exciting. Actually every time I arrive on a set it's exciting, whether it's for a movie or TV. But this was a first and I was shown to my room in the four-in-one trailer. I wasn't big enough for my own, but this was just great. The clothes I was to wear were hanging up, so I changed into them. Stephen Frears knocked on my door to say welcome and so did Roddy. Colm Meany was the star of the film; I had never met him but had heard great things about him. My first scene was to be sitting at the bar with three 'best friends'. I sat there so nervous; all I could think about was that if someone messed up a line, the director would shout 'Cut!' and we would have to start again. *Please don't let it be me that fucks up*, I prayed.

It wasn't. In fact, the day went extremely well and by the end of it I had become very relaxed. This was helped by the two leading men, Colm Meany and Donal O'Kelly, who went to great lengths to put me at ease. By day two of shooting I arrived on the set feeling as if I belonged there, and do you know what? I did belong there!

Stephen Frears was amazing. On days that I wasn't due on set and had no gig to go to I would arrive at the shoot just to watch him work. I learned so much by just watching him; he could have told the story without dialogue, just with pictures. But, of course, just as I was settling down and enjoying the work on the movie, as usual something popped up to not just surprise me but stun me. I was about to need my PMA more than usual. It began with a phone call from the Tivoli's owner and my co-producer, Tony Byrne. It seemed innocent enough. 'Let's have a game of golf,' he suggested. Yes, it *seemed* innocent enough.

It was on the ninth green on Hollystown golf course when he got round to it.

Tony Byrne had hit his ball straight down the fairway. I topped my drive and it dribbled about 120 yards into some light rough. I made it level with his drive with my second shot and hit the green with my third. He was on in two. He putted first and left it a good four feet short. I needed to make my twelve-footer to have a chance to halve the hole. I knew this green well. I knew it started right but broke a good eighteen inches left. I was confident that if I didn't sink the putt, it would at least be on the edge. I missed by a fucking mile. I picked up my ball and conceded the hole. Tony had a chuckle. As I fired my putter into my bag and made to head for the tenth tee, Tony put his hand on my arm.

I stopped. He needed to say something. I felt he had needed to say whatever it was he was about to say from the first hole. He had been very jumpy and ill at ease.

'I had a call from the Theatre Festival today.' He paused.

I was obviously expected to ask what it was about, but honestly I fucking couldn't care less. That putt on nine had been miles out and I was now two holes down. But I obliged. 'Oh, right, so what did they want?'

He cleared his throat, so I knew, whatever it was, it was a long story. 'Did you know that they have the *Circus Opera* coming in for the festival?'

I shook my head. The festival was nearly six months away, so how the hell would I know what they were bringing in?

'Well, it was supposed to go to Andrews Lane, but –' and now he waited to deliver the big one – 'they think that the Tivoli would be right for it.'

I smiled. This is what it was all about. Tony had made his money by selling shoes. He had bought the Tivoli when it was a virtual ruin and turned it back into the theatre it had been. For years he had courted the acceptance of the theatre 'clique' of Dublin to no avail. Unfortunately what Tony failed to understand is that he was twice the person any of them were. He also failed to see that no matter what he did, most of them would treat him as an outsider.

What Tony hoped for in that moment was that I would say, 'Oh, well, let's give it to them then.' *BUZZ!* Thank you for playing.

'It's just as well I got in there and booked it first then, isn't it?' I said instead. I moved on to the tenth hole and went on to win the match on the last hole and thought no more about it.

Earlier I mentioned Stephen Collins. Let me tell you why. Stephen Collins had trained for and went to London and fought Chris Eubank. Against all the odds he beat him too and became the world champion. A rematch was fixed for around mid-year to be held this time in Cork. Gerry and I had an invite from Stephen to sit ringside. The funny thing was that having beaten Eubank you would have thought that Stephen would now be the favourite, but no. The pundits felt that Eubank had not taken the first fight seriously enough and that this time he would annihilate Stephen. The pundits may know more than me about boxing, but they did not know Stephen Collins more than me. I fully expected Stephen to do the business.

Three days before the fight I had a phone call from Gerry. 'Have you seen the evening paper?' he asked.

'No, why?'

'Get it and look in the entertainment section.' I went out and got the paper and didn't open it until I was home with a cuppa. The headline read THEATRE FESTIVAL REJECTS BRENDAN O'CARROLL PLAY. That was bad enough, but the article said that the reason given by an anonymous source was that the play was not up to the standard required by the festival. Now this was unusual. Why? Because I hadn't even written the play yet! I knew what I wanted to write; I knew the framework I would use. But here's the thing – and this is me when I'm writing a book, a play, a movie script, a TV script or even a song – no matter what I'm writing, I can't start until I know my ending. It just doesn't make any sense to me to start. I mean, a pilot wouldn't take off unless he knew his destination, would he? I'm like that about most things. I wouldn't begin to negotiate a contract unless I knew where I wanted it to end up. And if it doesn't end up where you had aimed for, you don't sign it. If your plane doesn't have a destination, you don't take off. So it follows that if you don't have an ending, you don't start because you have no idea where you want the story to go.

The newspaper article threw me completely. The next day I got a call from Tony Byrne. He was pulling out of being co-producer. This meant that Gerry and I would have to find the £76,000 needed to 'turn the key'. Tony had also recommended a director for the play, and in that phone call he tells me that the director has pulled out as well. Gerry suggested that we just forget it and move on. I asked him to let me think about it. I don't like losing, and I never give up without a fight, but this time I felt beaten.

The following day I was due on the set of *The Van* for my final day's shooting. It was an early call, so by 7 a.m. I was in wardrobe ready for when I was called. We were shooting in Ardmore Studios in Bray, County Wicklow. I sat in the restaurant of the studio over a coffee, with a million thoughts going through my head. Roddy Doyle entered the room and made straight for me. He didn't sit; he just leaned on the table with both hands. 'You don't let anybody ever tell you that your work is not up to *their* standard. You are a writer; you are the person that originates the art. You do what you do and let an audience decide.'

I had no reply to offer except 'Thanks, Roddy.'

He then winked and I think he said, 'Keep it up, kid.' I say 'I think', because I was in such awe that I can't remember exactly.

I did my work that day with a clearer head, but by the next day I was back to self-doubting again. This was the day of Stephen Collins's return match with Eubank. We had a morning gig in the Submarine Bar in Walkinstown. Gerry had done the deal; we got paid, plus the owner would get us flown in his helicopter down to Cork for the fight. *A great deal, Gerry.* The gig was packed as the crowd would be staying to watch the fight on the big screen. The chopper flight down was a treat and, before we knew it, we were ringside watching the warm-up bouts.

The commentator for RTÉ that night was the wonderful Jimmy McGee. Jimmy heard that I was in the arena and sent a runner to ask if I would join him for a quick chat leading up to the main fight. I did and we waffled about previous fights and how much we admired Stephen. The lights went low and Jimmy, with that always excited and exciting voice of his, talked through the ear-splitting cheers as Stephen stepped out at the top of the stairs.

He was lit by a spotlight. One of his crew carried an Irish tricolour and music boomed out. There was a TV monitor in front of me, showing Stephen wearing headphones, and as the camera went in close on Stephen I could read his lips. 'I'm the champ, I'm the champ,' he repeated.

I started to say it out loud myself. 'I'm the champ, I'm the champ.' My head was now saying, *No headline or other people's opinion can shake me. I'm the champ. I believed the play would be a success last week, so why not this week? After all, I'm the champ.*

I stood now and in the throng of the massive cheers for Stephen Collins I screamed, 'I'M THE FUCKING CHAMP!'

Jimmy McGee looked at me, puzzled. 'What's that, Brendan?' he asked.

I smiled. 'I said here's our champ, Jimmy.'

Jimmy now stood too. 'Indeed he is, and we are about to see if he will still be the champ by the end of this historic night in County Cork.'

As the train to Dublin sped through the Irish countryside I stared out of the window, smiling. Stephen Collins had won the fight of his life and I was about to. He was still the champ . . . and so was I.

32

Here's what is crazy about the task I was about to undertake. I had decided long before then that the play I would write would be about that insurance training I had taken, the 'system' and, in particular, the PMA side of the course. I already had a title for it, *The Course*. Indeed, I had been writing *The Course* in my head for a few years. But PMA is not something you learn, it's something you practise. PMA is also like a treadmill. By this I mean that I know so many people who get a treadmill, work out on it every day for weeks or months. They get to the level of fitness they want to get to, then the treadmill gets folded up and slid under the bed or stuck away in the garage and rarely, if ever, used again. You cannot do that with a treadmill and expect to stay fit; it must be used. So must PMA. As it transpired, what was about to happen the rest of that year was an exercise in the application of a positive mental attitude. Every negative can be turned to a positive. The difference between a dream and a goal is a plan. And the main ingredient of any plan is action, doing something.

Over the following two weeks I wrote *The Course*. No, I didn't just write a play in two weeks. I had been writing this play in my head since the very first day I had stood in that room in Athlone singing 'It's a Long Way to Tipperary'. I typed it up. In the meantime, I was also kept busy at the keyboard, for I was committed to a third book in the Agnes Brown series, which I had named *The Granny*. Whereas *The Mammy* had been about Agnes's first years as a widow with five young children, and *The Chisellers* was about the Brown kids growing up, *The Granny* opens on the day Agnes becomes a grandmother. I was enjoying writing it, so it wasn't a chore.

Gerry and I and the OCS kept gigging too. He had written a couple of new songs that he added to the set and which were really well received, particularly one called 'Change of Heart', which was a beautiful song about the huge amount of young people Ireland was losing at that time to emigration and leaving the door open for them to return for ever. It remains one of my favourites. Gerry still wasn't sold on the play. But once we got to August that year and we stopped gigging to concentrate solely on *The Course*, Gerry got behind me a hundred per cent. And what a battle it was. I still had the Tivoli booked. I had the play written. I knew that Gerry and I would be in the play, but I still needed six more actors. Most importantly of all the play needed a director.

I have already said how much I love Roddy Doyle's books, but long before I read them, and I'm going back to my teenage years, there was *Goodbye to the Hill*, a hilarious book about growing up in Dublin city. I would read it on the bus to and from work and cry laughing. It subsequently went on to become a really successful play. The author was Lee Dunne. I had never met Lee, but I had seen him on TV many times and he came across as a warm and funny guy. I heard he was preparing to open his play *Return to the Hill* in the Eblana Theatre in Dublin. I got his phone number and called him. I told him briefly where I was at with *The Course* and asked him straight out if he would be interested in directing it. He was more than friendly. He said to get the script to him, and he would take a look.

The next thing we needed was money. Before pulling out Tony Byrne had given the stage and lighting design gigs to people he knew. I contacted them and they were still on board. I wanted a swinging wall included in the set so that the stage could be converted from a classroom to a hotel bedroom in thirty seconds. The designer was unsure at first but eventually did an amazing job. But all this was going to cost £76,000. Gerry and I had some money between us, but not enough to get us over the line.

I was now back in reasonable favour with my bank, so I met the manager. He said the only way he could give me the loan we needed was to add it on to my mortgage. I was adamant: 'I am not going to mortgage my home for this, no way!' I signed the second mortgage papers that afternoon.

I called Lee Dunne to see had he received the script and he had. He suggested that I meet him down at the Eblana Theatre that afternoon and we would talk about it. By two o'clock I was sitting at a table on the stage of the Eblana with the handsome, white-haired Lee Dunne sitting across from me. We should have met somewhere else. Lee was just days away from his opening night, so our conversation kept getting interrupted by cast and crew that needed answers to questions.

Eventually we got down to it. 'Well, what do you think?' I asked.

He was holding the script and flicking through the pages. He put the script on the table and placed his hand on it. 'This is very good . . .' There was a 'but' coming; I just knew it. 'But, seriously, who the fuck knows what PMA is?'

I wasn't expecting that and I was thrown for a second as a wardrobe person arrived on the stage, holding some fabric. 'Lee, is this OK for the opening scene?'

'That's perfect, darling, perfect.' He turned back to me now for an answer to his question.

'I do. I know what PMA is,' I answered.

'Yes, well, of course YOU do, but think of your audience,

who among them knows what PMA is?' He opened his arms and tilted his head the way people do when they are asking what they believe to be a rhetorical question.

A blonde with far too much hair arrived at the front of the stage. 'How is this wig, Lee? Is this OK?'

Lee stood for a moment. 'That's exactly what I want. Perfect, well done, love.'

I sat in silence for a moment. I had already answered the question, so I didn't know where to take the conversation.

'Look,' Lee began, and he rested his elbow on the table. 'Here's what we do. We teach them to sing.' He now opened his arms wide, smiled and tilted his head again, as if he had just solved a problem that frankly I didn't have. 'We make the premise of the play that if these students learn to sing a song their life will be changed.'

What I wanted to say would take too long. So I just got straight to the point. 'Lee, can you direct the play just as it is in the script now?'

He shrugged. 'Sure.'

I stood. 'Great, I'll get Gerry to talk to your agent and see if we can work out a deal.'

He smiled. 'Do that.' I had half stuck out my hand for a shake, but Lee had turned his attention to something else. 'Everybody on stage here for a line check, please.' He clapped his hands. He turned to me now. 'Hey, Brendan, why don't you come to the opening night next week?'

I was delighted. 'Sure. Thanks, Lee.' We now shook hands and I left.

For some reason I was in London on the day of the opening of Lee Dunne's play. However, my flight back to Dublin was due to land at 6.45 p.m. The curtain up wasn't until 8 p.m. I had a car waiting for me, so I would have plenty of time to grab a take-out coffee and head straight to the theatre.

But then my flight was delayed by nearly an hour. I landed at 7.25 p.m. and by the time I got to the car, with NO coffee waiting for me, it was 7.40 p.m. Then, of course, traffic. I called the box office to tell them that I would be late, say, eight ten, and not to give away my ticket.

The lovely girl on the phone said, 'Mr Dunne has told us to hold the curtain until you get here.'

Now I felt more pressure. *Fuck*.

The car pulled up outside the theatre at 8.05 p.m. and by the time I had collected my ticket and apologized to everybody I met it was 8.10. Ten minutes late. Not bad considering. I went through the first double doors into the space that was there for soundproofing purposes. Just another set of double doors and I was in.

There was an usherette standing between the doors. I handed her my ticket and said, 'I'm so sorry, where do I sit?'

The usherette snapped at me. 'Sit where you fucking like, just get in there.'

I was taken aback by the 'customer care' of the theatre staff but made my way to my seat. As I sat the lights dimmed and the overture began. When the music stopped the usherette I had encountered came through the doors and mounted the steps to the stage. *Fuck*, I thought. No wonder she had been snappy; I had mistaken this actress for house staff. She must have thought I was an asshole.

I was very glad to be there, though. We had yet to hear from Lee's agent, but I wanted to have a look at his work. Although I had read his stuff I had never seen any of his plays, so I wanted to see if his comedy rhythm and his pace were compatible with my sense of comedy. The play was very good, but by the end I knew two things. One, I could see why he wanted to change from PMA to a song and, two, he had a completely different style of comedy to mine. He would not be directing *The Course*. But the guy who played the barman was excellent, as was the barmaid who I had thought was a snarky usherette. I thought, *I'll have them if I can get them.*

When I got home my daughter Fiona went through the programme and saw the actor I was talking about: Brendan Morrissey. Fiona had seen him in a few things and raved about him. I made some calls and found out that he was represented by the Actors' Agency. This was an agency set up by a group of actors. They took turns at manning the phones. A great idea.

I called the agency and asked the guy who answered if he could give me an idea of Brendan Morrissey's availability. I was quite surprised when he answered, 'This IS Brendan Morrissey.'

I complimented him on his performance the previous night and told him who I was and why I wanted to know his availability. Rehearsals for *The Course* were due to start in three weeks' time, I told him. I had also made a decision on who the director was going to be. Me. We were too close to the wire now to start looking again so I had decided to do it myself. This meant that on opening night at the Tivoli I would be making my playwright, actor and director debut all at the same time. No pressure.

I offered Brendan the gig as assistant director too, as I would need someone who knew stagecraft. To my delight Brendan accepted and would give his three weeks' notice to a very disconcerted Lee Dunne that night. Meanwhile Lee's agent had called me with an offer. I said no thanks and that was that.

Brendan Morrissey called me the day after he had given his notice.

'I'm all yours,' he said.

'Good, now your first job as assistant director is to get me that barmaid in the play, Jennifer Gibney.'

He gave a gasp. 'Fuck, are you trying to get me killed?'

He did his gig and they both arrived on the afternoon of 9 September for the meet and greet. Everyone was given a script and told to go through it over the weekend and that we would see them all on the first day of rehearsal in Digges Lane studio on Monday. I knew they would all be stuck into their scripts over that weekend, learning lines and developing their characters, but when they arrived at rehearsals that Monday I had a surprise for them. They could put their scripts away for the first week of rehearsal. Because for that first week I had brought in John Douglas, and he was about to give them The Course.

I went out of the room to get a coffee and from the cafe below I could hear the strains of 'It's a Long Way to Tipperary'.

I smiled to myself. *'And so it begins.'*

33

I have a tendency to do this 'thing' and I have no idea why. I pick character names that are very close to each other, an example being in the TV series Dr Flynn and Father Quinn, which only leads to me confusing the two when I'm doing the show. I did it in *The Course* too and God only knows why. There was Ben Wilson, Bill Weston and Will Benson. I have no idea why I do this. There isn't even a gag about the confusion. Maybe when I started I thought there might be? Who knows? Anyway, they were the names, and once down on paper they remained a fixed item. So the cast line-up was as follows:

- Me playing Joe Daly, the course tutor.
- Gerry playing Will Benson, reformed alcoholic and sceptic. He is only there because a judge gave him six months to get a job or it would be prison.
- Brendan Morrissey playing Ben Wilson, farmer's son and innocent creature.
- Brendan Kealy playing Bill Weston, failed actor and grandiose character.
- Jenny Gibney playing Emily Beechmont. Once a committed housewife but now that the children have left the home her husband treats her like staff.
- Ciaran McMahon playing Tony Short. A stammer-inflicted guy, formerly a scheduler for a bus company.
- Esther Doorley playing a woman endeavouring to make the transition from call girl to insurance sales.

- Paul Lee playing Burt Rubenstein, a hard-nosed American from head office that has been sent to audit Joe Daly's work with the proviso that unless at least five of the six students pass the final exam Joe will be fired.

At the end of that week all the cast understood the pressure of learning the 'system' and the huge benefit of PMA. We could now begin rehearsals. It was a slow grind, but we had given ourselves two weeks to rehearse the show. The week before opening night was the toughest as I was also going between rehearsals to work with the set designer and the lighting designer, and in the evenings out to Andy O'Callaghan's Sutton Sound studio where Andy and I worked on the theme music, the transition music and the closing number 'PMA'.

Andy and I would work until late, and then it was into the rehearsal rooms early the next morning. We were due to finish rehearsals on the Saturday, have Sunday off, a dress rehearsal on the Monday and open on the Tuesday night. Instead I felt we were ready by Friday. So early that afternoon I sat everyone down. I told them that I was proud of them and the work they had put in. I said that I believed that we were ready and that all we could do was offer the show to an audience and see what happens. Then I asked whether anybody had anything they'd like to say.

Paul Lee put his hand up.

'Yes, Paul?' I asked with a smile in my voice. Not for long.

'I think that if this play doesn't get a proper director it is going to be a disaster.'

There was silence for a moment. Paul was actually sucking the PMA out of the room.

I smiled. 'Paul, do you have a director in mind?'

'Yes,' he answered very quickly. He said a director's name. I mused for a moment. 'Do you think he would be available to knock the show into shape by this Monday?'

He became enthusiastic. 'I'm not sure but I can check.'

I stood. 'OK, Paul, you do that and call me at home later when you know. Everybody else, have a nice weekend and I'll see you all early on Monday at the Tivoli.'

We all departed and Paul called me at home that evening.

'I spoke to him and he is available.' He was pretty pleased with himself.

Not for long.

'Paul, this play has a director and it's me. We will be opening "as is" this Tuesday night. We have a dress rehearsal on Monday and if none of that suits you, then don't come to the theatre. Are we clear?'

He mumbled a yes and our call ended.

He was the first to arrive on Monday. But before we got to then I had to handle something else that came up on Sunday. It was a phone call from Tony Byrne, the theatre owner. He wanted his rent up front. He said that sales weren't good, and he feared he would be left without his rent. I didn't have it. Both Gerry and I were drained of funds. I called my lawyer and he told me not to worry, that he would handle it.

Monday morning came and we all met in the pub across the road from the theatre, Ralph le Porter's. After coffees and hugs we went across to the theatre. They were still working on the lights and set so it would be an hour before we could rehearse on the stage. We all went to the main dressing room and did a speed run-through of the lines. This is where we go through the play's lines as quickly as we can. No thinking, no transitions between scenes, just the lines. It lasted about forty-five minutes and nobody missed a beat. Then we broke for coffee. During that break I went out to the box office to check how many tickets had been sold for the opening. The theatre seated 450, so I wanted to check that they had not oversold the capacity.

I very nearly dropped down with a heart attack when the lady running the box office told me the sales for the opening night. 'Fifty-six?'

She nodded.

'There are only fifty-six tickets sold for the opening night?'

She confirmed this with another nod and added, 'But Saturday night is better; there are a hundred and forty sold for Saturday.'

This was supposed to cheer me up. Tony Byrne had said that sales were not great, but fifty-fucking-six? I was gobsmacked. I went home quite disappointed. I had a hot bath to cheer myself up. It didn't work. So it was an uneasy sleep that night.

Next day I drove to the theatre at about six thirty. I had to drive past the front of the theatre to get to the car park. As I turned into Francis Street I could not believe the sight that awaited me. I had not allowed for the fact that my audience did not BOOK; they just turned up. The queue stretched as far as the corner. By 7 p.m. the theatre was full and a good 500 were turned away or, even better, booked for another night.

The mood was good in the dressing rooms – nervous, really nervous, but good. We got our call for beginners to the stage and went to our opening positions on the set. Standing there in the dark, listening to the mumbles of the crowd above the background music, my heart was racing. The theatre lights dimmed and the audience went silent. I could now *hear* the thump, thump, of my heart. The opening music started and the curtain slowly rose. We were in the dark and the audience couldn't see us, but we could see them. It was packed. Then the theme music stopped and the stage lights flared up.

I spoke the first line. 'Well done, everybody.' In that moment *The Course* was no longer just an idea, no longer threads of thoughts in my head; it was no longer just words on a page. It was, at last, a play. No matter what way things went from here – I was a playwright!

34

Let me say something about opening nights. I have had quite a few now and every single time they terrify me. *The Course* was my first. All I could think of was *Get to the end, just get to the song.* The play finishes with a song, the last three words of which are a stretched-out PMA, so it's: Peeeeee, Emmmmm, Aayyyyyyyy. Then the music comes to an abrupt halt. That first night, we finished the song, the music stopped and there was silence for what seemed like an eternity but was just a second or two, Then . . . there was the most unbelievably loud cheer and clapping. The stage went dark and we all made our way off, then the lights came up again on the empty stage as the theme music played and we went back on to take our individual bows.

Behind the set in the dark, Paul Lee, who had wanted a 'real' director, held my arm and whispered to me, 'Forgive me for doubting you.'

I replied with a whispered 'No'.

The Course ran at the Tivoli Theatre for eight weeks with every show sold out. We took a short break before moving it to a bigger 1,500 seat theatre, the Gaiety, where it broke the sales record for the eight weeks it ran there. Do you remember earlier when I told you that Gerry had said 'I can't act'? Do you? Well, he was dead wrong; he was, as I expected, fantastic. Paul Lee played the baddie so well that he would get booed as he came out to take his bow; he was great. It seemed like the part of Tony Short had been written for Ciaran McMahon. Esther Doorley played the call girl to a tee and Brendan Morrissey did not let the play down; he was super and hilarious too. But there were two cast members that stood out for me. Firstly there was Brendan Kealy. Brendan is a hilarious guy. All through rehearsals he pranked about, and he was full of energy and never seemed to get his lines right. He was always late for rehearsal. Yet his performance on the opening night was stellar, his comic timing was spot on and, as the night went on, I could see the other cast were also surprised by his performance. But not as surprised as they were when, at the end-of-the-show speech I gave, I offered a special congratulations to Brendan on his *DEBUT*. You see, Brendan Kealy had never stepped on a stage before.

The other actor that stood out was Jennifer Gibney. I have to be honest and say that we had not got on well throughout rehearsal. Jennifer takes the job of being an actor very seriously. Unfortunately for Jennifer she was being directed by yours truly and I don't take anything seriously. We had a couple of head-butting moments during the rehearsals and for a while I thought I had made a big mistake in casting her. But those thoughts vanished on opening night; she was magnificent. The biggest compliment a writer can pay any actor is that when the writer sees the actor perform the writer is thinking *That is exactly what I meant when I wrote that line.* Jennifer was a writer's dream. We still, however, were not bosom buddies, and when the play began to tour we would keep our distance. Until one morning in a hotel in Waterford . . .

The cast and crew were staying in the Bridge Hotel in Waterford. It's a lovely hotel and mine and Gerry's room overlooked Waterford Harbour where the rivers Barrow, Nore and Suir, or, as they are known, the Three Sisters, combine and end their journey, pouring into the Irish Sea. I woke about nine, late for me, as I am usually up and about at seven. The sun was shining as I made my way down to the restaurant for breakfast. We had opened *The Course* in the Theatre

Royal the previous night and it had been a cracker of a show, so I was feeling pretty good.

As I entered the restaurant I saw Jennifer sitting at a table alone. I made my way to a table on the far side of the room, nodding good morning to her as I passed. You could smoke in a restaurant, so I had a pot of coffee and a cigarette to start my day before making my way to the breakfast buffet. As I was sitting there I could see across the room that Jennifer had a broadsheet newspaper folded into a quarter. The only people who do this are those doing the crossword. I am a huge crossword fan. I have been doing the *Irish Times* cryptic crossword since I was about thirteen or fourteen, when I used to do it with my mammy. I still do it almost every day. Even in America I download *The Times* to my iPad and do it. So I was curious as to which paper's crossword she was doing.

When I got to the buffet I heard Jennifer order a fresh pot of coffee and she then left, I think for the bathroom. I sneaked over to her paper and saw it was the *Irish Times* cryptic crossword she was doing. I was impressed. I finished my brekkie and, as I was heading for the door, I stopped by her table and asked, 'How are you doing with the crossword?'

She smiled. 'It's a tough one today.'

'Really? Move over there and let me have a look.'

We finished the crossword and went our separate ways.

Next morning, when I passed her in the restaurant, she was again doing the crossword. I said good morning and headed for the table I had sat at the day before. When I sat down there was a photocopy of that day's crossword waiting for me. I looked over at Jennifer and mouthed a 'thank you' to her and she gave me a thumbs up. The message was clear: *Fuck off and do your own crossword.* I got it and was not the least bit offended – someone butting in on your crossword is like an onlooker telling you where to move when playing chess.

But I kept looking over at her. There was something familiar about her; I couldn't put my finger on it. But something about sitting there with her that previous morning felt, I don't know, comfortable? It took a few days but then I realized what it was. The last person I had sat beside doing the crossword, with a coffee in front of her and a Consulate cigarette between her red nail-varnished fingers, was Mammy. That's why it was comfortable – because I felt safe.

I'm not really a party boy, although I am a night owl. Most nights when the show ended I would head back to the hotel. There I would sit in the bar or residents' lounge with a large pot of coffee and either read or write depending on how I felt until one or two in the morning. On one such night Jennifer came down to the bar to get a bottle of water and saw me sitting reading. She came over to say hello and we then sat and talked for a good hour. We would mainly talk about the show, or I'd tell her what I had in mind to write next.

Jennifer hadn't known that I wrote books and when she eventually read *The Mammy* and I asked her what she thought of it her answer was funny. 'Well, you're either gay or you have a lot of sisters because you write the women so well.'

I laughed and assured her that I had five sisters and had been raised by, to all intents and purposes, a single woman. I would tell her about what I had in my head for what I wanted to do or write next. We became friends. This was wholly unexpected as I hadn't even liked her at the start.

We played *The Course* in virtually all the bigger theatres across Ireland. There were some theatres that we didn't get to play as the capacity was far too small to do so much as break even. In theatre the money comes in at a trickle but goes out in a gush. But that was to change following a phone call I got one morning from the assistant to one of Ireland's richest people.

Dermot Desmond was someone I knew of and who I had actually served when I was a waiter. I was quite surprised when his assistant called to say he would like to see me. I arrived at his building in the financial centre in Dublin a bit nervous and puzzled as to why I was there. I was taken into the lift by a nice secretary. This was my kind of lift; the walls of it were covered in PMA affirmations. I was then taken to an office to wait for Dermot to join me. I could see across the entire floor complex, and the thought struck me that when these offices had been finished there must have been a world shortage of walnut. Everything that wasn't glass or chrome was walnut. Dermot soon bounced into the room and ordered coffee for us both.

Dermot was just a gentleman to me. He chatted about Macroom in County Cork where he had been born and made me laugh with stories about his early years. All this time I was wondering why I was there. The thought had crossed my mind, knowing that Dermot was a huge investor, that he might think that I had more money than I did, and he was going to point out some investments I should make. He would have been very disappointed. I was wrong, so wrong.

Eventually I said, 'Right, well, thanks for the coffee; I'd better hit the road.'

He jumped up from his chair. 'Wait, Brendan, I went to see *The Course* at the Gaiety. It was amazing. I stood in the lobby afterwards watching people as they left and the show had given them such a lift. Your PMA message had them feeling like they could conquer the world.'

I was really flattered, not just by the compliment, but that he had even come to the show.

Dermot reached over to his desk, picked something up and handed it to me. It was a cheque. A cheque for a very substantial amount of money. 'Here,' he said, as I was taking in the amount. I, of course, was baffled. 'Look,' he began, 'I can imagine that you can't afford to bring the play to the smaller towns in Ireland. But as many people as possible must see this play. So use this money to subsidize any costs involved. Do the smaller theatres.'

I still wasn't sure what was happening. 'Sorry, Dermot, but what do you want for this?'

He laughed. 'Nothing, Brendan, just go and give this country of ours a lift.'

So I did. That cheque made it possible for us to play Letterkenny, Tralee, Dundalk, Drogheda and Derry without losing money.

As good as Gerry was as an actor, I could tell he was itching to get back to doing music. I think he had hoped that once we had finished the tour of Ireland we would go back to the OCS and leave the play stuff behind. That wasn't my plan. I wanted to take the play to the UK.

Gerry and I went across to the UK and visited so many places to try to sell the play. Eventually we managed to put together a small tour of one-week bookings in medium-sized theatres in Glasgow, Manchester, Liverpool and London. It flopped. Not the play but the tour. Let me explain. Wherever we would play the pattern was the same. Monday we'd have maybe sixty people at the show, then they would tell whoever they met. By Thursday we'd have half the theatre full and by Saturday we would be sold out and the venue would have asked us to extend, but because the bookings we had made were so close together we couldn't. I learned from that tour that nothing beats word-of-mouth sales. I do it myself. If I see an interesting advert for a show in the paper I always think, *I must go to that*, and then I don't. But if someone *tells* me they were at such and such a show and it was amazing, I

MUST go and see that show. I would correct this in later tours, but for now let's concentrate on this one: *The Course*.

On our return from the UK I was more than a bit down. Although all the Irish theatres had rebooked the play for the following few months the UK seemed to be beyond me yet again. But there was a nice surprise waiting for me, and I nearly let it go by accident. I was at home when my phone rang. I picked it up and a voice asked to speak with Brendan.

'Speaking,' I answered.

'Oh, good. I'm a film producer and I'd like to know if you would be interested in making a feature film of your book *The Mammy*?'

I smiled to myself. 'Fuck off, Gerry,' I said, and I put down the phone.

I swear, no coincidence, Gerry called just then.

'You're some wanker,' I said, laughing.

'Why, what did I do?' he asked.

'The call you made just then: would I like to make a movie of *The Mammy*?' I now laughed heartily.

There was silence on the other end. Then: 'What the fuck are you talking about, Brenny?'

I could tell from his tone that it hadn't been Gerry on that call. 'FUCK!!' I screamed. I ended the call with Gerry and sat staring at the phone, willing it to ring.

It took a good half-hour, but it did, and it was 'him' again. I apologized and told him my mistake.

He took it in good humour. The producers, he explained, had just finished making a Dickens movie for Disney and they felt there was a Dickensian feel to *The Mammy*.

I was more than flattered; I was so excited. So, I met them and, as flattered as I was, the deal they were proposing was way too small so I passed. They didn't give up. It took about a year but we eventually got to a deal that we could agree on. We shook on it and then I got a disappointing feeling when one of them said, 'Now, who do we get to write the screenplay?'

I spoke up, of course. 'Me. I'll write the screenplay.'

They literally scoffed at the suggestion. 'Oh, God, no. You have no experience. We don't doubt that you might be able to do it, but your name won't bring any money to the project.' It's always about money. They decided upon John Goldsmith. John was a great writer and had written the screenplay of their previous movie for them. I had no argument to make. The book was sent to him and I went back to touring with *The Course*. Within a few months the producers told me that they had Anjelica Huston interested in the project. I was delighted, even if they did not want me to write the screenplay. It was still my book and a movie of it would make a huge impact.

Then a meeting was called between the producers, and I was invited to attend. They were all very glum when I got there. 'We sent the screenplay to Anjelica. She hates it.' There was a general feeling of defeatism round the table. 'Anjelica feels that somewhere in the transcript the story loses its way.'

Nobody spoke for a few minutes. Then someone asked, 'So who would be best to replace Anjelica?'

They all thought for a moment and I decided to speak. 'Anjelica is right.'

This was met with a resounding 'Not at all' or 'No, it's lovely'. The script was lovely; it was beautiful. It just wasn't *The Mammy*. So I made a suggestion. 'Let me go out to Los Angeles to Anjelica and work with her on the screenplay. If it doesn't happen after my draft, then go with whoever you want to replace Anjelica.'

They looked from one to the other, deep in thought.

*

It was a beautiful day when I landed in Los Angeles. I checked into the Beverly Hilton and changed into shorts and a T-shirt. I was tired from the thirteen-hour flight, so I hit the bed early to get plenty of rest before my first day with Anjelica. I was starting yet another new adventure.

I had a great sleep and was up early the next morning, had breakfast and met the driver who would take me to Anjelica Huston's offices on Venice Beach. As it turned out her offices were attached to her house and the house included a studio for her husband, Robert Graham. Robert, a Mexican-born but American sculptor, was just an amazing artist. He created and cast the most beautiful bronze figures. His work was very much a celebration of the human form. The only works of his I have actually seen in real life were the figures he did for the 1984 Olympics in Los Angeles, and his amazing Joe Louis memorial in Detroit, which is a gigantic floating fist. What I cannot really get across on paper is that Anjelica and Robert owned the entire block in which they resided and how vast it was. The house itself was breathtaking. Anjelica was waiting for me when I got there; she is much taller than I had thought and yet had the confidence to wear high heels too. No crouching for her, for sure.

We started with a coffee and to my relief she smoked! She popped out the ashtrays and we chatted about the book for a while. I was blushing as she gushed about it. This was Anjelica Huston talking about a book written by a self-taught author from Finglas. I'm not being over-humble here, but, seriously, Anjelica *fucking* Huston!

Anjelica gave me a tour of the house, which I will not describe here as she is a very private person. What I will say is how I felt when she opened the door to her study and standing facing the doorway was her Oscar. I had only to gesture at it with my hand and she knew that I wanted to hold it. 'Sure,' she said to the unasked question. She actually giggled as I picked it up.

I know it's silly, and, yes, it seems to be just a statuette but when I held the heavy award there was an electricity that ran through me that was inspiring. I fondled it, turned to her and stupidly said, 'Congratulations.'

She replied with a simple 'Thank you'. That's what her mouth said, but her eyes were saying, *Put it down and step away from the fucking Oscar.*

We talked a lot that day. We went through what her vision of the story was and I went over what I meant when I wrote each chapter, so we came to an agreement. I suggested that during the time we had together I would earmark thirty events or so from the book that should happen in the movie and then go away and write my draft around those. My draft would actually be draft number four, as John Goldsmith had already done three.

Here's the thing, though. Although Anjelica had made the time and effort to work with me that week, she had not actually committed to the movie. On the final day, Greg Smith, one of the producers, joined Anjelica and me for lunch. Here's a little trick I noticed him do. It would be unprofessional for him to ask Anjelica outright if she would commit to the movie. This would have to be done between him and her agent, but he did want to get an indication of which way she was leaning. Because it would not come down to money – she didn't need money – it would come down to whether she wanted to do the movie or not. So he asked what seemed like an innocent enough question. 'Anjelica, should you decide to come to Dublin, do you think you might need a house in case you have visitors or would you prefer an apartment?' Her answer would tell him what way she was leaning. For instance, if she replied, 'Well, let's wait until closer to the time,' then she had not decided yet. But if she chose a house or apartment, she was *leaning* towards committing.

Anjelica thought for a moment. 'I think –' he waited – 'an apartment would be fine as long as it's big enough.'

Greg smiled from ear to ear.

That afternoon I let Greg take the car back to the hotel and I walked along Venice Beach, feeling on top of the world. I felt like a real writer for the first time, like I had the world in the palm of my hand. I walked as if I were holding my future by the hand, and it felt amazing. I walked to Shutters Hotel and had a pot of coffee and a smoke out on the deck overlooking the beach. When I left Shutters I was walking a little, looking to grab a cab, when I came across a shoe shop with some lovely examples in the window.

I strolled inside and had my first real Los Angeles moment. I was approached by a sales-guy. 'Can I help you, sir?' he asked ever so politely.

'Yes,' I answered, 'I'm looking for a pair of *fuck-off* shoes.'

Without hesitation he nodded. 'Follow me, sir.'

I did and he stopped at a shelf and pointed to a pair of crimson boots and said, 'Now, sir, these say *fuck off* to me. Would sir like to try them on?'

I bought them, by the way.

Within a week of returning to Ireland I had written draft four of the script. I sent it to the producers, and they sent it on to Anjelica. She loved it and committed to the movie. Everything seemed to be rosy in the garden . . .

Until it wasn't.

Gerry and I were still touring *The Course*. We were doing OK there. *The Mammy* was being made into a movie and I had made sure to write in parts for me and Gerry, as well as securing Gerry a credit as a producer. Alan Parker had just offered me a role in the movie of *Angela's Ashes*. Things were tickety-boo. All in all, 1999 seemed to have all the ingredients of being my best year yet.

As it transpired, 1999 would be a fucking disaster of a year.

OK, I won't deny that when the producers of *The Mammy* had rejected the idea of me writing the screenplay out of hand I was hurt. No, not just hurt, I was angry. So during the months in 1998 leading up to the producers eventually sending me out to Los Angeles to work with Anjelica, I had decided to write another screenplay, an original story. I dug deep into what I had learned from Syd Field's book *Screenplay*. The story was a simple tale about a boxer who gets a shot at greatness but fails to throw the winning punch, which he gets to throw years later. A kind of poor-guy-makes-good story. When my screenplay was finished I was more than happy with the end product. The screenplay was entitled *Sparrow's Trap*. (Even as I typed that a chill ran down my spine.) I just wanted to write it to prove to myself that I could. However, I fell into a trap that I had unwittingly set for myself.

You see, from that very first *Late Late Show* appearance with Gay Byrne, I had gone from strength to strength. I had conquered the stand-up scene in Ireland. I had written three novels that had all at some stage been number one on the bestseller lists. I had written, directed and starred in a play that had broken box-office records all over Ireland, and the first of my books was to be made into a movie starring and directed by Anjelica Huston. I began to think I was the guy on the poster. I began to believe my own press. I began to think that maybe I could walk on water. The Bible says, 'Pride cometh before a fall.' Yep, I can confirm that. Indeed, what a fall I was about to have, what a fucking fall. By the end of 1999 my marriage had ended, I would have no gigs, and I would be not just broke but two million pounds in debt.

35

When I gave the script to two of the producers of *The Mammy*
I expected them to dive on it. It wasn't a big budget and they
could release it on the back of *The Mammy*. Simple.

Not so simple. They asked who I had in mind for the role
of the detective and I told them I would like either Aidan
Quinn or Stephen Rae. They said that if I got either, then
they were in. I mistakenly took that as a go. Basically I heard
what I wanted to hear. I sent the script to Stephen Rae and
then I tracked down Aidan Quinn's agent in Los Angeles.
Aidan lived in New York at that time, but his agent was in
LA. In the meantime, I pressed ahead with pre-production.
I hired a first-class production manager, and even gave her a
producer's share in the movie. She set out the budget, put
together the schedule, arranged a buyout of the crew that
cost a little more but did away with overtime, she hired the
set designers, wardrobe designer, everybody. She was effi-
cient, by the book. She planned the shoot for January 1999,
as it would be cheaper and easier to get crew at that time of
year in Ireland. We had no big locations, the biggest being
the National Stadium for the final fight scene where we
would need a lot of extras. Other than that we built Sparrow's gym in an army barracks and Tony Byrne gave us the
use of the Tivoli for a dance scene.

The full story of the making of *Sparrow* is a book in itself,
but the crux of *my* problems I will relate here. Stephen Rae
invited Gerry and me out to his home; I saw this as a good
sign – however, it was just Stephen being nice. He wanted to

tell me face to face that he couldn't do the movie. He is a lovely man and his best wishes for the project were heartfelt. No worries, there was still Aidan Quinn. Having waited a month for a reply from his agent, I called his mobile phone to see if he had any news for me. He said that Aidan had not got back to him yet, but that we should have a sit down and talk about the movie. He said that the next available date he could meet me at his office in LA would be 1 January.

I flew to Los Angeles on 30 December and turned up at his office on 1 January. It was closed for the holidays. I called his mobile. 'Oh, I'm sorry, I meant the third,' he said.

I returned on the third. He shook hands with me and got straight to it. 'No.'

That was that. I was shattered. 'You brought me all the way from Ireland to tell me no?'

He was very calm. 'I didn't bring you anywhere. You came of your own accord.' I turned to leave but then turned back again. 'Someday I will walk in here and you will blow me to be a part of what I offer.'

He smiled. 'And if it's good enough, I just might.'

I couldn't get a direct flight home, so I went through New York. When I got to Fitzer's Hotel I was exhausted. All this time I had had Aidan Quinn's phone number, but I hadn't wanted to call him direct. Yet I was convinced that he had not even seen the script. So I called.

He was lovely on the phone. He said he didn't recall seeing the script but amazingly he offered to meet me the next day. We met, had a coffee and he took the script. He said he would love to do it, even just to have a few weeks in Ireland, 'but' – and it was a big but – Aidan's wife was expecting a baby. He said he would have a chat and call me within two days. As I boarded the Aer Lingus EI 106 that night for Dublin I really didn't hold out much hope of Aidan being my man.

I was right. He called and was unnecessarily apologetic.

I did get my man, though. Bryan Murray. Nobody could have played the part better. With just a few days to spare he signed on and we were ready.

Let me simplify the way the movie budget works. The production, us, get the money on loan from a bank. The loan is guaranteed by the distributors, as they will be the ones that take the money in. Once this is all in place, the budget cheque arrives on the first day of principal photography. About four days before we were to begin shooting, I called our distributors to make sure everything was in place. When they told me that they had decided NOT to go forward with the project I could have died. They had been a long time in the film business so I asked them for advice as to what I should do now. They said close it down. But I argued that then nobody would get paid – there were already people working, sets being built. The advice I was given was: 'It's a one-pound company. Close it down, and if they want to they can fight over the pound.'

Maybe I should have taken that advice. But instead – I don't know if it was working-class pride or my own ego, could be both – I went ahead. I had £37,000 in the bank and I spent it all, along with loans and gifts from anybody and everybody Gerry or I knew. Without the generosity of some of the most talented and hard-working people we couldn't have gone as far as we did. We nearly made it. We ran out of money in the very last week. I was stunned that the day after I told the crew and actors that I could no longer pay them they all turned up to finish the movie.

I have *Sparrow's Trap* in my vault. Nobody has ever seen it. It's a great little movie. But it nearly killed me.

When my marriage ended halfway through the making of *The Mammy*, I was living in an apartment in Dublin's Temple

Bar that I had bought a couple of years before. I was broke. Any money I had made from *The Mammy* went towards debts from *Sparrow*. I had no gigs in the diary and I was feeling very, very sorry for myself. At one point I didn't sleep for three days. I had the curtains closed for the three days, I did not switch on a light, and I did not eat. By the end of the third day I told myself that I must try to sleep, so I went to the bedroom in the apartment. Before I got into the bed I did something that I had not done since I was a child: I kneeled by my bed and prayed. Not a prayer kind of prayer; it was a prayer to my mammy. You see, my mammy always liked me to work things out for myself. She would guide me and goad me into finding the solution to whatever problem was facing me. So here was my prayer:

'Mammy, I know you would always want me to find the answer to things myself. But I can't this time. I am lost. I don't know where to turn, or what to do. Please, this ONE time, help me.'

When I opened my eyes there was no clap of thunder, no flash of lightning. Nothing. Except I slept at last and had the most amazingly real dream.

The dream: I was sitting in my office. (I didn't have an office any more.) The office door opened, and my secretary popped her head in. (I no longer had a secretary, and this girl was unknown to me.) She spoke. 'Mr O'Carroll, your mother is on line one.'

I snatched up the phone. 'Mammy?'

For a second there was silence then: 'Yes, I'm here, love.'

It was her voice. It was Mammy!

'Did you get my message?' I asked.

'Yes, I did.'

I waited for the solution. When she didn't answer, I asked, 'So, Mammy, what am I to do?'

'Brendan, if you want this so badly that you are prepared to get on your knees and pray for it, then get up off your forking knees and do something!' Then the phone went dead.

I cannot explain why but I awoke after twelve hours of sleep and I felt great! I made tea and ate two packets of biscuits. I called Gerry and we started to make calls to get gigs. We also called on Tommy Swarbrigg and he began to put a tour together for us. Within weeks we were earning again. I had been a hermit for some months, but I was seeing Jennifer, or now Jenny, on and off, so I started to loosen up a little.

I decided that I would take the kids to Orlando that September. The separation of Daddy and Mammy is hard on any children, and they were no exception. Fiona, now sixteen, was then dating Martin Delany, who worked for me as the sound engineer at my gigs. I think she took it the hardest; Fiona was convinced that I had left her mother for Jenny. I hadn't – I was leaving long before I even met Jenny, but I know that I cannot control what somebody thinks. Anyhow, I was *persona non grata* with Fiona for a long time. So when the Orlando trip arrived it was just me, Danny and Eric, now six years old. Fiona went on holiday with Martin.

We flew into Orlando on the hottest of September days. I hadn't enjoyed a holiday so much ever before. We had a ball. I loved every minute with my two sons. We 'did' Disney every day and on our second-to-last day there I took them to Epcot. I hadn't had a chance to take Danny there in 1994, although I had been myself. It would be a first for both of them. We had a wonderful day going from land to land around the lake, we did Soarin' and Future World, then – to top it all off – the fireworks.

The Epcot fireworks are the best I have ever seen, but a

strange thing happened that night. So, I'm standing in the dark – we had got a great viewing spot, the music was so beautiful and the fireworks were perfectly in time with the rhythm of the songs – and, as I stood there smiling, a thought flashed through my head ever so briefly. *Jenny would love this.* I have no idea why I thought that; I never expected to think anything even remotely like that. Jenny and I had been seeing each other all right but we were friends. She had been married before and we had both sworn that we would never do it again, but we were friends and she meant a lot to me, obviously even more than I had thought?

So the next day the boys and I went to breakfast. I was sitting in iHop having pancakes covered in maple syrup, but I could not get Jenny out of my mind. So now I need to tell you a little story:

It was about two years, maybe a little more, prior to that breakfast morning in Orlando. We were touring with *The Course*. We were staying in a dingy B & B in Manchester. One night a group of us were having a drink after the show when somebody asked me how a person gets ideas for writing. I said I didn't really know, but that honestly anybody that can use their imagination, I believe, can write. So I began a 'for instance' thing. I said to give me any two characters and a location and I'll come up with a story.

So here's what I got: 'A boy and a girl in Wales.'

I thought for a moment. 'OK,' I began, 'she's the daughter of the owner of a coal mine in Wales, and he is the son of the trade union shop steward. The fathers are bitter enemies. The boy and girl fall in love, but they keep their love a secret from everyone in the valley, especially their fathers, but soon they will both be eighteen and the girl must now leave for finishing school in Switzerland. And the boy, well, he is determined not to become a miner, and wants to go to America.

They have their last night together and she, through teary sobs, asks him will they ever meet again. He says, "Yes. Close your eyes. I want you to picture a beautiful meadow with wild flowers, with the scent of lavender drifting down from the surrounding hills. There's a stream running through it with water so clear you can see the fish at play."

'She keeps her eyes closed. "I can see it." Then she opens her eyes.

'He holds her in his arms and says, "Every year on this day I want you to close your eyes . . . and I will meet you there, in that meadow."'

They had all been silent as I was making this up, so I laughed. 'That's it. Yin and yang, black and white, with an ending full of hope.'

Fast-forward to the iHop on International Drive in Orlando. As the boys finish their pancakes, I went out back and called Jenny's home number.

Her father answered. 'Hello, Mr O'Carroll.' He was very formal.

I asked for Jenny.

'I'm afraid she's not here. She's at her sister's in California.'

Hopefully not sounding too disappointed, I thanked him and said I'd see him soon.

He then asked me, 'Would you like her sister's number?'

I stumbled over my words a little but got out, 'Sure, why not?' I took the number and, after a short debate with myself, I called.

A female answered, who I now know as Jenny's sister Joan. 'Oh, hello, Brendan, we've just dropped Jenny off at LAX. She's going back to Ireland today.'

I was disappointed but I told her that it was OK. 'I'll see her some time when I get home.'

Then Joan added, 'Jenny told me that if you should call, that she "would meet you in the meadow". Is that a help at all?'

I smiled to myself. 'Yes it is, Joan. Thank you.'

I hung up the phone and on my way back to the breakfast table I said aloud to myself, 'Brendan, my son, you just might be in love.' And it felt so good!

36

Although by 2000 we were back gigging with the OCS and making a living, it was around this time that everything that had happened in 1999 started to weigh on me. As I sit here, typing out my story, I cannot remember what it was about my state of mind that kept me going, what it was that stopped me from giving up, why I hadn't just thrown my hands in the air and said, 'Fuck it all.' I wonder was it PMA? I know for sure that once you begin to practise a positive mental attitude it becomes like the Catholic religion, ingrained. I may not go to mass, but every time a plane I'm on hits turbulence and starts bouncing around, I immediately call on Jesus and every saint I can fucking think of. Whatever it was that kept me afloat, I know only that I *didn't* give up. But truthfully I was hanging on by the flimsiest of threads.

Having spent virtually every day since 1989 moving forward, sometimes slowly, sometimes at speed, I now found myself in the doldrums. Just sitting there afloat, my sails sagging and going nowhere. It was a horrible feeling.

Now here's a thing. I believe that if you have a wonderful idea, all you need is for one other person to believe in you and your idea to make it happen. I tried and tried to come up with an idea that would move things forward, but here's the other thing: the idea you are looking for does not have to come from you. If you keep an open mind, that idea can come from anywhere – in my case out of a cup of coffee.

Denis Desmond is the top promoter in Ireland, probably one of the best in the world. Denis is the owner, along with his wife Caroline, of MCD. This book is not long enough to list his achievements and the exploits of MCD, and God knows it's long enough. The invitation to meet Denis for a cup of coffee seemed to come out of nowhere. I'm sure Denis was well aware of my failures of the previous year, as they had been well documented in the press. I cannot even remember where we met, but I got there before him and for some reason I remember feeling very nervous.

Denis arrived and sat down without a hello or anything. He ordered by pointing at my cappuccino. 'Whatever that is,' he said.

'Hi,' I said.

So before I get into the conversation, let me just give you some background on my relationship with Denis. Denis owns the Gaiety Theatre and the Olympia Theatre, both of which I had played in. The Olympia doing stand-up and the Gaiety doing *The Course*. I have played the Olympia many times and in all those times I have never had a deal with Denis. We just shook hands. I never asked what the split would be or if it was a fee. He just gave me a cheque at the end of the run and that was that. I never worried because Denis Desmond is among the most honourable business-men I know. OK, let's get back to that cup of coffee.

Once he had his coffee we chatted about trivial shit for a while, then eventually I asked, 'Denis, why am I here?'

He scratched his head. 'Oh yes,' he said, as if it were an afterthought, 'I have three weeks free in the Gaiety in two months' time. Scribble up something for it and put it on.'

Scribble up? What does that mean? So I tried to get out of agreeing to anything. 'Denis, I'm not feeling very funny right now, and when you don't feel funny it's hard to *write* funny.'

He ignored me. 'It's the first three weeks,' he said.

336

I promise you I really tried to resist. 'Denis, I'm serious. I wouldn't know where to begin.'

He looked right at me with what I now call 'that Denis smile', the smile that says *I won't take no for an answer.* 'Ah, you'll come up with something, Brendan. Why don't you write a stage play based on that radio thing you used to do?'

I had to think. Radio? '*Mrs. Brown's Boys*?' I said out loud, not really meaning it to be a question but that's how it sounded.

He stood. 'That's the one. I'll confirm the dates in a few days.' He dropped a five-pound note on the table for the coffees and was gone.

I sat there a bit shell-shocked.

On my drive home the casualness of Denis's request sank in. He believed that once he had told me what he wanted that I would produce it. He believed that. I realized something more important. He believed in ME.

That evening I sat at my laptop and decided to explore what a *Mrs. Brown's Boys* play would look like. When I looked up from my laptop the ashtray was overflowing and the clock told me it was 5 a.m. I had been 'exploring' for nine hours without a break. I went to the kitchen and made a coffee. I just sat in thought until 8 a.m. when it was time to wake Danny for school.

On the return from the school run I was feeling really tired, so I made the decision to hit the sack when I got back to the apartment. But I didn't. I made another coffee and proceeded to fill the ashtray all over again.

Danny had football training that evening so would be staying at his mam's. I typed, deleted and typed again, deleted again and typed again. I stopped only because I was bleary-eyed with lack of sleep. I barely made it to the bedroom, and

I think I was asleep even as I was getting undressed. I slept for twelve hours.

When I woke I went to the kitchen, on the way hitting the 'on' button on my laptop. I made a cup of tea and sat at the laptop. I opened up Scriptware, the programme I use for writing scripts, and it opened, as it always does, on the last page I had worked on. I was shocked that the page was blank but for two words: THE END. I couldn't remember typing those words, but when I read through the 150 pages I saw that I had done it. I had a *Mrs. Brown's Boys* play. I went to the title page, which was still blank, and typed out the title: *Mrs. Brown's Last Wedding*.

I was adamant that this time I would not play Mrs. Brown. Jenny tried to convince me that I should and even Denis Desmond said it would help sales. So here's what I decided to do. My daughter Fiona was attending film school in Dún Laoghaire. She gave me the phone number of the person who was charged with preparing the next movie make-up geniuses for the film industry. When I called I asked her if she had any upcoming 'stars' and she immediately recommended Tom McInerney.

I arranged for Tom to meet me with all his kit at Pat Baker's photography studio. When he arrived I was taken aback at how young he looked. I asked him if he knew the radio version of *Mrs. Brown's Boys*. It turned out that he did and had been a fan. 'Great, then I want you to make me up to what you picture in your mind Mrs. Brown looks like.'

I wanted no mirror. I did not want to see anything until the work was complete. I told Jenny that if, when I turned round to look in the mirror, I did not see Mrs. Brown I would not play the part.

Tom spent a good hour on the make-up, putting it on, then taking it off and starting again. Finally he said, 'Done.'

I made to turn the chair to the mirror, but then he stopped me.

'No, wait!' He looked me over again. 'There's just one more thing.' Tom reached into his bag and took out a tube, squeezing a small blob on to some card; as it was setting he painted it brown. He then carefully lifted it and for the first time placed Mrs. Brown's mole on to my chin. 'Now I'm done,' he announced.

I turned the chair to the mirror. There I saw, looking right at me, exactly what I had pictured in *my* head. Mrs. Agnes Brown had been born.

37

To test the play we took it to Cork City. We ran it in the Everyman Palace Theatre there. Cork is a wonderful place to try out a play. The Cork audience are the most honest you can find. If it's shit, they will let you know in short order. Thankfully it was a hit in Cork.

Mrs. Brown's Last Wedding opened and ran in the Gaiety Theatre, Dublin, and was sold out for eight weeks, breaking the box-office record previously held by *The Course*. We didn't have the money needed to put on the play, but Denis loaned us the money and we repaid him from the takings. That first touring cast were: myself playing Agnes, Jenny playing Cathy Brown, Simon Young playing Dermot, Claire Mullan as Winnie, Ciaran McMahon playing Mark Brown, Clyde Carroll playing Trevor, Derek Reddin playing Rory, and over time Gerry, as if to emphasize my opinion of how good an actor he was, played many of the characters, from Buster Brady to Mark Brown; he even played both Rory and Dino at some stage. However, as good as he was, his heart was in music. I could tell he was getting frustrated as we were moved further and further away from the OCS gigs.

Still, for now, we were back! We toured Ireland with *Mrs. Brown's Last Wedding*, selling out every venue we played. There are many stories from that time but one that always makes me laugh happened in Letterkenny in the county of Donegal. We were all staying in a B & B owned by a woman who was a religious tyrant. The place itself was clean and nice. There were religious pictures everywhere – more than you would see in a church. She laid down the law as we were checking in. NO smoking. NO food to be had in the room. NO alcohol in the room. We all stood and nodded dutifully, then went to our various rooms.

After three nights we were thrown out. Here's what happened. The woman one evening came into the hallway and smelled smoke. She followed her nose to the room of Simon Young. Without knocking she opened the door and went in. This is what she was met with: Simon was sitting up in the bed in his jocks and vest. He had a lit cigarette hanging from his mouth and a six pack of beer on his bedside table, one bottle open. He was preparing cream crackers and cheese. The crackers were already buttered and Simon was slicing the cheese using a picture of the Sacred Heart of Jesus he had taken down from the wall as a cutting board. I know it wasn't fair to our 'hostess', but even as she was herding all of us with our suitcases out of the place I cried laughing.

That first Irish tour of *Mrs. Brown's Last Wedding* was a huge success; we well and truly conquered Ireland. I know what you're thinking. What about the UK? Well, I'll be honest with you, I was terrified. My first foray over there with Tinkers Fancy had been a disaster, but I felt we had hit the bar with *The Course* – I was sure that if we had only stayed a little longer than one week in each city it would have taken off. I had to try again. Gerry and I flew to Glasgow. Why Glasgow? Well, for the very same reason we had chosen Cork City; it had an honest audience. If it worked in Glasgow, I was sure it would work anywhere.

The Pavilion Theatre on Renfield Street was built in 1904. It is a stunningly beautiful building that, despite all the odds, has consistently managed to remain the only private theatre in Scotland. The stage there has been graced by comedy legends from Charlie Chaplin to Billy Connolly. I have no idea who the owners are, but it is very much a one-man operation, that man being Iain Gordon. Iain himself takes anything to do with the theatre so personally that at times he can be a hard man to deal with, but once you understand that it's the Pavilion that comes first with him you begin to understand him.

Gerry and I sat across from Iain at his desk in the tiny room he called 'office'. Iain had received the script by post and agreed to meet us. 'I dinnae get it,' he said, as he tossed the script across the desk to us.

I tried to force the issue. 'I'm telling you, Iain, this play will sell. It already has all across Ireland.'

He smirked. 'That's Ireland, this is Scotland. Different places, different people, different audiences, don't you know?' He was giving us the brush-off.

I made one last push. 'I promise you that if you run this, you will take a million pounds at the box office. You will have at least one day when you take a hundred thousand pounds in bookings.'

He laughed then. 'If I had a penny for every arsehole that walked in that door and said that to me, I wouldnae need to work!' He picked up the script again. 'I just dinnae get it.'

Gerry looked at me; we knew we were finished. Gerry stood. 'Right, fair enough. Thanks for meeting us,' he said, and he put out his hand.

Iain still sat holding the script. 'I didnae say no.'

We both sat down quickly.

'I'll give you a week in March.'

Gerry smiled and was a bit surprised when I said no. Iain himself was a bit taken aback.

I explained. 'Look, we made this mistake before. We can't do less than three weeks.'

Why three weeks? Well, here's why. By the end of week

one, word of mouth would have spread and we should have a decent Saturday night. But by week three I just knew we would sell out. This was to be our new pattern. I don't know why but I was convinced it would work.

Iain eventually agreed and we set the date for the three-week run. Iain also agreed to build us a touring set in his workshop for a lot cheaper than we could have got it done elsewhere. We then went to Liverpool and did the same deal with the Royal Court Theatre there. Then on to Manchester and the Opera House Theatre and finally finishing in Birmingham's Alex Theatre. We came back from the week's trip having booked twelve weeks in the UK with a play that we didn't know would work in a country that had twice sent me packing. No pressure.

We finished the last of our bookings in Ireland and took a few weeks' break. The next time we were to step on a stage would be Glasgow. It was the Thursday before we were to leave for Glasgow that Iain called with some dire news. The play wasn't selling. We were due to open the following Tuesday and so far only around 500 seats had been booked for the 1,600-seat theatre. I asked him to comp out the night and the following night. Comp out is when you give free tickets to anybody and everybody just to fill the theatre. It creates a nice atmosphere and you hope that those people you comp will tell other people. However, on the night you're aware that those people are only there because it's free.

Iain wasn't happy about the suggestion. He said he wanted a guarantee of his three weeks' rent.

I said, 'OK, send me the papers then.'

I was surprised when he replied, 'No papers, your word will do.'

It was a gloomy ferry trip from Belfast to Glasgow. I was not looking forward to getting my ass kicked yet again by the UK audience. We opened on the Tuesday night to an audience of about 1,000. We did a great show, and the laughs were huge. We got a standing ovation and three curtain calls.

As I came off the stage Iain Gordon was standing at the bottom of the stairs that led up to the dressing rooms. When I reached him, he simply said, 'I get it.'

The next night, the Wednesday, had been comped to the tune of 500 seats, but we played to a full house. On the Thursday, when we arrived at the theatre, Iain was waiting outside the stage entrance. 'Here, you two,' he called to Gerry and me.

We walked over to him. He was smiling. 'Guess what?'

'What?' Gerry asked.

'The next three nights are sold out; we did over a hundred and twenty thousand at the box today. You fellas were right.'

Gerry and I high-fived and got ourselves ready for the now sold-out show. We came out of Glasgow with a healthy profit and Iain rebooked the play for the following October for another three-week run. I swear to you that the pattern repeated itself exactly in Liverpool, Manchester and Birmingham. It was a wonderful twelve weeks and we were booked to do it all again in October and November.

The ferry ride back from the UK this time was a very different one. As Holyhead began to fade in the distance, Bugsy, Jenny, Pepsi and I stood on the deck of the ferry having a smoke. I could not get the smile to leave my face. I had done it. I was going home victorious from the UK at last. I remembered that dismal night returning on this very same ferry feeling so downhearted. Pepsi it seemed remembered it too. I watched as he tossed his cigarette overboard and turned to go inside. As he passed me he winked. 'I told yeh.'

I stopped him and gave him a hug.

Jenny, smiling, asked, 'What was that about?'

I just said, 'History, Jenny. History.'

38

It took a while before the cast you see on the stage and on television became the core cast. We went through a few actors in some of the roles. Of what we have now, myself, Jenny as Cathy Brown and Dermot 'Bugsy' O'Neill as Grandad are the only members of the original cast. Derek Reddin started as Rory Brown but left for a long stretch and came back as Dr Flynn. The shortest length of time any of the cast has been with the show is about twenty years. Marty Delany, who began by playing a bit part fifteen years ago, took on the role of Trevor Brown and very quickly made it his own. So let's have a look at the cast, where they came from and the complex intermixing of who's who.

Obviously I'm Agnes Brown.

Cathy Brown is played by Jenny Gibney. Jenny had worked at the Revenue Commissioners and then the Bank of Ireland. After some years and many awards as an amateur actor and attending the Dublin Oscar Theatre School, she gave up the bank to give acting a 'shot'. I think it was her second-best move ever. Her best move ever came in 2005 when after a courtship that had lasted five years she married a strangely handsome writer. Me. Jenny's mother constantly reminds her that she 'can still go back to the bank' if it all doesn't work out!

Buster Brady is played by Danny O'Carroll. More below about Danny, but for now know this: nobody works harder to entertain an audience than Danny.

Fiona O'Carroll plays Maria Brown. Fiona attended Dún Laoghaire Film School's directors' course. She had no intention of acting when she graduated, but after a bit of cajoling and begging from me, she took the part of Maria. What you only get a glimpse of in the TV series is that Fiona has an amazing voice and actually had a chart hit in Ireland when she was only twelve years old.

Éilish O'Carroll plays Winnie McGoogan. My sister Éilish had worked for a long time in England, mostly in sales, and she was also an amateur actor; she has two beautiful sons there. Éilish first joined the crew as a wardrobe assistant twenty years ago. When Claire Mullan, the original Winnie, left through illness I asked Éilish to step in. She did and she was so good I left her there. She is a wonderful foil for Agnes as Éilish is up for anything.

Paddy Houlihan plays Dermot Brown. Paddy is Danny's best friend and has been since they were little boys. Back then Danny would bring what I thought was a quiet Paddy into the house and announced that this shy little boy was going to be an actor. I would tell Danny this: 'If ever I saw a kid that would never be an actor, it was Paddy.' After a lot of pushing from Danny, Paddy joined the crew as a general hand in 2000. Then in 2001 I was casting *The Course* for a limited run in Glasgow and Liverpool and I was stuck for the role of Ben, the character that carries most of the comedy. It was Jenny who suggested I give Paddy a run at it. I dismissed it out of hand, as I thought he was too young for the part, but Jenny persisted. Paddy was a magnificent Ben. Casting him as Dermot Brown was a no-brainer.

Pat 'Pepsi' Shields plays Mark Brown. Well, you know how he joined us, then left, then returned two years later. He had voiced Mark Brown on the radio version and just aces it on stage and screen.

Dermot 'Bugsy' O'Neill plays Grandad. I swear this is true. I walked into a theatre we were about to open in. Bugsy was building the set. As I passed him I said, 'Bugsy, I've written a grandad into the play; you're playing him.' Bugsy didn't stop what he was doing. He just simply said over his shoulder, 'OK.' That's Bugsy. He always has my back.

Amanda Woods plays Betty Brown. When you are an actor you need to be in a theatre. Most of the young ushers or the bar staff you see in theatres are aspiring actors or writers. Amanda was no different. She joined the team when we were performing in her home town of Letterkenny in Donegal, working on merchandise. Nearly two years later she stepped on to the stage in the Liverpool Empire to make her debut as Betty. It was full, over 2,000 people, and she did it! She is the perfect Betty.

From sound man to producer to actor. That is the route Martin Delany took to get to playing Trevor Brown. He is brilliant at it too. He is also a wonderful musician and singer. He was born in Cabra in Dublin but grew up in Wollongong, Australia. It is no coincidence that when we are touring Australia our warm-up gig is the arena there.

The hapless Barbara is played by Emily Regan. Emily joined us as a young girl, also in wardrobe. She went on to wardrobe design and made her debut as Barbara in the TV series.

Sharon is played by Fiona Gibney. Fiona started with us as assistant producer, moving from that to producer. She is a paralegal, which comes in handy too. If ever there was a person born to act, it's Fiona.

So what are the relationships? Well, most of them happened on tour but here's the rundown and, just to confuse you, I'm going to use their character names.

In real life:

Dermot is married to Barbara.

Buster is married to Betty and is Brendan's son.

Maria is married to Trevor and is Brendan's daughter.

Winnie is Agnes's sister, and Buster and Maria's aunt.

Bono is Agnes's 'real' grandson, and son of Betty and Buster and Blister's Brother.

Sharon is Cathy's sister and Brendan's sister-in-law.

Cathy is married to Agnes and is Sharon's sister and step-mum to Buster and Maria, as well as Granny to Bono and Blister.

SIMPLE.

By 2001 my own personal life was beginning to settle. Jenny and I had moved in together. I was very happy, and we had Danny and Eric living with us most of the time.

The previous year Danny had begun to worry me. He was then in secondary school but he didn't like school at all. He was really popular, played on the soccer team and on the GAA team, but he just couldn't get on top of the school-work. It was through a bizarre and maze-like way that I was to discover why.

You see, when Fiona had started school at just four years old it was at St Mary's school in Ashbourne. At the end of her first year there I went in for the usual parent–teacher chat. While waiting for the teacher to return from seeing some other parents out, I took a glance at Fiona's workbook. It was her maths book, but it wasn't really maths – each page or two had a single number written on it. I sneakily took a glance at one of the other kids' books and I noticed something. That child had written two pages of the number eight. Whereas Fiona's had only a half-page. I asked the teacher why this was, and she said that Fiona was too fast. She explained it something like this: the teacher would set out to teach the children to write the number eight and Fiona would do it straight away, and by the time the teacher had everyone doing it right Fiona would be bored. She said that one of her tasks now was to slow Fiona down to prepare her for mass education.

I left feeling worried that Fiona might need more of a challenge than the school could provide, so we enrolled her in the local Irish-speaking school. Believe it or not, Fiona would do more English in this school than a regular school, but everything was through the Irish language. As it happened, my mother and I spoke Irish as I was growing up. When I had started school I had to learn things like my colours in English, as I only knew them in Gaeilge. The reason I'm telling you this is that Danny followed Fiona into that school and Eric followed Danny into it. By the time Danny had finished his Junior Cert. exams (O level or GCSE) Eric was in second class. By the way, Danny did OK in his exams – not in the top thirty per cent but not in the bottom.

That's when I got a call to come to the school from Eric's teacher. Eric was having some difficulty, she explained, and she suggested that we get him assessed, as she felt he may have had a learning difficulty. I made an appointment with the child psychologist the teacher had recommended and went in with Eric. The lady who was to assess Eric said it would take an hour, so I went for a coffee and returned an hour later. 'Classic dyslexia,' is what she said. I was delighted actually because I could now get Eric the help he needed to read and write.

The lady said, 'I believe Eric has an older brother?'

I said yes, but that he seemed fine, although he did find school tough.

She said, 'Let me describe him?'

I waited for her to continue.

'He's good at art. He's probably the best footballer on his team and he is very popular. How am I doing?' I told her she had described Danny to a tee. (Glasgow Celtic had wanted Danny to try out.) She said she thought Danny should get tested for dyslexia too, then she added, 'It usually runs through the male side of the family.'

Then she asked whether I had had any difficulty in school. I explained that outside of primary I hadn't had much schooling, but that I was sure I wasn't dyslexic as by that time I had written three plays, four books and was a member of Mensa with an IQ in the top one per cent.

She smiled. 'Michelangelo was dyslexic. Einstein was dyslexic.'

I laughed. 'Well, I'm no Einstein.'

She opened a book she was holding. 'Read that page there,' she said, pointing to a random page. I began to read, thinking, *She's picked the wrong person to read this page. If she wants to ask me questions about what I'm reading, I have a wonderful memory. Fuck, I could tell her where the full stops and commas were.*

When I handed her the book back, she asked, 'Did you read it once or twice?'

Proudly I said, 'Just once.'

Then she held up her hand in which she had a stopwatch. 'You have the reading speed of about a twelve-year-old.'

I always knew that as much as I loved reading, it did take me longer than others to finish a book, but I would remember everything I read. Anyway, never mind me, the next week I'm sitting in the waiting room at the Irish Dyslexia Association with Danny. Danny is now sixteen and he's uncomfortable about being here.

I put my arm round him. 'Are you worried about finding out that you might be dyslexic?' I asked.

His answer surprised me. 'NO. I'm worried that I might not be.' He folded his arms. 'Because if I'm not, then I'm just a fucking dope.'

I squeezed him. 'You are NOT a dope. You're one of the smartest kids I know.'

He shrugged in response, and soon after that the door opened and Danny went in.

'Classic dyslexic,' the tester said.

Now what to do? I went to Danny's school and they told me that he was too far into things to get him remedial teaching now. On the drive back from that meeting Danny said, 'Dad, I can read well enough to read a script. That's all I need. I'm going to be an actor.' This was not the first time he had said this.

'Do you know what an actor spends most of his time doing, Danny?' I asked.

'Learning scripts, I suppose?'

'No,' I snapped. 'An actor spends most of the time looking for work. He will spend more time looking for work than working. Is that the life you want?'

He smiled. 'Yes.'

I shook my head. 'Shut the fuck up,' I said, and we had a quiet trip home.

Danny left school and joined the crew of *Mrs. Brown's Last Wedding* that summer. Over the following three years he would sweep the stage, load and unload the truck, learn the lighting controls and learn about sound. He helped build and paint the set and he ran all kinds of errands. All that before he stepped on a stage and made the character of Buster Brady his unforgettable own. (He still reads his scripts slowly.)

Fiona at just fifteen wanted to play the role of the ex-prostitute Tina Lovejoy in *The Course* and she could not understand why I wouldn't let her. She was so annoyed with me. When she finished film school she too joined the company. She also began by sweeping the stage and working in the wardrobe department and running errands before she nailed the role of Maria Brown.

After film school in Ballyfermot Eric would join us as the

show's vision mixer. Eric always had a great eye for a scene or a shot; he's the first to pull me up if I make a mistake, not that I ever do. So it was now the family business.

At the end of 1999 Gerry and I eventually went our separate ways. He is still a brilliant singer-songwriter and has also become a successful entertainment manager.

We had struck gold with *Mrs. Brown's Last Wedding*. We now had an audience in Ireland and the UK bookings were coming in fast, too fast. Let me explain what I mean by that. One thing Jenny and I have in common is love for our families. Jenny calls every member of her family every day and I would walk through fire for my three children. Understanding that may help you understand what I am about to tell you: the greatest gift you can give is time. We made the decision very early that we would not work when Eric was off school. So with Christmas, mid-term, Easter and summer holidays it actually worked out that he was off school twenty-six weeks a year, which meant we would only work twenty-six weeks of the year. Well, with Glasgow, Birmingham, Manchester and Liverpool taking six weeks each year that only left two weeks, which we would usually do in Dublin. Obviously we couldn't just keep going back with *Mrs. Brown's Last Wedding*, so I wrote more Mrs. Brown plays. Here is the running order:

Mrs. Brown's Last Wedding
Good Mourning Mrs. Brown
Mrs. Brown Rides Again
For the Love of Mrs. Brown
How Now Mrs. Brown Cow

We were really doing fine.

39

We had a long break between October 2000 and 2001. During that break I decided to put Jenny to the 'magic' test. Let me explain. I believe in fairies. I believe in Santa and the spirit of Christmas and I believe in the power of happy things to not only lift your spirits but to clear your head. I believe in magic. It was time to take Jenny to Disney. Jenny had never been to Florida and even before we went to any Disney park she was amazed by the beauty of the place. The sun and cleanliness of Orlando would impress anyone. Jenny passed my test. She is as fairy- and magic-minded as I am. If we see a fairy ring of mushrooms, we will both step in and do the required spin, making a wish. I never asked Jenny what her wish was (you have to keep it a secret), but I knew mine. What I didn't know was that eventually mine would come true.

The long break we took during 2000–2001 had drained our resources. I should mention that even though we only worked for twenty-six weeks of the year, we paid everyone for fifty-two weeks. So it was that when Gerry departed in 1999 we were left with some unique problems. Some of them financial and, of course, some administrative. I set up a new company to tour our plays, BOC Productions Limited. We had a tour planned for Ireland and the UK, and to finance that tour we needed to raise £70,000. My bank, although happy with my seeming recovery, were dubious about lending any money for a 'show', as they would refer to it. They would not lend money to BOC Productions Ltd because it was a limited company; instead I would have to borrow it personally and the most they would sanction would be £10,000. So here's what we did. Jenny, Danny, Fiona, Martin, Paddy, Amanda and I *ALL* took out a £10,000 personal loan and pooled them to put the tour together.

The result of that is that each of them to this day are profit-share recipients. That sounds great, but it also meant that if we had a loss at a venue, they didn't get paid. But, as I have said, we were all doing fine and continued to do so. Tour after tour was successful and the following four years were a bonanza for all concerned. The cast and crew were now earning triple what they had been. It was a joy for Jenny and me to see them getting married, buying new homes and taking holidays far and wide around the world. Jenny and I took our holidays with Eric in Orlando, sometimes maybe twice a year.

Penguin USA had the American rights to my Mrs. Brown books – *The Mammy*, *The Chisellers* and *The Granny* – and they had all done surprisingly well in America, so I did a couple of US book tours in 2003 and 2004 that I greatly enjoyed. A new book that I had written, *The Scrapper*, was doing really well in Ireland and across Europe for the O'Brien Press, particularly the Italian and French versions. When it was out of contract with the O'Brien Press I was offered a book deal by Penguin for a prequel to *The Mammy*. It was quite a substantial deal and financed my share of Jenny and I buying our first home together in Orlando, Florida. It was our 'happy place'. The book would become *The Young Wan*. Jenny and I were very happy and life was good.

With both Jenny and I having been married before we had discussed whether we would ever do it again. We had both agreed that no, we would not, as we wanted each other to be free to walk out of the door at any time if this thing of ours was not working for either of us. But then . . .

I was writing *The Young Wan*. I often write into the early hours of the morning when the house is quiet and I'm not going to get any interruptions. One particular night in December 2004 I had started writing about 10 p.m. and I was so into it that I didn't even see Jenny heading off to bed. When I stopped writing it was 4 a.m. and I was exhausted, so off I went to bed. I climbed into the bed and Jen was fast asleep. I stared at her for a long time. I just loved that she was there by my side. A thought ran through my head: *What if she wasn't there?* So I decided that the only remedy was to make her legally obliged to be there.

We married on 1 August 2005 on the steps of our local golf course. We had fought like cats and dogs right up to the week of the wedding. The night before I had told Jenny that when I turned round at the altar to see her in her wedding dress if I had the slightest doubt I would stop the ceremony. We would still have a party, we would still live together, just not get married. Amazingly Jenny had been having the same thoughts. I assured her that if she wanted to stop it at any time, I would back her a hundred per cent.

Jenny arrived the next day at the bottom of the steps in a golf cart with her father, Michael, and her mother, Annie, whom Jenny had chosen to be her bridesmaid. I had my back to the steps. When I heard the families clap, I turned round and looked down those steps at my bride. I promise you, I was never more sure of anything in my life as I was at that moment that I wanted to grow old and live out my days with this powerhouse of a woman. Nothing has changed since that moment.

So back to the tour. As I said, we were doing really well on tour and everybody was hunky-dory. However, if you remember, I also said that in theatre the money comes in dribbles and goes out in gushes. Well, we were about to get a wallop. The UK part of the 2005 tour took place in the most wonderfully sunny April and May there had been in years. That dropped attendances for a start. Also, the company we were dealing with, who owned the theatres, had insisted that we expand to other theatres, two in particular – one in Oxford and one in Hull. To facilitate two weeks in each of these venues they cut our other four 'bankers', those bankers being three weeks each in Glasgow, Liverpool, Manchester and Birmingham, by a week each. This had a disastrous result. We lost the income of four 'banker' weeks and neither Oxford nor Hull had sales over thirty per cent of capacity in any performance. In Oxford, a 1,500-seat theatre, we even played the show on one evening to fifty people. This was devastating. We had a cash-flow problem.

The tour finished in Hull. Before the last show I gathered the cast and crew together and I explained where we were regarding finances, although they all knew or had guessed from the audience size. I was bitterly disappointed to tell them that we could no longer afford to pay them when they were not working. The second part of the tour would take place in October and November that year and although we could not yet pay the cast, we would double their fees when we started that October. They all took it very well and commiserated with me, which I found a little embarrassing, but when we came back to do the second half of the tour we had eliminated the two losers, Oxford and Hull, and extended the bankers back to three-week runs, all of which sold out. With double their money the cast were happier than ever. We continued touring through 2006, 2007 and 2008, and the wind was in our sails. Things couldn't get any better. Or could they?

It was an ordinary evening in 2008 when we opened the

play *For the Love of Mrs. Brown*. A miserably cold and rainy night at the Pavilion in Glasgow. We were due to play there for three weeks and, as bad as the weather was, the three weeks had sold out. When we had finished the play that first night and I was back in my dressing room, the stage-door guy tapped on my door. He popped himself in and said, 'There are a couple of "suits" at the stage door asking to see you.'

I frowned, trying to think whether there was someone I'd invited and forgotten about. 'What do you mean "suits"?'

He shrugged. 'Suits. In or not?'

I told him 'in'.

There were two of them; one of them did the talking and the other stayed silent for the entire visit. The talker was quite a handsome man with a very Etonian accent. He said that he had come to see the show because Ian Pattison, writer of *Rab C. Nesbitt*, had recommended it to him. He went on about how he had not seen such a diverse audience with such a common reaction to comedy. He praised my performance. During this I had been changing from Mrs. B to Brendan, and I would usually be fast doing this and would then wait for Jenny to come down from her dressing room. But his talking delayed me and when Jenny arrived she gave me a look that asked *Who are these?* I returned the look with a *The fuck if I know* raise of my eyebrows.

The talker saw this and spoke up. 'Look, I won't beat around the bush. I'm Stephen McCrum, BBC comedy. Would you be interested in making a sitcom of the show?' He handed me his card.

Over the years I had been approached by many TV production companies. Once I said I was interested they would begin to recast the show. That then would be me saying no. Or they would point out that the show was funny but we

357

couldn't use that language. So I was prepared for the same conversations with Stephen. So, to take a feather from his cap, I didn't beat around the bush.

'What do you think about the cast?'

He was quick to answer. 'I don't believe it would work with any other cast. There seems to be a chemistry there.'

I was impressed, but not as much as I was about to be. 'What about the language?' I asked, waiting for him to give it the elbow.

'What language?' he asked, and I smiled. 'I saw nothing offensive there tonight. I presume that's the way the characters speak. An audience will make the leap.'

Stephen McCrum was about to become the shepherd that would carefully navigate the politics and maze that is the BBC to try to bring this merry bunch of gypsy performers to the television screens of the United Kingdom. Good luck with that!!

40

In Glasgow Stephen McCrum had said that he would like to get his boss to come and see the play. We were moving on to Manchester Opera House in a few weeks so he thought that this would be a good place for her to see it. I doubted if things could happen that quick and was not surprised when he called me to say that he couldn't get the people he needed to see the show to Manchester and that maybe it would be later in the year or early next year? I just said, 'Sure, whatever.' I held out little hope.

He surprised me yet again with a call the day after the opening night in Manchester. 'My boss happened to be in Manchester to attend some award thing and went to see the show. She only saw the first half and had to go, but she's commissioned a pilot script.'

'We're making a pilot?!'

'Eh, no. She wants a script first, and then she'll make a decision on making a pilot. But this is good, really good.'

I hung up the phone. *A pilot script? What does a pilot script look like? What does any television script look like?* I had written by this point two movie screenplays, five novels and six plays. Each format was different, but I had been able to adjust to each one. I was sure I could make the television adjustment happen easily enough.

I was so wrong.

McCrum called me a few times over the next couple of weeks. He had a plan. He would not reveal it to me as a whole but asked me to trust him. I did, implicitly. Stephen McCrum wanted to make a small video movie using snippets of the show and vox pops from the audience leaving the show. He wanted to submit this along with the pilot script. The reason he wanted to do this, he said, was that the show itself was not easy to visualize on the page. It needed something the commissioners could look at. In the meantime, he pushed for me to 'get the script done'.

I wrote the first script like it was a movie, using the usual measure of a page being a minute of screen time. The show was to be twenty-nine minutes long, but I did thirty-five pages just to be sure and to leave room for editing. McCrum sent it back to me with the comment *Too light*. It needed to be twice that number of pages.

I was baffled. Still I ploughed on. The second draft I sent in was fifty-five pages long, and was, I thought, a decent script. Again it came back. *Not good enough*.

By the time I had sent in the ninth draft from Florida I was numb. The comments coming back from Stephen were *Not funny enough, More physical comedy, Not enough of Agnes*.

I was flummoxed. I sent him the tenth draft and I was so sure I had got it.

He returned it with a compliment. *This is good, very close, see attached notes*. I printed off his email and there were SIX PAGES of notes. Very fucking close? I didn't even look at those notes. I just went out with Jenny and played eighteen holes of golf and forgot all about McCrum and his six fucking pages of 'very close' notes.

I went to bed early that evening, setting my alarm for 4 a.m. I rose with the alarm and, as I was leaving the bedroom, Jenny woke briefly. 'Are you OK?'

'Yeh,' I answered, 'I'm just going to take another crack at this script.'

She turned over. 'Good luck.'

'Good luck is right, you wouldn't believe it but he sent me six pages of notes, six fucking pages!'

Jenny did not hear a word. She was back asleep before I had even begun that sentence.

I went out to the kitchen table where I do all my writing. I flicked on the kettle and took McCrum's notes and placed them beside my MacBook. I turned them face down. The kettle boiled and as I was pouring the boiling water over the teabag . . I got it. I don't know where it came from but it came to me. I suddenly knew how to turn the stage show into a TV show.

I sat and typed and typed. By 9 a.m. I had finished the script. I pressed print on the laptop and made my fourth cup of tea as the printer was spitting out the morning's work. Then I sat down and turned over McCrum's notes. One by one I ticked the relevant ones off. I just ignored those I didn't agree with.

I sent the script at 9.45 a.m. Orlando time so it would arrive with him at 2.45 a.m. his time. I was wide awake now and pretty pleased with myself.

At 2 p.m. Orlando time a text arrived from McCrum. It read simply: *Eureka!*

The next move was to make the short video that was to accompany the script. We made it in the Empire Theatre in Liverpool. McCrum was delighted with the footage he got, particularly the vox pops. He assured me that he would get a great edit out of it, and he did. All that was to be done then was to present it to the commissioner. Stephen planned to do this on Monday 20 October. Well, that was the plan, but that was not the outcome. You see, something happened that made McCrum slow down the plan.

Russell Brand is a hilarious comic and I am a fan. On Saturday 18 October he and the great Jonathan Ross made a prank call to actor Andrew Sachs. Andrew did not pick up the call so they left a lewd message on his answering machine. The UK went into a spin and uproar ensued. It was naughty but not exactly fatal. The BBC were fined £100,000 and both the lads were disciplined, severely!

McCrum called me on the following Friday. 'Well, how did the presentation go?' I asked.

He was silent for a few moments. 'I didn't make the presentation. I'm holding everything back for now. The place is in a tizzy and if I present this now all they will see is "fuck", nothing more. I'm going to wait until things calm down.' I left it at that. Stephen McCrum knew the workings of the BBC better than anybody. I was sure it would calm down in a matter of weeks.

It was six months before I heard from Stephen McCrum again. I was at home in Florida and, if I'm not mistaken, it was April Fool's Day. He asked me if I was still OK to make the pilot? I, of course, said I was, and he said he was moving forward. He said he would be making the presentation to BBC Two the following Tuesday.

Stephen called me on the Monday. There was a union strike on the underground and nobody could get into work at the BBC, so the appointment had been cancelled. He'd keep me in touch.

He called me again on the Tuesday. 'I've been told that I'm to make a presentation to BBC Two and BBC One.'

I asked the obvious question: 'Is that good?'

He was puzzled. 'I don't know. This has never happened to me before.'

Well, I thought, *maybe we should think about it as having two bites at the cherry.*

On the Thursday morning I woke early enough at eight

thirty and made my way to the kitchen. As I passed my mobile phone, I noticed it was flashing with a text message that had come in. I made tea and lit a fag before I looked at my phone. The message was from Stephen McCrum.

It read: *Just had to make one presentation. BBC One would like to see a pilot. We are go for the pilot.*

Funnily instead of jumping in the air and screaming I quietly went into the bedroom and woke Jenny.

I turned the phone to her. 'Look at this.'

She read it and she too stayed very calm. 'We have a pilot,' she said ever so softly.

I cannot explain it, but we walked around in a daze all that day.

We had a pilot.

Obviously I expected that we would make the pilot the very next week, but Stephen had other plans. He said he wanted a particular director, Gareth Carrivick, an Academy Award-winning director that Stephen believed was perfect for the pilot. However, Gareth would not be available for two months, but Stephen assured us it would be worth the wait.

So we waited and went back to work touring all over the UK. Two months later the date was set to rehearse and shoot the pilot. Stephen was right to wait for Gareth Carrivick; he was brilliant. The BBC had offered me a choice as to where I wanted to record the show. London, Belfast, Manchester or Glasgow. Without hesitation I selected Glasgow. (Remember the psychic? She had been right so far.)

When we arrived in the Pacific Quay, or PQ as they call it themselves, we were welcomed with open arms. The staff gym became our rehearsal room and the floor was taped out in a floor plan of Agnes Brown's house. We worked and worked up to ten hours a day. Gareth would always make us go faster and faster. We got to the stage where we were performing at breakneck speed. Gareth assured us that on TV it would look normal. He was right, but I remember being totally exhausted at the end of every day. Here's the thing also: long before we had got the date of the pilot I had booked us into the Pavilion with a new play, *How Now Mrs. Brown Cow*. The dates didn't clash but we were due to open the play two days after recording the TV pilot. So during the day the cast were working on the TV show and in the evenings we were learning the lines for the new stage show. We would only have Monday and the Tuesday morning on which to rehearse the new play.

The television rehearsals came to an end on the Thursday morning. On the Friday afternoon they were to bring in the 'adults', the crew from every department, to see a run-through of the show, so we would rehearse on the set in the morning. We had not yet seen the set. We met that morning in the gym and Iain McDonald, the set designer, guided us over to the studio proper.

It was magic as we walked into Mrs. Brown's house for the first time! It took my breath away. It was exactly as I had imagined it. I looked to Jenny, and she was crying. I joined in. What was also extraordinary was that the cushions on the couch had a dragonfly pattern on them. Iain didn't know about the dragonfly being lucky for me; it was a complete accident. We sat in the chairs, on the couch, at the kitchen table and checked out every nook and cranny of the set. Magic!

That afternoon, when the 'adults' arrived, there was tension in the air. Apparently Stephen and Gareth had brought a crew from London to work with the local crew on the show, particularly as heads of department, which did not go down well with the local crew. Tony Keene was head camera man, Martin Hawkins lighting designer, Nick Roast head of sound and Jo Kennedy-Valentine floor manager; they had all come from London to make Gareth's show. Within hours any tension was gone. Why? Because we did the show for them. They all laughed loud and long and nothing bonds people quicker than shared laughter.

The cast were dismissed and we went back to our apartments. Stephen said he would drop in later for a glass of wine. He did and we half talked about what would be going on the next day, Saturday. I say 'half talked about' because nothing could have prepared me for how hard we were to work the following day.

It was gruelling. Camera rehearsal was new to us. So it would be: deliver a line. Stop. 'Step six inches left. Good.' Then do the next line. 'Hold it, keep standing where you are, but can you shift your weight on to your left side? That's it! OK, carry on.' Next scene. 'Eh, Brendan, I know Cathy is over there, but can you look at the biscuit tin when you are talking to her? It's better for the camera angle.' It felt fucking bizarre and it went on for ten hours. We were wasted.

When Stephen asked if we'd like to go for a drink afterwards my answer was: 'You must be fucking joking.' We went back to the apartment and fell into bed.

The next day, Sunday, was show day. I was as nervous as fuck. The audience were packed into the 400 seats in the studio a good hour before we were due to start. That hour disappeared in what seemed like minutes. Before I knew it, the warm-up guy had introduced me to the floor. I walked out to great applause that I was so grateful for. I really was terrified. Then I took the mic from him and turned to the audience. Suddenly I felt OK. Calm even.

The picture that ran through my head was a young Dublin woman sitting on a stool. *I don't care . . . as long as he has a big cock.* For a split second I was back there in the Rathmines Inn, the cash register dinging in the background. I could feel myself smiling and all the nervousness left me. I was home.

The show was over in what seemed like the blink of an eye. The entire cast were so nervous that, as the title music ran, I made a decision. I would deliberately fuck-up my lines in the opening scene. Once I did it they could relax and they wouldn't feel that they were the only ones if they did too.

Before we knew it we were all out in the scene dock, hugging and kissing. The show had run so smoothly. Gareth had really knocked us into shape. I asked Stephen McCrum when he expected to hear if the pilot had worked or not. He said not to expect to hear anything before Christmas. I didn't know if the BBC would like the pilot, but for sure I knew that we could not do any better. We had a small wrap party afterwards and I left the studios legless and so happy.

We began rehearsals for *How Now Mrs. Brown Cow* at 9.30 a.m. the next day. There were more than a few sore heads. The rehearsal went really well, and we were ready for opening the next evening. Here's a funny thing. We performed the show on that opening night at television speed not stage speed. The curtain went up at 7.30 p.m. and by 9.15 we were in the pub next door. Iain Gordon the theatre manager said to me in the dressing room afterwards, 'Don't get me wrong, it's a very funny show, but, fuck, it's wild short!' That night I wrote a new scene into the play and the next evening we slowed the show down to a proper delivery speed.

It worked. The new play was up and running and thankfully the rest of the three-week run sold out. God bless

Glasgow. We toured again: Birmingham, Liverpool, Manchester and finally Dublin. The new play was a hit, and we were easily due our break. Whatever would happen the other side of Christmas I was so proud of my family, my extended family (the cast and crew) and my wife, Jennifer Gibney. She did not take my name on stage, but she brought everything else.

On the afternoon of Friday 13 November I got a phone call on my mobile. I was at home in the kitchen where the signal was shit. The voice on the other end was garbled and I couldn't make it out. 'Hold on,' I said loudly, as if speaking louder would help, 'I'm going outside to get a signal.'

I went out into the garden. Just then Jenny came into the kitchen. She had been putting away the washing. She could see me out in the garden and hear me shouting. When I walked back into the kitchen she said quite matter-of-factly, 'Who was that then?'

I barely got the words out. 'It was Stephen McCrum. We have a series on BBC One.'

Jenny and I sat down and cried.

Afterword

I'm sure you are wondering what the coincidence was about the Johnny Seven OMA. It was this: We were sitting round our kitchen table. The 'we' was myself, Jenny, Jenny's dad Michael and her mother Annie. We were talking about the coming Christmas and I was going on about how children's expectations were so high nowadays. Michael, a retired fire chief, said, 'You are so right. I remember one Christmas about forty years ago. We were attending a fire at a warehouse in Phibsboro, I think it was, and I watched a young kid staring at a half-burnt pallet that was stacked with toy guns. I went to him and said, "Go on, son, help yourself." The kid went over and took one from the bottom where they weren't burned. As he passed me I told him you can take as many as you like, and he said something like, "No, thanks." You see that? HE wasn't greedy.'

It took me a few moments to speak. 'Michael, it was a Johnny Seven, and that kid was me.'

And the world turns.

THE END
(Or is it?)

Acknowledgements

I would like to thank the following for their contribution and help in putting this book together.

From *Mrs. Brown's Boys*:
Fiona Gibney, Marian Sheridan, Aly Aly Mahmoud, Éilish O'Carroll, Graeme Hunter, Conor Gibney, Dean McNevin, Evan Rogers, Eric O'Carroll, Danny O'Carroll, Fiona O'Carroll, Paddy Houlihan, Dermot O'Neill, Patrick Shields and, of course, Mark Sheridan.

Penguin Random House/Michael Joseph:
Jenny Roman, Paula Flanagan, Ella Kurki, Lee Motley, Emma Henderson, Ella Watkins, Jen Harlow, Mubarak Elmubarak, Jen Breslin, Cliona Lewis, Deirdre O'Connell, Alice Mottram and, of course, Louise Moore.

I would most especially like to thank two people.

Firstly, Daniel Bunyard. Daniel conceived this book and was very much the energy behind it. It is rare to find someone who knows how to push, but not too hard. How to compliment, but not to lie and to know the right words to say at the right time. Daniel is none of those things (just kidding).
This is the third book I have worked on with Daniel and he has become a friend whom I value very much.

Finally, my muse and partner in everything I try to achieve, Jenny Gibney O'Carroll. I am what I am because you love me.